ECONOMIC INTEGRATION AND ASIA

T0305139

Economic Integration and Asia

The Dynamics of Regionalism in Europe, North America and the Asia-Pacific

Mordechai E. Kreinin

Department of Economics, Michigan State University, USA

Michael G. Plummer

Associate Professor of International Economics, Graduate School of International Economics and Finance, Brandeis University, USA and Visiting Professorial Lecturer, Johns Hopkins University Bologna Center, Italy

Edward Elgar
Cheltenham, UK • Northampton, MA, USA

Published by
Edward Elgar Publishing Limited
Glensanda House
Montpellier Parade
Cheltenham
Glos GL50 1UA
UK

Edward Elgar Publishing, Inc.
136 West Street
Suite 202
Northampton
Massachusetts 01060
USA

A catalogue record for this book
is available from the British Library

Library of Congress Cataloguing in Publication Data

Economic integration and Asia / edited by Mordechai E. Kreinin, Michael G.
   Plummer.
      Includes index.
      1. Asia—Economic integration. 2. Pacific Area—Economic integration.
   I. Kreinin, Mordechai Elihau, 1930– II. Plummer, Michael G., 1959–

   HC412.E2177 2001
   337.I'5—dc21
                                                      00–052067

ISBN 1 84064 483 4

Printed and bound in Great Britain by MPG Books Ltd, Bodmin, Cornwall

Contents

PART III   ECONOMIC INTEGRATION IN ASIA

Acknowledgements

The publishers wish to thank the following who have kindly given permission for the use of copyright material.

Elsevier Science for: 'Effects of Economic Integration in Industrial Countries on ASEAN and the Asian NIEs', *World Development*, **20** (9), 1345–66; 'Motives for Japanese DFI: Survey, Analysis, and Implications in Light of the Asian Crisis', *Journal of Asian Economics*, **10** (1), 385–94; 'The Trade-Investment Nexus' in Farok J. Contractor (ed.), *Economic Transformation in Emerging Countries: The Role of Investment, Trade and Finance*, Chapter 5, 59–70; 'Export and Direct Foreign Investment Links: A Three-Country Comparison' in Mordechai E. Kreinin, Michael G. Plummer and Shigeyuki Abe (eds), *Asia-Pacific Economic Linkages*, Chapter 3, 47–64, references; 'Determinants of Inter-Asian Direct Investment Flows' in John H. Dunning (ed.), *Globalization, Trade and Foreign Direct Investment*, Chapter 9, 194–203.

Institute of Southeast Asian Studies for: 'Economic Co-operation After 30 Years of ASEAN', *ASEAN Economic Bulletin*, **14** (2), November, 117–26; '*Ex Post* Estimates of the Effects of the European Single Market Programme on the Exports of Developing Countries', *ASEAN Economic Bulletin*, **15** (2), August, 206–14.

International Economic Journal for: 'Structural Change and Regional Integration in East Asia', **8** (2), Summer, 1–12.

Journal of Economic Integration for: 'Economic Effects of the North American Free-Trade Area on Australia and New Zealand', **9** (1), March, 1–28.

Taylor and Francis for '"Natural" Economic Blocs: An Alternative Formulation', *International Trade Journal*, **VIII** (2), Summer, 193–205.

United Nations for: 'Regional Economic Integration and Dynamic Policy Reform: The "Special" Case of Developing Asia', *Asia-Pacific Development Journal*, **4** (1), 1–26.

Every effort has been made to trace all the copyright holders but if any have been inadvertently overlooked the publishers will be pleased to make the necessary arrangements at the first opportunity.

PART I

INTRODUCTION

[1]

Overview: economic integration and East Asia

Over the past decade, the authors of this volume conducted and published numerous studies concerning the effects of regional economic integration and East Asia. This book contains 14 articles that were deemed by the authors to be representative of their work in this area. It is divided into three parts. Part I consists of an overview of the selected chapters, and a short summary of a forthcoming empirical book to be published by Edward Elgar (Chapter 1); and an historical review of ASEAN economic integration (Chapter 2). Part II includes seven chapters that consider the effect on Asian countries of regional integration in Europe and North America, while Part III contains five chapters dealing with the integration of the Asian economies themselves.

I. Summary of this book

Chapter 2 provides an historical overview of economic integration in Asia, with particular emphasis on ASEAN. Starting with innovative approaches in the 1980s and early 1990s, ASEAN leaders began to develop more ambitious means of economic cooperation, at the same time that political imperatives were declining in importance. This culminated in the creation of the ASEAN Free-Trade Area (AFTA), at the Fourth Summit in 1992. Since then, ASEAN has expanded coverage of AFTA, expedited the liberalization process, and has embarked on deeper regional economic cooperation. Since publication of this chapter, the Asian Currency Crisis of 1997–99 occurred. This financial shock slowed down the movement toward more ambitious regional projects, such as the multilateralization of AFTA tariff cuts, unified investment policies, and agreements on harmonization. However, the implementation of a free-trade area continues apace, and cooperation in other fields resumed in 1999–2000.

As Asian countries have been developing through export-oriented strategies, they have become more sensitive to any developments that could be detrimental to their exports and the inflow of DFI to their economies. Prominent among those concerns are the discriminatory effects of preferential trading arrangements in their key export markets and sources of DFI. The chapters in Part II consider the effects of regional integration in industrial countries on Asia.

Chapter 3 is an *ex-ante* assessment of the effects of the proposed NAFTA, the second enlargement of the EC, and EC-92 (Single Market Program) on ASEAN and South Korea. By matching the commodities exported by ASEAN or South Korea to an integrating market (such as the United States) with those exported to the same market from 'internal' sources (such as Canada) and considering the level tariff and non-tariff barriers on external imports, it identifies the industries that would bear the brunt of the discrimination. Total trade diversion is estimated (as a terms of trade effect) at 4 per cent of ASEAN exports and 5 per cent of South Korean exports to North America; and 8 per cent and 5 per cent of their respective exports to the EC. EC-92 is expected to have further discriminatory influences. The effect of integration on DFI in ASEAN and South Korea is evaluated qualitatively. Chapter 4 essentially repeats the exercise, using the same technique, with respect to the effects of NAFTA on Australia and New Zealand.

Chapter 5 revisits a topic of Chapter 3 by estimating *ex-post* (after the fact) the effect of EC-92 on developing countries. For example, trade diversion can occur by induced internal liberalization in the EC, or enhanced competitiveness of EC firms resulting from the Single Market Program. While the Program directives appeared to be outward-looking in their orientation, developing countries feared that they might lead to considerable trade diversion, a concern that is consistent with the *ex-ante* assessment of Chapter 3. According to our *ex-post* results, EC-92 Directives appear to have had a negative effect on the exports of ASEAN and China, but not on those of the Asian NIEs. As expected, the effects were concentrated in light manufacturing and in electrical machinery. Our estimates are based on control-country and gravity-model approaches.

In contrast to the three earlier chapters that deal directly with formal integration, the next chapter is unique both in this book and in the literature. It assesses the motives for Japanese outward DFI drawing on a comprehensive *private-sector survey* (Toyo Keizai) of Japanese parent companies of foreign subsidiaries. It shows that the reasons behind Japanese DFI outflows are many and varied, with 'securing market share' constituting the most salient motive. Direct foreign investment as a means of avoiding trade frictions is relevant only in outflows to developing countries in five industries, including transportation equipment, machinery, and electronics. As expected, motivations are found to differ between developed and developing host economies.

There follows a chapter on the trade-investment nexus. Between 1973 and 1995 (estimated) annual flows of DFI expanded by over twelve-fold and the annual flows of exports eight-fold. A question that is often posed in the literature is whether DFI is a substitute for exports or, conversely, is it reinforced by, and in turn promotes, exports. Translated into statistical language, the question is whether the correlation between DFI and exports is negative or positive. Chapter 7 shows definitively that this relationship, although complicated, is positive. Rather than being a substitute for trade, DFI and exports are complementary. Given current trends of globalization, it is likely that this relationship will be reinforced over time. Further evidence of this is provided in the subsequent chapter, where we estimate econometrically the trade–investment nexus of three important markets: the United States, Japan, and South Korea. Our regressions in this chapter also provide strong support to the *positive* correlation between trade and DFI and *vice versa*. In both chapters, we ran causality tests between the two variables but failed to discover a unidirectional causal relationship, suggesting that the two variables are determined simultaneously and are mutually reinforcing. Perhaps there exist some underlying variables that are important determinants of both trade and DFI outflows.

Chapter 9 examines the pattern and structure of DFI flows inside East Asia. Such flows have followed a consistent and unidirectional pattern, first from Japan to the NIEs and subsequently from Japan and the NIEs into other less-developed East Asian economies. The regression results suggest that the more similar an East Asian country is to Japan, in terms of its population, openness, and relative wages in the manufacturing sector, the greater will be the flow of investment from Japan to that country. Furthermore, an appreciation of the yen relative to the host country's currency also resulted in greater flows of Japanese DFI to that country. Similar results hold for the NIEs' DFI flows into other Asian countries.

Part III contains five chapters that deal with economic integration in Asia itself. Chapter 10 addresses a general question in the literature of what constitutes a 'natural' economic bloc, a topic that has been discussed extensively in the 1990s. Using Asia as a case study, it offers a new formulation of what has become the traditional definition of a natural regional grouping. Instead of focusing on the total value of intra-regional trade or its share in the region's total trade, it concentrates on the *pattern* of trade prior to integration. Employing revealed-comparative-advantage indices, it assesses the degree to which joining a regional group would distort the ranking of a country's industries by comparative advantage. A 'natural' grouping is one that would preserve the comparative advantage of the constituent countries. It occurs if each country's exports to the world as a whole has a commodity mix similar to its exports to the integrating region. We found that while ASEAN is not a natural bloc in this sense, the whole of East Asia (which include the 'East Asian Economic Caucus' countries) does meet our criterion, though an Asia-Pacific-wide agreement (such as APEC) would be even less distortive.

Chapter 11 uses the same technique to estimate structural change *over time* of individual countries or groups of countries. The results show that: (1) sizable changes in the structural patterns of developing East-Asian trade occurred over the past decade; (2) the manufacturing sector has been restructured at a faster pace than primary commodities; and (3) ASEAN development consists largely of upgrading the industrial structure as against expansion of traditional exports.

There follows a chapter on regional economic integration and dynamic policy reform. It considers the implications of regional economic integration for the outward-oriented development strategy in Asian developing countries. Existing studies strongly underestimate the usefulness of regional economic integration in the development process by ignoring its most important dimensions: the salutary effects obtained through reinforcement of policy reform, as well as the 'dynamic' benefits, are far more important than traditional (static) effects. Hence, regionalism is not merely a 'building block' for unilateral liberalization but also a catalyst for the economic development process. The chapter demonstrates how this 'open regionalism' is being played out in ASEAN and APEC.

Chapter 13 also focuses on policy determinants, but from the perspective of DFI. An outward-oriented development strategy embraces not only trade – as traditionally formulated – but also incoming DFI. In turn, properly directed DFI can be a catalyst for trade reform. This chapter first develops a theoretical model, adopted from the endogenous protection literature, designed to explain how inward DFI can be a liberalizing force for a country's trade policy. Second, this approach is applied to developing Asia, and an empirical analysis of DFI in Asia is undertaken, with a focus on China and South Korea.

In the final chapter, the authors consider the multilateralization of regional preferences in the Asia-Pacific region. Controversies surrounding the desirability of regionalism frequently contrast the economic merits of such an approach with those of nondiscriminatory multilateral liberalization. The chapter focuses on the effectiveness of regionalism as a means of achieving the goal of multilateral trade and investment liberalization in a political-economy model. A series of analytical propositions are developed and applied to the experience of regional groupings within the Asia-Pacific region (ASEAN, Australia–New Zealand, and APEC). The chapter concludes that, rather than being a stumbling block to multilateralism, outward-looking regionalism is an effective stepping-stone towards non-discriminatory global free trade.

II.   Has regionalism delivered for developing countries?

In a book entitled, *Economic Integration and Development: Has Regionalism Delivered for Developing Countries?*, to be published by Edward Elgar in 2001, we cover the following topics: ASEAN Economic Cooperation; MERCOSUR and Other Regional Groupings in the Developing World; Effect of EC-92 and NAFTA on Developing Country Trade Flows; and Effect of EC-92 and NAFTA on Direct Foreign Investment in Developing Countries. In one word, our answer to the questions embodied in the book's title is a qualified 'NO'! What follows is a short summary of the book.

In the last two decades, concern in the developing world over the possibility of trade and investment diversion caused by regional groupings among industrial countries intensified. This was due in part to the potential closing of existing markets, especially in view of the new outward-oriented development strategy that many of these countries began to adopt over this period. In turn, there has been an enhanced tendency towards regionalism in both Europe and North America, where regional groupings are embracing not only industrial but also industrial and developing countries.

Examples are the widening of the EU towards Eastern Europe and its deepening as evidenced by the Single Market Program (EC-92) and the European monetary union; the creation of the Canada–US Free-Trade Area (CUSTA) and the North American Free-Trade Agreement (NAFTA), which for the first time brought together a major developing country and developed countries. In fact, Japan and Korea are the only major countries that have not joined in any regional grouping.[1] This trend has been intensified partly because of the fragility of the WTO, where the 1999 Seattle Ministerial Meeting failed to launch the anticipated Millennium Round. In large measure, this failure was due to US insistence on labor and environmental standards which developing countries, in particular Brazil and India, felt would deprive them of their comparative advantage (as well as infringing on their national sovereignty).

As a counterpart to regional groupings in the developed world, there do exist customs unions and free-trade areas among the developing countries, such as the Common Market of the Southern Cone, or MERCOSUR – a customs union in Latin America – and the ASEAN Free-Trade Area (AFTA), a free-trade area between the ASEAN countries. MERCOSUR consists of Brazil, Argentina, Uruguay, and Paraguay, along with certain special and preferential trading arrangements with other Latin American countries. AFTA was originally composed of six countries (the resource-rich 'ASEAN-4' – Indonesia, Malaysia, the Philippines, and Thailand – Singapore, and Brunei Darussalam); and lately expanded to include Vietnam, Laos, Myanmar – formally Burma – and, eventually, Cambodia. However, these groupings are too small to be considered serious counterweights to the EU and NAFTA. Moreover, their trade and investment orientation is directed outside their respective regions.

For these reasons, there is no concern in industrial countries regarding the impact of regional groupings in the developing world, but the reverse is not true. There is intense concern in the developing countries regarding trade and investment diversion in Europe and North America. During 1997–99, this concern has been exacerbated by the global financial crisis originating in Southeast Asia and spreading elsewhere. The idea that the internal growth effects of the EU and NAFTA will promote imports from the developing countries and offset the diversionary effects is also being widely questioned.

This is the topic to which this book is devoted. In particular, the next two chapters describe the formation and economic implications of ASEAN, MERCOSUR, and other regional groupings. There follows two chapters that address the two questions mentioned in the previous paragraph: (1) the effect of industrial groupings on the developing-country exports; and (2) the impact of industrial groupings on direct foreign investment patterns. We employ a variety of statistical techniques and empirical approaches to assess the aforementioned effects. While studies undertaken in the 1990s examine these questions *ex-ante*, our focus is on what has actually happened, that is, *ex-post* analysis.

In short, what we found is a significant amount of trade diversion in specific manufacturing categories, in particular, electronics. These are commodities that constitute an increasing share of Asian exports. The negative effect of the Single Market Act appears to be stronger than that of NAFTA. With respect to direct foreign investment, the data do not permit us to reach a definite conclusion. However, we could not discern any diversionary effect to justify the concern of developing-country observers.

It is because of the trade impact that we offer a qualified 'no' to the question raised in the title of this book. It would appear that developing countries have an abiding interest in minimizing discrimination against them. And that can be accomplished only in the context of WTO negotiating rounds. Hence, it is not only the industrial countries that have an interest in a Millennium Round concentrating on services, agriculture, and investment questions. Rather, developing countries have at least an equal if not greater interest in participating actively in negotiations on liberalizing commodity trade. The Seattle fiasco was a failure not only from the point of view of the United States – though it is often portrayed as such in the press – but also from the point of view of the developing world.

In past years, economists have urged developing countries to participate actively in GATT/WTO negotiations, rather than rely on 'free' concessions exchanged between the industrial countries, for that is the only way they could achieve trade liberalization in products of export interest to them. Now we add another reason to emphasize their stakes in global negotiations: to minimize the discriminatory impact of the regional movements, even though such a movement is probably here to stay.

If these conclusions are correct, then why was the answer given in the first sentence a *qualified* 'no'? Because regional integration occurs not only among industrial countries but also among developing countries. Indeed, Chapters 2 and 3 survey in detail the two major preferential trading arrangements in the developing world: MERCOSUR, a customs union, and AFTA, a free-trade area. Here evidence of the effects on trade and investment flows are scanty in the main because not many studies have been devoted to the topic, and too few years have elapsed since the inauguration of these new regional arrangements. Such as it is, there is *ex-ante* evidence to suggest trade creation by AFTA, although that was not borne out by preliminary *ex-post* data analysis. Likewise, MERCOSUR was probably responsible for changes in trade flows, but in certain areas (such as automobiles) these changes appear to have been due to trade diversion. This is because the common external tariff in these sectors was high and actually increased recently.

In this sense, the ASEAN and MERCOSUR experiences are quite different. Most ASEAN countries began a comprehensive liberalization of their trade regimes in the mid to late 1980s, and AFTA was superimposed upon a liberalized regime. In other words, AFTA was a regional expression of an export-oriented development strategy that had been recently adopted by its member-countries. By contrast, in certain sectors, the MERCOSUR customs union was superimposed upon an import-substitution strategy and, therefore, intensified discrimination against outsiders. In these areas, trade diversion could easily swamp any trade-creating benefits of liberalization in other sectors.

The conclusion to be drawn from this experience is that regional integration between developing countries is welfare-enhancing only if it is outward-looking and minimizes discrimination against outsiders.

In sum, this book leads to three important policy conclusions. First, in designing preferential trading arrangements, developed countries should recognize and try to minimize the possible adverse effect on developing countries that might result from discrimination. Second, the developing countries have an abiding interest in the success of WTO negotiations that would minimize the discriminatory impact upon them of regional groupings in Europe and North America. And third, any customs unions or free-trade areas among the developing countries themselves should be outward-looking if they are to enhance the welfare of developing countries.

Note
1. This will likely change in the future because: (1) Japan and Korea are both members of APEC, and it is not clear yet if the 'Bogor Vision' of open trade and investment in APEC by 2010 (2020 for developing countries) will be nondiscriminatory; and (2) Japan and Korea are currently exploring the feasibility of a bilateral free-trade area.

[2]

Economic Co-operation after 30 Years of ASEAN

Seiji F. Naya
Michael G. Plummer

ASEAN has made remarkable strides in economic co-operation since its very humble beginnings. Starting with bold and innovative approaches in the late 1980s and early 1990s, ASEAN leaders began to develop more ambitious means of economic co-operation, at the same time that political/diplomatic imperatives were falling in importance. This culminated in the creation of an ASEAN Free Trade Area (AFTA) at the Fourth Summit in 1992. Since then, ASEAN has expanded coverage of AFTA, expedited the liberalization process, and has embarked on deeper regional economic integration accords. While many of these latter initiatives are only now being developed, they are indicative of the intentions of the ASEAN leaders to create a unified marketplace in a wider Southeast Asian region.

I. Introduction and Overview

Exactly 30 years ago, ASEAN leaders created what was to become the most vibrant regional grouping in the developing world on the eve of the new millennium. ASEAN continues to confound the critics and pessimists by reaching ever-higher levels of economic co-operation. The "deepening" of ASEAN economic integration, which began in 1992 with the creation of the ASEAN Free Trade Area (AFTA), is now being complemented by substantial "widening": in July 1995, ASEAN's former nemesis, Vietnam, joined the grouping, and in July 1997, so did Laos and Myanmar, with Cambodia temporarily on the sidelines. Hence, ASEAN has grown to comprise all of Southeast Asia and is moving in fits and

starts to reach its ultimate goal of a united, integrated Southeast Asian marketplace.

To attain its current state of integration and prosperity, ASEAN has had to overcome many political/diplomatic and economic obstacles. In our March 1991 lead article of the *ASEAN Economic Bulletin*, we suggested that there were four major economic policy challenges facing ASEAN:

First, the most effective, and in the long run the most promising, path to economic development in ASEAN is for all countries to continue to pursue trade and investment liberalization policies at the national level. ... Second, ASEAN member-states, individually and as a group, should continue to pursue their interests at the Uruguay Round of GATT. ... Third, while ASEAN should continue to press for "first-best" solutions by

9

promoting international trade and investment liberalization, ASEAN can supplement this process by expanding more vigorously its intra-regional trade and investment links to pool markets and resources and stimulate economic growth. ... Fourth, ASEAN can continue to explore economic co-operation agreements with its trading partners, based on the concept of open regionalism, i.e. agreements which do not cement ASEAN into various trade blocs. (Naya and Plummer 1991, pp. 271–73)

We thought that this agenda was, in fact, a fairly ambitious one, and while it may seem uncontroversial today, it certainly was deemed so at the time of its writing (1989–90). ASEAN economic co-operation had not developed significantly and many scholars felt it couldn't (because of the dominance of politics in the Association) or that it shouldn't (due to the potential effects of trade diversion in a region characterized by low levels of intra-regional trade). We were even warned at this time that our policy-advising work for ASEAN officials would lose its credibility if we used the term "free-trade area", for this would conjure up fears of a fledgling European Community (EC) with its strong supranational bureaucracy and common market. An additional argument against formal regional co-operation was that preoccupation with intra-ASEAN integration would detract from its efforts in the far-from-finished Uruguay Round.

Instead, the ASEAN leaders exceeded these challenges; in many ways, the Fourth Summit in January 1992 went even further than what we dared recommend. Trade and investment liberalization continues to deepen in the region, and additional co-operative measures taken at the Fifth Summit in December 1995 are providing fresh momentum. The Uruguay Round was concluded successfully in 1994 and the World Trade Organization (WTO) Ministerial Meetings — the first of which was held in Singapore in December 1996 — are targeting liberalization in important sectors. Hence, while a free-trade area in ASEAN was derided as being impossible a short time ago, the creation of AFTA in 1992 and "AFTA Plus" arrangements taking off beginning in 1995 testify

to the great strides made in economic integration based on "open regionalism" in ASEAN. These changes signal a new era.

As deepening and widening take place in Southeast Asia, more complicated problems will no doubt arise. Moreover, this intensification of economic integration in ASEAN is taking place at an important time in the history of Southeast Asian development: former centrally-planned Mekong countries are rapidly changing to market-based economies, and the original ASEAN countries are hitting possible bottlenecks along the road to economic development, as evidenced by the growth slowdown, financial difficulties, and currency problems of 1997 in some of the member states. But while the challenges to economic integration are considerable, so are the potential rewards. ASEAN has made the decision to push forward jointly; market-driven processes and economic integration policies such as AFTA will reinforce the interdependence of the region.

The purpose of this Special Anniversary Issue of the *ASEAN Economic Bulletin* is to take stock of accomplishments in ASEAN and suggest how new theoretical and conceptual breakthroughs in the international economics, international relations, and business literature can contribute to the future of ASEAN economic integration and development. While we cannot hope to cover all relevant developments in these disciplines, a number of key areas are highlighted. Contributors include some of the most prolific and influential scholars on ASEAN economic development and integration.

In this introductory chapter, we first survey progress made in terms of ASEAN economic integration to date with a eye on the future, including recent economic co-operation initiatives, membership expansion, and other developments. This hopefully will provide sufficient background information to give an up-to-date overview of how ASEAN economic co-operation has progressed and where it stands today. In Section III, we review briefly individual contributions to this special issue and end with some concluding remarks.

II. ASEAN Economic Cooperation at the Turn of the Century

ASEAN economic integration started modestly in the mid-1970s with the first two ASEAN Summits. At that time, political instability in the region was the driving force behind ASEAN, and it has been argued that much of the attraction of regional economic integration was merely its use as a "cover" for political co-operation, in particular, *vis-à-vis* instability in Indochina (see Morrison, this issue). First attempts at co-operation in trade — the Preferential Trading Arrangement (PTA) — were piecemeal and voluntary; they began with a product-by-product approach to integration which allowed for the exclusion of almost all items that would be important in stimulating trade. Even improvements in the PTA to embrace an across-the-board approach and deepen margins of preferences were not sufficient to increase intra-regional trade.

Industrial co-operation was even more modest. The first programme established to promote industrial co-operation was called ASEAN Industrial Projects (AIPs). These projects were designed as government-owned entities based on the premise of an "import-substitution" approach to economic development, which had been hitherto followed by many ASEAN countries. Not surprisingly, AIPs were slow to develop; in fact, only several are in existence today, and they originated as national projects. The ASEAN Industrial Complementation (AIC) scheme was developed to support vertical integration of industrial production in ASEAN, but it was stagnant until the "Brand-to-Brand Complementation" (BBC) scheme was created. The BBC is devoted to the automobile industry and has had some success, but only in this industry and with Japanese joint ventures. The ASEAN Industrial Joint Ventures (AIJVs) were more flexible and became far more attractive (and less bureaucratic) over time, but by the early 1990s, the number of AIJVs had been very disappointing to ASEAN leaders.

Modest though they were, these initial agreements were essential to the creation of a strong base on which to build deeper ASEAN economic integration. In the mid-1970s, the import-substitution orientation of ASEAN governments probably would have led the region to adopt the same kind of regional economic integration programmes popular in Latin America, where regional economic integration was used as a means of furthering their (often extreme) inward-looking paradigms. These all failed. If ASEAN had moved too quickly in terms of regional economic integration, economic co-operation in Southeast Asia would have likely met the same fate. In fact, the consequences may have even been worse, as the over-riding political imperative in ASEAN, whose nation-states — unlike in Latin America — were young, could have been negatively affected by a poorly-developed economic co-operation agenda.

Many scholars who have criticized the gradualism of economic co-operation in ASEAN frequently fail to understand the need for a go-slow approach at the time. The "ASEAN Way" is one of consensus; the regional organization was only able to move forward when all countries were ready. Thus, when economic shocks in the mid-1980s and other developments pushed inward-looking countries to accept the logic of an outward-oriented development strategy, the region was ready to consider new avenues of "deep" integration. Moreover, the diminished external threat allowed ASEAN to concentrate fully on economic issues and integration. Moreover, regional economic integration in key ASEAN export markets (North America and Europe) in the late 1980s and early 1990s threatened the region with possible trade and investment diversion, underscoring the need to render ASEAN countries more competitive. ASEAN economic integration could be used as one means to achieve this.

Deepening of ASEAN Economic Integration

Since the Fourth Summit in January 1992, ASEAN economic integration has progressed on a number of fronts. In addition to the more traditional elements of a preferential trading arrangement, it has expanded into a number of important areas characteristic of the most highly-developed regional integration accords. Many of these areas are just being developed and, no doubt, it will take a long time before a truly-integrated ASEAN market is realized.

1. ASEAN Free Trade Area

As the ASEAN countries adopted outward-oriented development strategies in the late 1980s and early 1990s, they became more dependent on the international marketplace and vicissitudes therein. Hence, the threat of protectionism in Western markets, as well as the emergence of new, competitive developing countries such as China, served to generate interest on the part of the ASEAN countries as to which vehicles could be used to increase the attractiveness, efficiency, and competitiveness of ASEAN countries. The positive elements of the European experience showed what might be gained from closer economic integration; however, the small-size and "openness" of the ASEAN markets (that is, the high proportion of trade with extra-regional partners relative to GDP) suggested that an inward-looking trade bloc would not be useful. Hence, ASEAN leaders sought to create a closely integrated market in which multinational corporations and domestic firms could minimize transactions costs. This required keeping ASEAN outward-looking in every sense. ASEAN countries have not wavered in this commitment, be it in APEC, where they have led the push for "open regionalism", or in the WTO, to which they are firmly committed.

The first, significant leap in this direction came with the agreement to form AFTA in January 1992 at the Fourth Summit. Rather than overly-commit to regional integration in sensitive areas, the Fourth Summit kept the scope and nature of AFTA somewhat ambiguous and only manufacturing categories were to be included in its 15-year transition plan. Since then, the ASEAN leaders have increased the scope of coverage to essentially all goods and shortened the period of implementation, such that AFTA should be fully implemented by 2003 (2006 for Vietnam), and there are proposals to speed up the process even further (for example to 2000 for most goods).

Moreover, the Philippines has tabled a proposal, backed by Singapore and Indonesia, that would allow any regional liberalization to be also extended to outsiders, thereby "MFNizing" cuts within AFTA and minimizing (or abolishing completely) trade diversion, whose costs, after all, fall primarily on the host market.

AFTA is to be implemented through cuts under the Common Effective Preferential Tariff (CEPT) scheme, in which tariffs on all manufactured and processed agricultural goods are to be brought down to 0–5 per cent within the 2003 time frame.[1] All quantitative restrictions and other non-tariff barriers are also scheduled to be abolished. While ASEAN countries were given several years before they were required to begin reducing tariffs, a Fast Track Programme, initially covering tariffs in 15 product groups and accounting for almost 40 per cent of ASEAN trade, was created under which tariffs were to be brought down to less than 5 per cent before 2000.

In 1995, the share of CEPT products in intra-ASEAN exports was high at 82 per cent, and while the share of intra-ASEAN exports in total exports accounted for only 20 per cent that year, intra-ASEAN CEPT exports grew at an annual rate of 19 per cent, from US$57 billion in 1994 to US$56 billion in 1995.[2] Any exclusions from the CEPT list are intended to be temporary. The rules of origin on CEPT products is an across-the-board 40 per cent, less than certain sectors in some other free-trade areas such as NAFTA in which, for example, the rules of origin on automotive trade is 62.5 per cent.

ASEAN has been trying to expedite the inclusion of CEPT products in order to ensure that AFTA will be realized in a short period of time. This is to reassure businesspeople that ASEAN is dedicated to reducing transactions costs, as well as to keep "one step ahead" of other regional initiatives such as APEC. In fact, the Green Lane System for CEPT Products, launched at the Fifth ASEAN Summit, has substantially improved the clearance of intra-ASEAN preferential trade; for example, reviews in Malaysia and Thailand showed that processing time for CEPT products were reduced by 60 per cent and 40 per cent, respectively, compared to non-CEPT products.[3]

In short, AFTA is well on the way to full implementation by 2003. In fact, by the year 2000, ASEAN will already be a significantly-integrated market. However, the ASEAN leaders have also noted the importance of trade facilitation measures to complement trade liberalization, and they have been working to improve the co-ordination and co-operation in the general field of international trade and investment. Though more difficult to quantify, these trade facilitation and "non-border" measures can be even more important than trade liberalization. We discuss a number of such items in which ASEAN has been active below.

2. ASEAN Industrial Co-operation Scheme and Investment Promotion

Direct foreign investment (DFI) inflows are often paramount to an outward-looking development strategy (see Montes, this issue). DFI brings in new (non-debt creating) capital flows, foreign exchange, easy access to foreign markets, and technology transfer. Increasingly, ASEAN countries have been placing a stronger emphasis on technology transfer in their multilateral and bilateral relationships. Evidence of this is ubiquitous, from the preponderance of requests for technical assistance in development aid and co-operation programmes to the "virtuous cycle" of policy liberalization stemming from the desire to promote DFI capital inflows as a means of private-sector led technology transfer. Regional economic integration accords such as AFTA can promote DFI inflows through reductions in transactions costs (be they border- or non-border in origin). In doing so, they establish an attractive business environment within which multinationals can easily profit from a vertical division of labour, as well as facilitating the emergence of multinationals within the developing region itself. In fact, some have argued that the most important benefit of AFTA is not its effects on trade but rather its ability to attract more DFI to the region at a time when competition for such flows is increasing (Ariff 1996 and Petri, this issue).

As ASEAN countries developed increasingly outward-oriented development strategies, they placed a higher emphasis on luring DFI. Hence the greater perceived need for such schemes as the BBC and the AIJV. However, with the advent of AFTA, industrial co-operation in these areas is becoming less important, as their main attraction has been greater margin of preferences granted on intra-regional trade. Cognizant of this, the ASEAN leaders created the ASEAN Industrial Co-operation (AICO) Scheme, which offers more in terms of tariff (0–5 per cent) and non-tariff incentives.[4] Operationalized in November 1996, it is based on CEPT commodities and is designed to promote inward investment in technology-based industries. It is essentially an intermediate step giving favoured industries a "head start" in attracting DFI before the full implementation of AFTA.[5] The AICO is part of an on-going process within ASEAN to create an ASEAN Investment Area (AIA), the details of which are being developed at the time of this writing.

Thus, the AICO and the AIA are new concepts but constitute vital components of the efforts within ASEAN to create a more attractive business environment. Moreover, the extent to and facility with which foreign investment is allowed into one ASEAN country will affect the others, as the concept of the AIA underscores the "public good" nature of investment laws in the region. In September 1996, the ASEAN countries created the The ASEAN Agreement for the Promotion and Protection of Investments, which includes the simplification of investment procedures and approval processes, as well as enhanced transparency and predictability of DFI laws.[6]

3. Other Initiatives

In order to take advantage of new technologies, developing countries are finding that they must establish strong intellectual property protection laws and means of enforcement. Without an attractive, stable environment in which multinationals can operate and in which domestic firms can invest in new innovations, the process of technology transfer is significantly inhibited. Moreover, lack of effective intellectual property laws and implementation has often caused frictions with developed countries. For example, when ASEAN countries appear on the U.S. "watch list" under Super 301, it is usually because of intellectual-property-related issues. Formal regional co-operation agreements can help in creating a strong underlying framework for the protection of intellectual property and "peer pressure" in the implementation of associated laws.

In December 1995, the ASEAN countries agreed to the ASEAN Framework Agreement on Intellectual Property Co-operation. This Agreement commits ASEAN countries to strengthening co-operation in protecting intellectual property and creating ASEAN standards and practices which are consistent with international standards, and in doing so promote technological innovation and the transfer and dissemination of technology.[7] The Agreement also notes that ASEAN countries should explore the possibility of setting up an ASEAN trademark system, including an ASEAN Patent Office, in which ASEAN countries could promote region-wide protection of patents.

The EU's Single Market programme in the EU was aimed largely at integration in "non-border" areas. Perhaps one of the most important areas of European co-operation can be classified under the rubric of "harmonization issues", such as in product testing, professional certification, standards conformance, and so forth. ASEAN countries are characterized by greater diversity in these areas than the EU, not only because of the colonial history of the region (that ended up reflecting varied European differences plus the addition of others) but also because nation-state building has often meant taking pride in creating such differences.

In the area of "harmonization", which is a critical area of trade facilitation, ASEAN has created a (non-binding) Memorandum of Understanding Concerning Co-operation on Standards and Conformance and the ASEAN Agreement on Customs, including harmonization of tariff nomenclature, customs valuations, and customs procedures. These are the first steps in a long process; while many of the related items are included in developed-country agreements such as the EU, they are rare in developing-country regional accords and are often difficult to find in comprehensive agreements such as the North American Free Trade Agreement (NAFTA).

As countries develop, the role of the services sector becomes increasingly important, both in terms of its share of total output/employment and in its complementary, symbiotic relationships with other sectors. For example, while often thought of as an agricultural and industrial giant, the United States is overwhelmingly dependent on the services sector, which accounts for approximately 80 per cent of GDP. The important role of services is also highlighted by the General Agreement on Trade and Services (which emerged from the Uruguay Round), subsequent discussions on formulating framework agreements in financial and information services, and the important role placed on services in modern free-trade areas.

Realizing the emerging importance of services to ASEAN economic co-operation — and the commitment at the Fourth Summit to pursue co-operation in "non-border" areas — ASEAN countries agreed to an ASEAN Framework on Services in December 1995 and a Ministerial Understanding on ASEAN Co-operation in Finance in March 1997. With respect to the Framework on Services, member states dedicated themselves to strengthening existing co-operative efforts in services sectors and developing co-operation in areas not covered by existing agreements. This included, *inter alia*, establishing or improving infrastructural facilities; joint production, marketing, and purchasing arrangements; research and development; and exchange of information.[8] It also commits ASEAN countries in a "substantial number of sectors over a reasonable period of time" to eliminate existing discriminatory measures and market access limitations among member states, and prohibits new or more discriminatory measures and access limitations. Finally, it takes the first steps towards outlining "mutual recognition" in services.

Until the 1990s, scholars implicitly assumed that "real" economic integration through free-trade areas and common markets could be separated from "financial" economic integration (Plummer, this issue). This is not the case in the contemporary economic system. The EU discovered that creating a truly integrated market required closer co-operation in the area of finance and macroeconomics, especially exchange rates. The Mexican Peso Crisis, which exploded the year that NAFTA was implemented, was a reminder of the need to stress the role of stable financial and macro policies along with the real sector. ASEAN countries have been slowly embarking on means to strengthen regional co-operation by bringing in the financial sector. The Ministerial Understanding on ASEAN Co-operation in Finance (March 1997) sets out the broad goals of co-operation in diverse areas of finance and macroeconomics, including banking, capital markets, insurance matters, taxation and public finance, as well as exchanging information on developments affecting ASEAN countries in various multilateral and regional organizations.

While the agreements on services and finance are ambitious, in reality they have had little time to develop and, in fact, much needs to be done before they reach the same level of co-operation as the real sector. Nevertheless, negotiations on tourism and telecommunications were to be concluded by July 1997, while financial services, maritime transport, air transport, construction and the business services sector are scheduled to be completed by end-December 1998.

As noted above, the key to ASEAN's success has been the stress placed on diplomatic harmony and peace. In fact, AFTA would have never materialized if the ASEAN leaders and lower-level government officials had not created previously an atmosphere of trust and ease of dialogue. ASEAN meetings are often characterized as highly "amicable", but this has been a long-established and delicately-balanced tradition. If ASEAN economic co-operation initiatives were to generate strong ill feelings between member states such that bilateral relations were strained, this could be highly detrimental to regional development and the basic over-riding objectives of ASEAN.

Therefore, as economic deepening proceeds, the need for a dispute settlement mechanism beyond that existing at the WTO is important. The Protocol on Dispute Settlement Mechanism (20 November 1996) develops such an approach, in which it outlines: coverage and application, establishment and functions of a panel, treatment of panel results, the appeal process, compensation, and the maximum time frame. The specifics of the dispute settlement mechanism still need to be worked out; however, the framework has been established as a first, important step in the process.

In sum, beginning in the early 1990s, economic deepening in ASEAN picked up considerable momentum and continues to flow into new areas. Uncertainties arising in mid-1997 may pose a challenge to the speed of integration. Still, ASEAN countries have committed themselves to outward-oriented development, and regional economic integration forms a part of this strategy. The region has learned that the costs of import-substitution are, indeed, high; no country seems poised to turn back the clock. This commitment to outward-oriented development explains the preoccupation in ASEAN with "open regionalism" in AFTA as well as in APEC. Trade diversion may benefit specific industries under certain conditions and, arguably, for a short period of time. But from an economy-wide perspective it is costly to the host (import-receiving) country, which ends up paying more for its imports, and creates distortions in partner countries. Inward-looking policies, at the national and regional level, cannot be consistent with overall economic liberalization and, in fact, put a country at a disadvantage in international competition. Open regionalism, then, is seen more as a necessity than an ideal.

Widening of ASEAN

In July 1995, Vietnam became the newest member of ASEAN, the first expansion of the grouping in over 10 years. As part of ASEAN, Vietnam is the second largest member in terms of population but has by far the lowest per capita GDP and, as a "transitional economy", is faced with tremendous policy challenges in approaching the ASEAN norm. Laos and Myanmar joined ASEAN in July

1997, and once Cambodia also accedes, the Southeast Asian economic space will be completed. But this will add even more difficulties to the grouping in terms of economic divergence (see Langhammer, this issue).

Vietnam's accession to ASEAN has important real as well as symbolic value, since ASEAN was created in many ways as an organization opposed to Vietnam. A main motivation for allowing Vietnam to accede is this political importance; however, Vietnam is a large and potentially dynamic country which could well complement ASEAN's factor endowments. From Vietnam's perspective and that of the other acceding Mekong countries, the accession to ASEAN reflects a key component of their emerging economic reform strategies: that of integrating into the global marketplace. As part of ASEAN, Vietnam will find it easier to join APEC and the WTO. While Vietnam still has a long way to go before its external trade, investment, and related policies will satisfy the requirements of the WTO, the push being given by ASEAN membership and the rigours imposed on it in order to meet AFTA are leading the country in this direction. The same will no doubt be true of the other Mekong countries, even though the exact conditions and arrangements are not yet known for their accessions.

The embrace of the Mekong countries completes an important goal for ASEAN in that it settles the issue of economic widening and essentially closes the question of expansion: the ASEAN 10 comprises all of Southeast Asia and it is unlikely that, at least geographically, other countries could join. This presents both a comfort and a challenge: a comfort, in that ASEAN, unlike the EU or NAFTA, has completed its boundaries (once Cambodia is fully on board) and it can begin to work on deepening integration; a challenge, in that these new countries have a long way to go in order to have economic systems and markets consistent with the rest of ASEAN.

A number of additional questions arise from ASEAN's perspective. First, ASEAN is now embarking on by far its most ambitious economic deepening initiatives. Is this the right time to

handle simultaneously the widening issues? The EU did not agree to its Third Enlargement (that is the accessions of Austria, Finland, and Sweden) until its Single Market Programme was essentially complete, and it appears to be avoiding concrete steps in favour of the applications of Central and Eastern European countries until Phase III of Economic and Monetary Union.[9] Second, is the region ready to deal with the complications associated with a "two-tier" ASEAN? Third, to what degree will ASEAN's acceptance of countries with controversial political regimes affect its role in the international community?

In short, the decision to expand to 9 was not an easy one. In doing so, the ASEAN countries committed themselves to the long-run responsibility of helping the Mekong countries stabilize their respective domestic economies, establish markets, and integrate them into the subregional, regional, and international economic systems. Efforts along these lines will vary from general co-operation, such as sharing of development experiences, exchanging macroeconomic information, and inviting these countries to trade fairs, to more technical assistance, such as AFTA-related customs procedures and codes, data gathering, investment measures consistent with ASEAN practices, and so on. The ASEAN-Mekong Basin Development initiative is an integral part of this process. In this sense, the relatively-developed ASEAN countries will be engaging in "technical co-operation between developing countries" (TCDC) *par excellence* and will need strong support in the process. After all, a stable and prosperous Mekong region is not only an ASEAN dream but a global one as well.

III. Summary of the Volume's Contributions

This Special Issue will address many of the questions outlined above. It is mainly interested in addressing the conceptual and theoretical-rather than empirical-issues associated with economic deepening, ASEAN enlargement, and regional economic development. The issue begins with a short survey by Dato' Ajit Singh, the first ASEAN Secretary General, of the policy issues associated with the ASEAN Enlargement to include the Mekong countries. In addition to highlighting many of the challenges and opportunities associated with the creation of an ASEAN 10, he calls on the academic community to assist ASEAN in developing its economic reform agenda.

Hal Hill of the Australian National University begins the academic contributions with a survey of the origins and determinants of rapid economic growth in ASEAN. In addition to reviewing the large and growing literature related to economic growth, he considers the experiences of individual ASEAN countries from a political-economy perspective. He concludes that the ASEAN countries succeeded in adopting correct development policies more than anywhere else outside East Asia by focusing on macroeconomic orthodoxy and openness. Next, Charles Morrison of the East-West Center explores the origins of ASEAN economic co-operation from an international-relations perspective. In particular he considers issues of incentives for integration in Southeast Asia and political-economic co-operation in the context of wider regional groupings, such as APEC. Rolf Langhammer of the Kiel Institute of World Economics focuses explicitly on difficulties associated with the integration of the Mekong countries into ASEAN. He assesses how long and under what conditions the newly-acceding member states will be able to "catch up" to the rest of ASEAN, using the example of the European Union and its proposed expansion to include Central and Eastern European countries as a yardstick. Manuel Montes of the Institute of Southeast Asian Studies (ISEAS) considers the important issue of direct foreign investment and technology transfer in ASEAN, and stresses the usefulness of economic co-operation as a catalyst.

The last two contributions by Peter Petri and Michael Plummer, both of Brandeis University, relate explicitly to regional economic integration in the more traditional sense. Petri considers ASEAN economic co-operation as an economic policy strategy parallel to — rather than in competition with — economic liberalization under APEC and the WTO, with a stress on the importance of open regionalism. He develops a computational general equilibrium model with the additional characteristic of direct foreign investment to highlight the potential gains from various regional configurations. Plummer surveys developments in the theory of regional economic integration and applies them to the case of ASEAN economic deepening and widening.

As the premier journal dedicated to Southeast Asian economic integration and development issues, the *ASEAN Economic Bulletin* continues to be an important forum for the exchange of ideas. Moreover, its parent institution, ISEAS, is at the cutting-edge of research into new issues and challenges facing the region. In this sense, ISEAS has played an important role as catalyst of ASEAN economic development and co-operation. As we celebrate 30 years of ASEAN, we should also recognize ISEAS for its contributions to the region's success. ASEAN counts many hard-earned diplomatic and economic victories during its existence and in doing so has supported the goals of peace and prosperity, not only for its citizens but also for the world. Challenges await the region in the next millennium which are no less daunting; we will continue to count on ISEAS as a central "think-tank" to facilitate the exchange of research and ideas as well as to generate its own contributions to the academic, policy-making, and private-sector-based communities.

NOTES

This opening survey was written in part while Michael Plummer was visiting at the Research Institute of Economics and Business Administration at Kobe University. The authors would like to acknowledge their appreciation for the financial assistance of Kobe University, the United Nations Development Programme, and the Japan Foundation's Center for Global Partnership. Chia Siow Yue and Joseph Tan offered excellent advice at all stages of this project; Yuri Muraguchi provided stellar research assistance, and the staff at the *ASEAN Economic Bulletin* was extremely competent and patient in helping us put together the finishing touches on this Special Issue.

1. *AFTA Reader*, March 1995.
2. *Joint Press Statement*, The Tenth ASEAN Council Meeting, 11 September 1996.
3. Ibid.
4. ASEAN Secretariat, *ASEAN Industrial Co-operation Scheme*, 1997.
5. Ibid.
6. *Protocol to Amend the Agreement* among the ASEAN Countries, Jakarta, 12 September 1996.
7. *ASEAN Framework Agreement on Intellectual Property Co-operation*, Bangkok, 15 December 1995.
8. *ASEAN Framework Agreement on Services*, Bangkok, 15 December 1995.
9. Certainly, waiting to bring on board selected Central and Eastern European countries is a function of other things as well, including which countries should be accepted. But this is exactly the point: the complications implicit in the decision to include new countries at highly-variable levels of economic development compared to the EU (see Langhammer, this issue) when it is placing a priority on Monetary Union are great.

Seiji F. Naya is Director, Department of Economic Development, Business, and Tourism, State of Hawaii, and Professor of Economics, University of Hawaii at Manoa. **Michael G. Plummer** is Assistant Professor of Economics, Brandeis University.

PART II

EFFECTS OF ECONOMIC INTEGRATION IN INDUSTRIAL COUNTRIES ON ASIA

World Development, Vol. 20, No. 9, pp. 1345–1366, 1992.
Printed in Great Britain.

Effects of Economic Integration in Industrial Countries on ASEAN and the Asian NIEs

MORDECHAI E. KREININ
Michigan State University, East Lansing, Michigan

and

MICHAEL G. PLUMMER*
*Monterey Institute of International Studies, Monterey, California, and
East-West Center, Honolulu, Hawaii*

Summary. — This paper assesses the effect of the proposed North American Free Trade Area, the second enlargement of the European Community (EC) and EC-1992 on Association of Southeast Asian Nations (ASEAN) and South Korea. By matching the commodities exported by ASEAN or South Korea to an integrating market (such as the United States) with those exported to the same market from "internal" sources (such as Canada), it identifies the industries that would bear the brunt of the discrimination. Total trade diversion is estimated (as a terms-of-trade effect) at 4% of ASEAN exports and 5% of South Korean exports to North America; and 8 and 5% of their respective exports to the EC. EC-1992 is expected to have further discriminatory influences. The effect of integration on direct foreign investment in ASEAN and South Korea is also evaluated.

1. INTRODUCTION

With the advent of the unified European market (EC 1992) and the US-Canada free trade area (FTA), there is an ever-increasing discourse about "regionalization" of the world trading system. In Europe, the European Community (EC) may expand in future years to incorporate the European Free-Trade Association (EFTA) countries, and even Eastern Europe, perhaps in a looser form of association. In North America, the US-Canada FTA is likely to have adverse trade-diversionary effects on Mexico (Weintraub, 1990), leading it to seek an FTA with the United States, thereby creating a North American FTA. Moreover, President Bush has even raised the notion of a hemisphere-wide FTA, however remote this possibility may be. These developments,[1] along with the US-Israel FTA and the US-Caribbean Basin initiative, discriminate against other parts of the world, such as Asia, and may lead the countries of East Asia to form a regional bloc of their own. The possible evolution of a tripolar world is a source of concern in some quarters, seen as a rival to the General Agreement on Trade and Tariffs (GATT) system of multilateral trade.

This paper investigates one component of these "building blocks," namely the impact of regional integration among industrial nations on the six Association of Southeast Asian Nations (ASEAN) countries — Malaysia, Indonesia, Thailand, the Philippines, Singapore, and Brunei Darussalam[2] — and on South Korea.[3] ASEAN was established as a regional organization by the Bangkok Declaration of 1967, originally composed of five countries and enlarged to six with the inclusion of Brunei Darussalam in 1984. While ASEAN is best known for its cooperation in the diplomatic realm, it introduced a series of economic cooperation programs in the mid-1970s. These programs have been enhanced and expanded in recent years. But economic cooperation remains at a rudimentary level, consisting of preferential trading arrangements (PTAs) and

*The authors are grateful to the East-West Center for financial support and the International Business Center of Michigan State University for a supplemental grant. They wish to thank the seminar participants of the Institute for Economic Development and Policy (East-West Center), Richard Pomfret, and anonymous referees for their useful comments, Sherry Bushnell for superb computational assistance, and Cynthia Nakachi for her excellent clerical assistance. Final revision accepted: March 31, 1992.

some industrial cooperation programs. The agreements fell well short of an FTA, until an ASEAN FTA was agreed to at the Fourth Summit in January 1992.

In the 1980s, all ASEAN countries, as well as South Korea, have experienced economic growth based on an outward-looking development strategy. Policies of trade liberalization and export promotion, as well as measures to attract direct foreign investment, have been implemented, leading to a boom in international trade and investment, particularly in manufactures. Success of this policy depends on reasonably free access to the markets of industrial countries; hence, changes in the global trading environment are of great significance to them.

Based on the theory of economic integration, we can expect the Asian countries to be affected in several important ways by regional groupings among industrial countries:

(a) Trade diversion, the extent of which depends on the degree to which commodity exports to an integrating country (such as the United States) overlaps that of a partner country (e.g., Canada), and on the degree of discrimination against outsiders in the "overlapping," or "matched," commodities. The price elasticity of import demand would in part determine the amount of third country or "external" exports excluded by the discrimination.

(b) Investment diversion, as domestic and foreign investment shift away from East Asia and to countries within an FTA or a customs union zone. This effect would be particularly pronounced in industries sustaining acute trade diversion.

(c) A positive indirect dynamic effect, as the growth rate in the integrating area accelerates because of expanded market size. Thus, if market unification increases the annual growth rate of the EC or North America by, say, 0.5% per year, then imports into the regional grouping would rise, the size of the increase depending on the income elasticity of import demand. Along with other sources, Asian exports to the EC also would expand. But that effect may be offset in whole or in part by the dynamic counterpart of trade diversion, which implies shrinkage of the Asian market as its exports contract.

(d) Other effects resulting from special features of the Unified European market and the North American FTA.

Table 1 offers a bird's-eye view of the Asian economies considered in this study. Their combined Gross Domestic Product (GDP) in 1989 was $480 billion, of which $268 billion was accounted for by the ASEAN group. Per capita GDP was $471–$10,582 per year (excluding Brunei), while their annual growth rate were 1.3–10% over the past decade. Clearly, the group includes first-tier newly industrializing economies (NIEs) (South Korea and Singapore) and second-tier NIEs (Thailand and Malaysia). With the exception of the Philippines, these are rapidly growing economies. The composition of their output reflects movement of resources out of agriculture and into manufacturing and services, a typical feature of dynamic economies. A substantial part of their exports is destined for North America and Europe, and thus may be affected by regional integration in these areas.

2. NORTH AMERICAN INTEGRATION

A US-Canada FTA was negotiated in 1985–88 and went into effect on January 1, 1989. It will become fully operational in 1997 after an eight-year transitional period. While the agreement contains numerous provisions, the most important ones for the present study are the removal of tariffs and nontariff barriers (NTBs) on commodity trade and of various restrictions on service transactions. Negotiations between the United States and Mexico concerning an FTA commenced in 1990, and were broadened in 1991 to include the United States, Canada, and Mexico with the aim of establishing a North American FTA. The level of attention paid to this issue in the midst of a major war in the Persian Gulf attests to the importance attached to it by policy makers. Inasmuch as trade restrictions between the three countries would be eliminated, all other countries, including ASEAN and South Korea, would be discriminated against in the North American market when competing against "internal" sources.

A caveat concerning the above statement is the General System of Preferences (GSP) granted by the United States (the "donor" country) and Canada to most developing countries (known as the "beneficiary" countries), including ASEAN. South Korea and Singapore were "graduated" from the US GSP scheme in 1988, so they are no longer eligible for preferential status. But the four major members of ASEAN continue to receive GSP benefits. Indeed the ASEAN grouping enjoys a special status through a provision in the US GSP known as the "rules of 'cumulative origin.'" Under the GSP, manufacturing exports (and some nonmanufactures) from the beneficiary countries enter the United States duty free. To qualify for such treatment, a commodity must be wholly produced within that particular developing country, or if imported materials are

Table 1. *Basic statistics of ASEAN countries and South Korea*

Country	GDP (US$m) 1989*	Per capita GDP (US$) 1989†	Real GDP‡ growth 1983–89	Share of GDP in 1990§			Exports to: (1989, US$m)			Imports from: (1989, US$m)		
				Agriculture	Industry	Service	North America¶	EEC 12	Rest of world	North America	EEC 12	Rest of world
Brunei	5,773	25,512	−2.6‖	2	51	43	73	278	1,581	72	538	884
Indonesia	82,726	471	5.0‖	20	41	40	3,583	2,321	16,032	2,526	2,594	11,347
Malaysia	37,452	2,047	5.3	19	42	39	4,872	3,858	16,319	4,020	3,137	9,356
Philippines	44,348	738	1.3	27	33	40	3,061	1,319	3,373	2,311	1,251	7,603
Singapore	28,360	10,582	6.6	0	36	64	10,829	6,036	27,904	8,787	6,218	34,689
Thailand	69,676	1,257	7.0	14	35	50	4,561	3,810	11,658	3,141	3,603	18,552
Total ASEAN	**268,335**	**859**	—	—	—	—	**26,979**	**17,622**	**76,867**	**20,857**	**17,341**	**82,431**
South Korea	211,879	5,000	10.0	8	46	46	22,861	7,441	32,069	17,475	6,678	37,403

Sources: Asian Development Bank (1991, 1989). Key indicators of Developing Member Countries of ADB, July 1989. Brunei, Ministry of Finance (1977, 1987). International Monetary Fund (Yearbook 1990, December 1990). World Bank (1990).
*1986 for Brunei and 1988 for Indonesia.
†1986 for Brunei and 1988 for Malaysia and Indonesia.
‡Growth of real GNP for the Philippines.
§1986 for Brunei.
¶United States and Canada.
‖1983–86 for Brunei and 1983–88 for Indonesia.

used, they must be subject to "substantial transformation" within the country. At least 35% of
the value of the commodity exported to the
United States has to be accounted for by the
beneficiary country in question. This is known as
the "rules of origin." In the case at hand, the
entire ASEAN region is considered one country
for the purpose of meeting this requirement.

The GSP, however, is not as liberal and
comprehensive as it might sound. It is subject to
a variety of product and country restrictions as
well as possible "graduation" (elimination of
GSP treatment), and the entire program is
"temporary" in the sense that it needs to be
renewed by Congress in eight-year intervals and
is revised annually.[4] Moreover, some studies
show that in the aggregate GSP benefits are
marginal at best.[5] Still, ASEAN, except for
Singapore, does have GSP access to the US and
Canadian markets, while South Korea does not.

How does this status affect the newly formed
discrimination to be created by the North American FTA? Of the two "internal" countries
competing with ASEAN in the US market,
Canada does not have GSP status. *The FTA will
give it restriction-free access that did not exist
before*, and ASEAN will have to cope with this
new situation. Mexico is a US GSP beneficiary,
but its benefits were highly limited, and many
commodities were excluded from this status,
prior to 1989.[6] Indeed it will be seen that many
commodities in which ASEAN and Mexico
compete in the US market were not eligible for
GSP treatment. Canada and Mexico would now
enjoy free access to the US market, contributing
to discrimination against ASEAN. On the other
hand, the US tariff is reasonably low, and hence
the margin of discrimination against ASEAN is
expected to be low. For that reason, attention
must be paid to NTBs, which would also be
eliminated in the case of an FTA. In addition, the
US-Canada FTA agreement provides that in
taking any administrative action to restrict trade
(such as the imposition of anti-dumping duties)
the two partners would exempt each other unless
the partner country is a major source of the
disruption. Given the large and increasing number of such actions, that exemption could add
significantly to the discrimination against outsiders, including Asian countries.

Our approach is disaggregative in nature,
based on the four-digit SITC commodity groups.
For each such industry, we determined whether
ASEAN (or South Korea) competes directly with
an internal FTA source (e.g., Canada or Mexico)
in the market of another FTA member (e.g., the
United States) by matching exports to the latter
markets at a disaggregative level. To accomplish

this it was necessary to establish a minimum
dollar cut-off for the exports of each country or
country group in each four-digit industry, for its
inclusion in the analysis. While such a cut-off is
necessarily arbitrary, we set it at a low level
because in the case of developing areas
(ASEAN, South Korea) the FTA discrimination
is not only harmful to existing industries; rather it
may also thwart the growth of emerging new
industries. Even a low cut-off point does not
capture those industries that are not now en-
gaged in exports in North America, but may be
prevented from doing so by the discrimination. A
low cut-off point could capture incipient exporting industries. Thus any four-digit SITC industry
in ASEAN *or* South Korea whose annual exports
(in 1987 or 1988) to the United States, Canada,
or Mexico was $250,000 or more was retained for
the analysis. Information about ASEAN was
broken down further (for each commodity
group) by the percentage of the ASEAN total
exports accounted for by each individual member
country during 1985–88. For competing exporters
the minimum cut-off points (in thousands of US
dollars) were as follows:[7]

EC9	500	PORTUGAL	250
EFTA	500	SPAIN	250
CANADA	250	USA	500
GREECE	250	CARIBBEAN BASIN	100
MEXICO	250	ISRAEL	100

While the detailed tables for all four-digit
SITC groups are available from the second
author upon request, it was necessary (in order to
conserve space) to condense many categories
into three- or even two-digit groups. Thus if and
only if most four-digit items that comprise a given
three- or two-digit group fell into our "matched"
set, were they aggregated into that respective
level.

Table 2 (A) shows ASEAN exports to the
United States that compete directly with commodities exported by Canada and/or Mexico.
Two other areas that have a preferred status in
the US market — Israel (an FTA) and the
Caribbean basin (the Caribbean Basin Initiative)
— export some of the same commodities to the
United States. These preferential arrangements
came into being in the mid-1980s, so that the
effect on Asia of the newly contemplated FTA is
superimposed upon these earlier effects. For
each "matched" commodity group the table
shows 1988 (or 1987, if the 1988 data are not
available) ASEAN exports to the United States,
the two main exporters among the ASEAN
group (if exports of the commodity are spread
over several ASEAN exporters the table indicates: "more than two"), the competing sources
within the FTA (Canada and/or Mexico), and the

Table 2. Discriminatory effects of North American integration on ASEAN

SITC	Description	1988* ASEAN exports (US$m)	Main ASEAN exporters	Internal competition	Range of average tariff (%)	Nontariff barriers Industrial countries	Developing countries	GSP status†
	A. ASEAN exports to the United States							
512	Organic chemicals	147.8	>2	Canada/Mexico	7–11	Low	Low	Y
513	Inorganic elements	1.5	>2	Canada/Mexico	2–5	Low	Low	Y
5310	Synthetic dyes	0.6	>2	Mexico	17	Low	Low	Y
541	Medicines	11.1	Singapore	Canada/Mexico	4–5	Low	Low	Y
5511	Essential oils	17.5	Indonesia	Canada/Mexico	2	Low	Low	Y
5530	Perfumes and cosmetics	17.5	Singapore	Canada/Mexico	5	Low	Low	Y
554	Soaps	0.8	Sing/Phil	Canada/Mexico	4–5	Low	Low	Y
581	Plastic materials	14.1	Sing/Malay/Phil	Mexico	4	Low	Low	Y-M
599	Chemicals, n.e.s.	22.1	>2	Canada/Mexico	3–5	Low	Low	Y
611	Leather	6.6	>2	Canada/Mexico	4–12	Zero	Zero	Y
6129	Leather manufactures	17.3	Thailand/Phil	Canada/Mexico	4	Zero	Zero	Y
6210	Materials of rubber	4.1	Malaysia	Canada/Mexico	2	Low	Low	Y
629	Rubber articles, n.e.s.	33.3	Sing/Thailand	Canada/Mexico	3–4	Low	Low	Y
631	Veneers, plywood	446.1	>2	Canada/Mexico	0–7	Low	Low	Y-M
632	Wood manufactures	55.2	>2	Canada/Mexico	4–5	Low	Low	N
642	Articles of paper	14.5	Sing/Thailand	Canada/Mexico	0–4	Low	Low	N
65	Textiles	206.8	>2	Canada/Mexico	5–16	Avg	High	Y-M
6624	Brick	5.6	Thailand/Sing	Canada/Mexico	13	Low	Low	Y
665	Glassware	3.7	Sing/Thailand	Canada/Mexico	7–15	Low	Low	Y
666	Pottery	13.7	>2	Mexico	6–16	Low	Low	Y
667	Precious stone	95.9	Thailand/Sing	Canada	0–9	Low	Low	Y
673	Iron and steel shapes	61.1	Singapore	Canada/Mexico	5	High	High	N
678	Iron and steel tubes	82.8	>2	Canada/Mexico	4–7	High	High	Y
6822	Copper	1.8	Thailand/Sing	Canada/Mexico	3	Zero	Zero	N
684	Aluminum	30.0	>2	Canada/Mexico	1–3	Zero	Zero	N
6871	Tin	78.5	Singapore	Mexico	0	Zero	Zero	N
689	Nonferrous metals	3.0	Phil/Sing	Canada/Mexico	4–5	Zero	Zero	Y
69	Metal manufactures	60.2	>2	Canada/Mexico	1–7	Low	Low	Y
711	Power machinery, nonelec.	47.9	Singapore	Canada/Mexico	2–6	Low	Low	Y-M
714	Office machines	3,145.4	Singapore	Canada/Mexico	2	Low	Low	Y-M
715	Metal-working machinery	12.8	>2	Canada/Mexico	3–4	Low	Low	Y

cont.

Table 2. Cont.

SITC	Description	1988* ASEAN exports (US$m)	Main ASEAN exporters	Internal competition	Range of average tariff (%)	Nontariff barriers Industrial countries	Nontariff barriers Developing countries	GSP status†
7171	Textile machinery	0.3	Singapore	Canada/Mexico	5	Low	Low	Y
718	Machines for specialized ind.	22.2	Sing/Phil	Canada/Mexico	3	Low	Low	Y
719	Machines, n.e.s., nonelec.	305.8	Sing/Malaysia	Canada/Mexico	1–5	Low	Low	Y-M
72	Electrical machinery	4,663.9	Sing/Malaysia	Canada/Mexico	2–5	Low	Low	Y-M
7316	Freight cars	1.0	Malaysia/Phil	Mexico	13	Low	Low	Y-M
732	Road vehicles, motor	25.9	Sing/Thailand	Canada/Mexico	1–4	Low	Low	Y
733	Road vehicles, nonmotor	4.7	Malaysia/Sing	Canada/Mexico	3–7	Low	Low	Y
734	Aircraft	77.7	Singapore	Canada/Mexico	1–2	Low	Low	Y
7353	Ships and boats	34.1	Singapore	Canada/Mexico	1	Low	Low	Y-M
812	Plumbing, heating, lighting eq.	6.0	>2	Canada/Mexico	6–7	Low	Low	Y-M
8210	Furniture	169.3	Philippines	Canada/Mexico	4	Low	Low	Y
8310	Travel goods	35.3	Phil/Thailand	Canada/Mexico	12	Low	Low	Y-M
841	Clothing, not of fur	1,618.6	>2	Canada/Mexico	7–13	Low	High	N
8510	Footwear	60.3	Thailand/Phil	Canada/Mexico	17	Zero	Zero	Y-M
861	Instruments	128.3	Sing/Malaysia	Canada/Mexico	4–8	Low	Low	Y-M
862/863	Photographic films	8.8	Sing/Thailand	Canada/Mexico	3	Low	Low	Y
864	Watches and clocks	5.7	Singapore	Canada/Mexico	2–8	Low	Low	Y
89	Misc. manufactures	701.6	>2	Canada/Mexico	1–9	Low	Low	Y-M
Nonmanufacturing exports (SITC 0-4) where ASEAN exports to the United States exceed $10 million‡								
03	Fresh fish	128.5	>2	Canada/Mexico	1–3	High	Low	Y
0517	Fresh nuts	34.9	Phil/Indo	Canada/Mexico	Specific	High	Low	Y
053	Preserved fruits	110.8	Phil/Thailand	Canada/Mexico	11–13	High	Low	Y
0611	Raw sugar	60.2	Phil/Thailand	Mexico	Specific	High	Low	Y
0990	Food preparation	17.9	Thailand/Phil	Canada/Mexico	7	High	Low	Y
332	Petroleum products	179.4	Brunei/Sing/Indo	Canada/Mexico	6	High	High	Y
B. ASEAN exports to Canada								
5128	Chemical compounds	12.3	Singapore	U.S./Mexico	12			Z
5714	Ammunition	0.4	Phil/Malaysia	United States	7			Z
5812	Products of polymer	0.5	Phil/Thailand	U.S./Mexico	12			Z
5999	Chemical prod. preparation	0.6	Singapore	United States	8			Y
6114/29	Leather manufactures	4.1	Thailand	U.S./Mexico	10			Z
6210	Materials of rubber	0.9	Malaysia	United States	9			Z
629	Rubber articles	2.1	Malaysia/Sing	United States	13			Z
631	Veneers, plywood	15.3	Sing/Indo/Malay	United States	9			Z
6324/7/8	Wood manufactures	3.5	All	United States	9			Z
6423	Exercise books	1.0	Singapore	United States	9			Z

Code	Product					
6513/6	Yarn	10.0	Sing/Malaysia	U.S./Mexico	12	Y
6521/2	Cotton	8.3	Malaysia/Sing	U.S./Mexico	12	Y
6535/6	Synthetics	16.7	Malay/Thai/Sing	U.S./Mexico	28	Y
6540	Lace	1.0	Phil/Indo	United States	18	Y
6556	Cordage	0.6	Phil/Thailand	United States	15	Y
6569	Other textiles	1.0	Sing/Thailand	United States	22	Y
Other 6	Other metals	9.6	All	United States	7	N
7114/5	Aircraft	5.3	Singapore	U.S./Mexico	4	N
714	Office machines	81.4	Singapore	U.S./Mexico	3	N
7184	Construction, mining, mach.	1.8	Malay/Thai/Sing	U.S./Mexico	4	N
719	Other nonelectrical mach.	29.1	Singapore	United States	6	Y
72	Electrical machinery	98.4	Malaysia/Sing	U.S./Mexico	7	N
732	Road vehicles, motor	2.9	Sing/Malay/Thai	U.S./Mexico	8	N
733	Road vehicles, nonmotor	4.0	Sing/Malaysia	United States	10	N
7349	Aircraft parts	2.8	Singapore	United States	5	N
8210	Furniture	7.8	Phil/Sing	United States	15	Y
8310	Travel goods	0.8	Phil/Thailand	United States	12	Y
841	Clothing	50.6	All	U.S./Mexico	23	Y
8510	Footwear	2.6	Phil/Thailand	U.S./Mexico	15	Y
861	Instruments	3.1	Sing/Malaysia	United States	5	N
8642	Clocks	0.4	Singapore	United States	11	N
89	Misc. manufactures	31.1	Sing/Thai/Phil	U.S./Mexico	10	N

Nonmanufacturing exports

Code	Product					
031	Fresh fish	5.5	Thai/Phil/Sing	U.S./Mexico	2	Pref
0320	Prepared fish	10.0	Thailand/Phil	United States	7	Pref
053	Preserved fruit	5.8	Phil/Thailand	U.S./Mexico	8	Y
4223	Coconut	7.4	Malaysia/Phil	United States	14	Y

C. ASEAN exports to Mexico

Code	Product			
2311	Natural rubber	16.5	Indonesia	United States
5	Chemicals	2.4	Sing/Indo	United States
71	Nonelectrical machinery	8.0	Singapore	U.S./Canada
72	Electrical machinery	19.0	>2	U.S./Canada
7353	Ships and boats	0.8	Singapore	United States
8210	Furniture	0.4	>2	United States
841	Clothing	3.2	>2	United States
8619	Measuring instruments	0.8	Singapore	U.S./Canada
89	Misc. manufactures	0.4	Singapore	U.S./Canada

Sources: See data-sources appendix.
*In cases where 1988 data were incomplete, 1987 data were used.
†Y denotes yes; Y-M denotes yes for ASEAN, but not for Mexico; and N denotes no. For Canada, Pref denotes nonzero preferential treatment for GSP recipients. Preferential treatment of ASEAN exports to Canada, but tariff rate is still above zero.
‡Coffee, cocoa, tea, pepper, spices, animal feed, natural rubber, lumber, crude petroleum, and natural gas face no or very low tariff.

US tariff rate. The last item refers to nominal rates; in many cases the effective rate of protection (namely, protection accorded to the domestic value added) is considerably higher.

Next the table shows the level of NTBs facing exports to the United States from industrial and developing countries, based on the data compiled by a World Bank-UNCTAD study.[8] That study shows the number of tariff line items within major commodity groups that are subject to NTBs.[9] Based on that information we classified the NTBs into zero, low (below the average level for all commodities) and high (above the average level for all commodities). The NTB information is provided only for the United States, EC, and Japan; similar data for Canada and Mexico are not available. Finally, the right-hand column indicates the presence (Y for yes) or absence (N for no) of the commodity on the US GSP list. Mexico is *excluded* from the beneficiary list for some commodities, and those are shown as Y-M.

While many ASEAN export categories are represented on the "matched" list, it is possible to identify a score of *major* items that are competitive with "internal" FTA sources. But some of the potentially impacted commodity groups face a rather low US tariff rate as well as a low level of NTBs, so that the expected degree of discrimination against ASEAN would be low. The following subset contains the major matched commodity categories, where the US tariff rates and/or NTBs' levels are high: organic chemicals, textiles and clothing, precious stones, iron and steel, footwear, travel goods, instruments, fish, preserved fruits, fresh nuts, raw sugar, food preparations, and petroleum products.

Most ASEAN countries are involved in the export of these commodities. Because the US market is reasonably "open," the main discriminatory impact of an FTA on ASEAN is concentrated in very few commodity categories. Indeed many important "matched" items appear in the machinery group (SITC 7) where the US tariff rate is under 5% and NTBs are low. It is, however, possible that other exports, such as glassware, leather, and pottery would be prevented from growing in future years.

Although the partial-equilibrium approach adopted here is best suited for the identification of the heavily affected industries, we also attempted to measure the aggregate effect of trade diversion. Can the aggregate effect of the FTA on ASEAN be measured? Because NTBs cannot be quantified accurately, the answer must concentrate on the effect of the tariffs. Two approaches were employed yielding roughly similar results in terms of dollar value. The first one

assumes that ASEAN exporters to the United States would attempt to maintain their share of the market, and would therefore absorb the new degree of discrimination and reduce their export price to the extent needed to remain competitive. Since the United States is a "large" country, we assume a two-thirds pass-through of the tariff (Kreinin, 1977), so that the reduction in the ASEAN export price would be equal to two-thirds of the tariff. In other words, the cost of a discriminatory North American FTA (in the US market) to ASEAN is quantified as a deterioration in ASEAN's terms of trade by two-thirds of the US tariff. Calculated in that fashion it amounts to $434 million.

An alternative approach is to apply elasticity coefficients to the price reduction engendered by the internal tariff cut, and multiply the results by Asia-Pacific exports. A recent study (Reinert and Shields, 1991) of the elasticity of substitution between US imports from Mexico, Canada, and the rest of the world for two- and three-digit commodity groups shows the overwhelming majority of the estimates cluster around one, thereby confirming the estimates in the previous paragraph.

One reason why the above quantitative estimates understate the expected trade diversion is that they relate only to tariff removal within the grouping. Since US tariff rates are very low, except for occasional spikes, the main diversionary impact would come from removal of NTBs. A recent study (Roland-Horst, Reinert and Shields, 1992) assesses the effect of removing all impediments to trade by assuming that all price differentials between the United States, Canada, and Mexico are due to some form of trade restrictions. It finds the diversionary impact of NTBs plus tariffs to be *10 times* greater than that caused by the removal of tariffs alone. Multiplying our estimates by 10, however, would no doubt lead to gross overestimation for several main reasons: Considering the role of transport cost and product differentiation, not all price differentials can be attributed to trade restrictions; not all NTBs will be removed by NAFTA; and the multiplication factor mentioned above is likely to vary greatly by commodity groups and may not be so high in the heavily affected categories. Also, in many cases removal of NTBs within the region would merely make restrictions on outsiders more binding. The rise in imports from Mexico may be at the expense of domestic (US) rather than Asian producers. But without assigning a specific number, it is possible to conclude that the diversionary impact is likely to be several times the estimates generated above for mere tariff elimination. Even a factor of 2–3 would bring the trade diversion to the 10–15% (of Asian exports to NAFTA) range.

Table 2(B) shows ASEAN exports to Canada in commodities that "match" US and/or Mexican exports in the sense described above. The main items affected are: chemical compounds, veneer, textile and clothing, and certain machinery items. In most cases the internal FTA competition comes from both the United States and Mexico. While several ASEAN countries are affected, Singapore appears most frequently on the list. Since Canada is a "small" country we assume 100% pass-through, and the effect of the FTA on ASEAN terms of trade is estimated at $43 million or one-tenth that in the US market.

Table 2(C) shows ASEAN exports to Mexico, a country which has undergone a radical liberalization policy in its protective structure. The average tariff rate in Mexico has fallen from 29% in December 1985 to 12% in December 1987, and quantitative restrictions have been reduced to cover only a few sectors of the economy (Trigueros, 1989). As expected, the matched commodities in the Mexican market are few in number and small in magnitude. The terms of trade effect amounts to only $6 million. In total, North American integration is estimated to divert $484 million of ASEAN trade, or 4% of ASEAN exports to North America in 1988.

Table 3(A) shows the results for South Korean exports to the US market. The leading industries that would be affected by an FTA (where US tariff is above 5%) are: organic chemicals, leather manufactures, textiles and clothing, iron and steel, metal manufactures, nonmotor road (railway) vehicles, travel goods, furs, footwear, instruments, and fish. In most cases the internal competition originates in both Canada and Mexico. Using the same methodology, we estimate the deterioration in the terms of trade at $821 million. South Korean exports to Canada would be affected generally in the same industrial sectors, with the notable addition of machinery items, by competition from the United States and Mexico, and the terms of trade loss would amount to $179 million. In the case of South Korean exports to Mexico only electrical machinery looms as an important category, and the terms of trade loss comes to $15 million. Total trade diversion from South Korea is estimated at $1,015 million, or 5% of Korean exports to North America in 1987.

3. EUROPEAN INTEGRATION

European integration is a process that commenced over 30 years ago. In the late 1950s, the original "six" members started the formation of a customs union and Common Agricultural Policy (CAP), a process which was completed ten years later. During the 1960s and 1970s the EC set up a web of preferential arrangements with various countries: an association agreement with Greece and Turkey was negotiated in the early 1960s; an FTA with the seven EFTA countries in Europe came into being in the 1970s; and a preferential trading zone with the Associated States in Africa (mainly Francophone Africa) and the Caribbean (ACP) and with countries in the Mediterranean basin was set up in the 1960s. In the 1970s, the EC was enlarged from six to nine members, with the accession of the United Kingdom, Ireland, and Denmark, and the Associated States were expanded to include Anglophone Africa. All these preferential agreements: The EC and its enlargement, the FTA with EFTA, the preferential treatment accorded the Associated States and mediterranean countries, discriminated against other parts of the world, including ASEAN and the Asian NIEs. In fact, the complicated web of EC preferences can be viewed as a pyramid structure in which developing Asian countries would be near the bottom, just above the non-European developed countries. The Asian countries are beneficiaries of the EC GSP; but the GSP is subject to numerous restrictions and is far less liberal than the various EC association treaties.

In the 1980s, the EC was further enlarged to 12 countries with the accession of Greece (1981), and then Spain and Portugal (1986). And on December 3, 1992 the Unified Market ("EC 1992") is scheduled to come into being.[10] Our present concern is with the impact of these final steps on Asia, recognizing that they were superimposed on the earlier integration measures that had already discriminated against nonmember countries. Because ASEAN is not a major exporter of services, and is unlikely to become so in the near future, the main impact of EC 1992 is likely to be in the area of nontariff barriers on commodities, as those are shifted from country barriers to EC-wide barriers to cope with the abolition of border checkpoints, and special features of the Unified Market. Likewise, the remaining intra-EC NTBs would be abolished.

(a) *The second enlargement of the EC*

Using the same format as in previous sections, Table 4 and 5 present the relevant data for ASEAN and South Korean exports to the EC and to the three countries acceding to the EC in its second enlargement. It should be noted,

Table 3. *Discriminatory effects of North American integration on South Korea*

SITC	Description	1988* Korean exports (US$m)	Internal competition	Range of average tariff (%)	Nontariff barriers Industrial countries	Nontariff barriers Developing countries	GSP status
A. South Korean exports to the United States							
512	Organic chemicals	62.7	Canada/Mexico	6–10	Low	Low	
5133	Inorganic acids	1.0	Canada/Mexico	2	Low	Low	
514	Other inorganic chemicals	2.7	Canada/Mexico	2–5	Low	Low	
5310	Synthetic dyes	5.2	Mexico	17	Low	Low	
5331/3	Paints	2.7	Canada/Mexico	4–5	Low	Low	
5417/9	Medications	4.9	Canada/Mexico	4–5	Low	Low	
5530	Perfumes, cosmetics	2.7	Canada/Mexico	5	Low	Low	
5541	Soaps	2.3	Mexico	4	Low	Low	
5714	Hunting ammunitions	8.8	Canada/Mexico	4	Low	Low	
5811/2	Plastics	59.3	Mexico	4	Low	Low	
5992/9	Chemicals, n.e.s.	1.6	Canada/Mexico	5	Low	Low	
6114/9	Leather	8.8	Canada/Mexico	4	Zero	Zero	
612	Leather manufactures	36.4	Canada/Mexico	11	Zero	Zero	
6130	Fur skins	1.1	Canada	3	Zero	Zero	
6210	Materials of rubber	7.3	Canada/Mexico	2	Low	Low	
629	Rubber articles	201.0	Canada/Mexico	3	Low	Low	
6312	Plywood	4.5	Canada/Mexico	7	Low	Low	
632	Wood manufactures	10.8	Canada/Mexico	5	Low	Low	
6419	Bulk paper	31.6	Canada/Mexico	2	Low	Low	
642	Articles of paper	12.8	Canada/Mexico	2–4	Low	Low	
6513/67	Textile yarn	14.0	Canada/Mexico	9–11	Avg	High	
652	Cotton fabrics	67.7	Canada/Mexico	11–12	Avg	High	
6532/5/7	Noncotton woven textiles	275.0	Canada/Mexico	16	Avg	High	
6540	Lace	9.2	Canada/Mexico	9	Avg	High	
6554/6/8	Special textile products	21.5	Canada/Mexico	7–10	Avg	High	
6561/6/9	Textile products	101.3	Canada/Mexico	6–12	Avg	High	
6624	Brick	8.3	Canada/Mexico	13	Low	Low	
663	Other minerals	12.9	Canada/Mexico	3–7	Low	Low	
6664/7/8/9	Glass	15.1	Mexico	3–4	Low	Low	
665	Glassware	9.2	Canada/Mexico	10	Low	Low	
666	Pottery	73.0	Mexico	6–16	Low	Low	
6674	Synthetic stone	13.2	Canada-	7	Low	Low	
6725	Iron and steel slabs	3.2	Canada/Mexico	5	High	High	
6732/4	Iron and steel bars	48.1	Canada/Mexico	2–5	High	High	
6741/8	Iron and steel plates	105.2	Canada/Mexico	6	High	High	
6750	Iron and steel strips	2.8	Mexico	6	High	High	
6761	Railway rails	1.7	Canada/Mexico	6	High	High	
6770	Iron and steel wire	8.7	Canada	2	High	High	
678	Iron and steel tubes, pipes	225.5	Canada/Mexico	5	High	High	
679	Iron and steel castings	20.7	Canada/Mexico	2	High	High	
6822	Copper alloys	4.2	Canada/Mexico	4	Zero	Zero	

cont.

Code	Description	Value	Country	Rate	Tariff	Tariff	Flag
6842	Aluminum alloys	2.3	Canada/Mexico	3	Zero	Zero	N
6861	Zinc, unwrought	4.9	Canada/Mexico	10	Zero	Zero	N
6895	Base metals, n.e.s.	1.0	Canada/Mexico	4	Zero	Zero	N
69	Metal manufactures	682.5	Canada/Mexico	1–7	Low	Low	N
71	Nonelectrical machinery	1,402.0	Canada/Mexico	3	Low	Low	N
72	Electrical machinery	3,329.6	Canada/Mexico	3	Low	Low	N
731/4/67	Railway vehicles	262.6	Canada/Mexico	14	Low	Low	N
732	Road vehicles, motor	2,436.7	Canada/Mexico	0–1	Low	Low	N
733	Road vehicles, nonmotor	104.1	Canada/Mexico	6	Low	Low	N
734	Aircraft	42.7	Canada/Mexico	1	Low	Low	N
7353/9	Ships and boats	98.3	Canada/Mexico	1	Low	Low	N
812	Plumbing, heating, lighting eq.	49.5	Canada/Mexico	5	Low	Low	N
8210	Furniture	76.6	Canada/Mexico	4	Low	Low	Y
8310	Travel goods	459.5	Canada/Mexico	13	Low	Low	Y
841	Clothing	2,974.6	Canada/Mexico	13	Low	High	Y
8420	Fur clothing	142.4	Canada	7	Low	High	N
8510	Footwear	1,803.7	Canada/Mexico	17	Zero	Zero	N
86	Instruments, watches, clocks	262.4	Canada/Mexico	3–8	Low	Zero	
89	Misc. manufactures	1,986.5	Canada/Mexico	2–7	Low	Low	

Nonmanufacturing exports — $5 million cut-off

Code	Description	Value	Country	Rate	Tariff	Tariff
031	Fish	208.9	Canada/Mexico	1–3	Low	High
0320	Canned fish	71.3	Canada/Mexico	7	Low	High
0539	Fruit and nuts, preserved	11.6	Canada/Mexico	13	Low	High
055	Vegetables, preserved	11.4	Canada/Mexico	13	Low	High
0620	Sugar preparations	3.3	Canada/Mexico	10	Low	High

B. South Korean exports to Canada

Code	Description	Value	Country	Rate
0990	Food preparations, n.e.s.	15.7	Canada/Mexico	7
1210	Tobacco	12.3	Canada/Mexico	Specific
2662	Synthetic fiber	7.3	Mexico	7
332	Petroleum products	44.0	Canada/Mexico	6
5121/5/7/8	Organic chemicals	6.6	U.S./Mexico	10
5310	Synthetic dyes	1.0	United States	3
5333	Paints	0.4	United States	10
5811/2	Plastic materials	8.9	U.S./Mexico	12
6122	Harnesses	0.3	United States	9
6123/9	Leather goods	2.6	United States	11
6130	Fur skins	0.4	United States	5
6210	Materials of rubber	1.0	United States	9
6291/449	Rubber articles	26.6	United States	10
6312/27	Wood	1.6	United States	9
6419/23	Paper, books	2.8	United States	7
6513/6	Yarn	64.7	U.S./Mexico	12
6521/2	Cotton	11.8	United States	18
653	Woven, textiles, noncotton	51.3	U.S./Mexico	25
654/5/67	Other textiles	22.1	United States	19
6624	Brick	1.0	United States	11
6631/2	Other mineral manufactures	0.8	United States	10

Table 3. *Cont.*

SITC	Description	1988* Korean exports (US$m)	Internal competition	Range of average tariff (%)	Nontariff barriers Industrial countries	Developing countries	GSP status
664	Glass	2.0	United States	8			N
67/68/69	Other metals	94.8	U.S./Mexico	9			N
71	Nonelectrical machinery	55.9	U.S./Mexico	5			N
722/3	Elec switch gear pow mach	8.9	U.S./Mexico	10			N
724	Telecommunication equipment	137.6	U.S./Mexico	6			Y
7250	Electrical equipment	57.7	United States	10			N
729	Other electrical machinery	39.4	United States	7			N
7316	Freight cars	0.7	United States	13			N
732	Road vehicles, motor	143.0	U.S./Mexico	9			N
733/4/5	Other vehicles	3.6	United States	10			N
8123/4	Plumbing and lighting equipment	8.4	United States	9			N
8210	Travel goods	3.1	United States	15			Y
8310	Clothing	52.5	United States	12			N
841	Fur	283.5	U.S./Mexico	23			Y
8420	Footwear	28.7	United States	20			Y
8510	Instruments	89.6	U.S./Mexico	15			Y
861	Watches, clocks	8.2	United States	5			N
864	Sound recorders	5.5	United States	11			N
891	Toys, outdoor games	57.6	United States	5			Y
8942/4	Misc. manufactures	60.8	U.S./Mexico	10			N
Other 89		13.2	U.S./Mexico	12			N
Nonmanufacturing exports — $2 million cut-off							
031	Fresh fish	1.5	U.S./Mexico	1			Pref
0320	Prepared fish	6.0	United States	7			Pref
0990	Food preparations	4.8	United States	11			Pref
3329	Coal	9.1	United States	2			Y
C. South Korean exports to Mexico							
5	Chemicals	1.4	United States				
6291	Rubber and tires	0.2	United States				
65	Textiles	5.9	United States				
67	Iron and steel	1.9	U.S./Canada				
6960	Cutlery	0.4	United States				
71	Nonelectrical machinery	5.5	United States				
72	Electrical machinery	102.8	U.S./Canada				
841	Clothing	5.0	U.S./Canada				
8510	Footwear	1.1	United States				
8641	Watches	0.6	United States				
89	Misc. manufactures	4.1	U.S./Canada				

Sources: See data-sources appendix.
*In cases where 1988 data were incomplete, 1987 data were used.

however, that the EC-9 abolished its tariffs on manufacturing imports from Spain, Portugal, and Greece in the late 1970s and early 1980s. So the 1987 exports, except for agriculture, shown in Tables 4(A) and 5(A) already embody the effect of that market-opening step, and the estimated terms-of-trade effects shown below are only suggestive. This reservation does not apply to parts (B)-(D) of the tables, as Spain and Portugal would eliminate tariffs on imports from the EC-9 by 1996 (Tovias, 1990), at the end of a 10-year transitional period. Yet, as a result of their respective association agreements, Greece, Spain, and Portugal did give preferential treatment to some EC exports, and these rates, rather than the most-favored nation rates, became the relevant tariffs in the tables. Moreover, the accessions of the three will require substantial changes in their respective trade regimes. In addition to granting duty-free access to EC exports of all commodities, the three must (by 1996): (i) adjust their external tariff schedules to conform to the level of the EC Common Customs Tariff law,[11] (ii) adopt the CAP, (iii) abide by the EC preferential arrangements with EFTA, Israel, relevant Mediterranean nonmember countries, and ACP countries, and (iv) eventually adopt the EC GSP and the EC textile agreement.

In compiling the data set, the EC, Greek, Spanish, and Portuguese tariff rates were available to us on a much more aggregative basis than those of the United States (see data-sources appendix), and to a certain extent these schedules dictated the level of commodity aggregation in the analysis.

In sectors other than manufacturing, ASEAN would sustain a discriminatory impact in fish, fruits and vegetables, other foods, and tobacco all of which are subject to moderately high tariffs *and* a restrictive CAP, and vegetable oils which is subject to a high tariff. (Cork and wood are major ASEAN exports, but EC tariffs and NTBs, and hence the degree of discrimination, are low). In the manufacturing sector, a significant discriminatory impact would be felt in the following industries: rubber manufactures, veneer and plywood, textiles and clothing, precious stones, metals, machinery, transport equipment, footwear, and instruments. In most cases, internal competition comes from all three acceding countries, and most of the ASEAN countries would be impacted by the discrimination. Following the approaches adopted in the case of NAFTA, and considering the EC as a "large country," the adverse effect on ASEAN exports is estimated at $468 million. ASEAN exports to the three acceding countries are rather small, but

their tariff rates are high. Fruits and vegetables, machinery, and transport equipment are the main affected categories. The aggregate effect on ASEAN would add up to $41 million. Hence, the total effect of the Second Enlargement of the EC on ASEAN is about half a billion dollars, or 8% of ASEAN exports to the EC in 1988. As in the case of NAFTA, these figures may rise by a factor of 2–3 if the effect of removing NTBs were included.

In the case of South Korea, only two non-manufactures are impacted to any significant degree: fish and tobacco. Among manufactured goods, significant detrimental effects would occur in: chemicals, articles of rubber, textiles and clothing, iron and steel, metal manufactures, machinery and transport equipment, travel goods, footwear, and instruments. The aggregate effect is estimated as follows: EC-9, $324 million and the Acceding-3, $40 million, for a total of $364 million, or 5% of South Korean exports to the EC in 1987. Again, including NTBs would raise this number considerably.

(b) *EC-1992*

While it is possible to estimate the effect of the second enlargement of the EC on Asian countries, the impact of the Unified Market Program (EC 1992) is more difficult to assess empirically. Still, several qualitative observations might be offered,[12] listing both negative and positive effects on ASEAN and Korea. To begin with the negative effects, the removal of border check-points in the EC means that all intracommunity NTBs will be abolished, including technical barriers to trade which result from differential product standards between member states.[13] Following is a list of products where such technical barriers are regarded as important (Lundberg, 1990):

Electrical engineering products	Foodstuffs
Mechanical engineering equipment	Metal articles
Instruments, medical equipment	Mineral products
Pharmaceutical products	Rubber products
Motor vehicles	

Most of these items are included in our "matched" lists of severely affected exports from ASEAN and South Korea to the EC. Clearly, the abolition of intra-EC NTBs will enhance discrimination against Asian countries. In general, the creation of a single market in Europe, with the attendant benefits of scale economies, would make EC firms more formidable competitors in global trade, and would affect adversely non-European firms including Asian ones.

Second, national quotas on several sensitive

Table 4. *Discriminatory effects of European integration on ASEAN*

SITC	Description	1988* ASEAN exports (US$m)	Main ASEAN exporters	Internal competition	Average tariff (%)	Nontariff barriers on developing country exports	GSP status
A. ASEAN exports to the EC							
11	Fresh meat	10.0	Thailand/Indo	Spain/Greece	8.0	High	Y
22	Dairy products	1.2	>2	Spain	20.0	High	Y
3	Fish	364.4	Sing/Thailand	Spain/Port/Greece	13.0	High	Y
42/4/8	Cereals	29.2	Indo/Thailand	Spain/Port/Greece	9.0	High	Y
48	Cereal preparation	9.4	Indo/Thailand	Spain/Port/Greece	15.0	High	Y
05	Fruits and vegetables	828.9	>2	Spain/Port/Greece	7.0	High	Y
Other 0	Other food	702.4	>2	Spain/Port/Greece	10.0	High	Y
11	Beverages	3.6	Singapore	Spain/Port/Greece	15.0	High	Y
12	Tobacco	67.9	>2	Spain/Greece	30.0	High	Y
21/2218	Hides and skins, oil seed	38.5	>2	Spain/Port/Greece	4.0	Low	Y
24/2515	Cork and wood	526.1	>2	Spain/Port/Greece	3.0	Low	Y
26-9/32-34	Other nonmanufactures	121.1	>2	Spain/Port/Greece	7.0	Low	Y
42/43	Vegetable oils	233.0	>2	Spain/Port/Greece	15.0	Low	Y
51-3	Organic and inorganic chem.	55.4	>2	Spain/Port/Greece	12.0	Low	N
541	Medicinal, etc. products	14.9	>2	Spain/Port/Greece	7.0	Low	Y
55	Perfume, cleaning, etc. prod.	15.0	Indo/Sing	Spain/Port/Greece	10.0	Low	Y
56/57	Fertilizer	7.2	Malaysia	Spain/Port/Greece	12.0	Low	N
581	Plastic materials, etc.	5.9	Singapore	Spain/Port/Greece	8.0	Low	Y
599	Chemicals, n.e.s.	21.7	>2	Spain/Port/Greece	7.0	Low	Y
61	Leather	39.6	Indo/Thailand	Spain/Port/Greece	8.0	Low	Y
62	Rubber manufactures, n.e.s.	656.9	>2	Spain/Port/Greece	6.0	High	Y
63	Veneers, plywood, etc.	366.1	>2	Spain/Port/Greece	12.0	High	Y
64	Paper, paperboard, and manuf.	7.3	Sing/Thailand	Spain/Port/Greece	11.0	High	Y
65	Textile yarn, fabric, etc.	368.7	>2	Spain/Port/Greece	7.0	High	Y
66	Glass and pottery	21.1	>2	Spain/Port/Greece	7.0	High	Y
667	Pearls, prec & semi-prec stones	112.9	Malay/Thai	Portugal	4.0	High	Y
67-9	Metals	253.0	>2	Spain/Port/Greece	6.0	High	Y
71	Nonelectrical machinery	822.5	>2	Spain/Port/Greece	5.0	High	Y
72	Electrical machinery	1,719.1	>2	Spain/Port/Greece	4.0	High	Y
73	Transport equipment	85.9	>2	Spain/Port/Greece	7.0	High	Y
812	Plumbing, heating, lighting eq.	3.4	Sing/Indo	Spain/Port/Greece	4.0	High	Y
8210	Furniture	56.2	Thailand	Spain/Port/Greece	5.0	High	N
8310	Travel goods, handbags	39.7	Thailand/Sing	Spain/Port/Greece	7.0	High	N
841	Clothing, not of fur	983.2	>2	Spain/Port/Greece	13.0	High	Y
8510	Footwear	108.3	Thailand	Spain/Port/Greece	10.0	High	Y
86	Instruments, watches, clocks	100.2	>2	Spain/Port/Greece	6.0	High	Y
89	Misc. manufactured goods, n.e.s.	407.5	>2	Spain/Port/Greece	7.0	High	Y

B. ASEAN exports to Greece

Code	Product				
03	Fish	1.6	Thailand/Sing	EC9/Spain/Port	6.1
05	Fruits and Vegetables	0.5	Thailand/Sing	EC9	17.6
51/53/59	Chemicals	5.2	Singapore	EC9/Spain	13.9
62/2311	Rubber	11.2	>2	EC9/Spain	17.2
65	Textiles	1.5	Thailand	EC9/Spain/Port	6.3
71	Nonelectrical machinery	6.5	Singapore	EC9/Spain	3.6
72	Electrical machinery	8.8	Singapore	EC9/Spain/Port	5.7
73	Transport equipment	39.5	Singapore	EC9/Spain/Port	9.0
8210	Furniture	0.2	Philippines	EC9/Spain	28.8
83/84	Clothing	1.9	>2	EC9/Spain	33.2
8510	Footwear	5.2	Thailand/Phil	EC9/Spain/Port	20.0
86	Instruments	7.8	Thailand/Sing	EC9/Spain	0.0
	Other nonmanufactures	9.8	>2	EC9/Spain	
	Other manufactures	11.4	>2,	EC9/Spain	

C. ASEAN exports to Spain

Code	Product				
03	Fish	13.9	Thailand/Sing	ECP/Port/Greece	7.6
05	Fruit and vegetables	50.1	Thailand/Phil	ECP/Portugal	2.5
5	Chemicals	2.2	Indo/Sing	EC9/Port/Greece	9.7
62/2311	Rubber	20.1	Malaysia/Sing	EC9/Port/Greece	16.2
63	Wood and cork	2.8	>2	EC9/Portugal	4.1
65	Textiles	6.0	>2	EC9/Portugal	16.0
66	Minerals	3.7	Thailand	EC9	10.7
67	Iron and steel	5.2	Indo/Sing	EC9/Greece	13.8
71	Nonelectrical machinery	18.1	>2	EC9/Portugal	9.3
72	Electrical machinery	78.0	Singapore	EC9/Portugal	12.5
73	Transport equipment	2.6	Sing/Indo	EC9/Portugal	19.7
8210	Furniture	2.5	Phil/Indo	EC9/Portugal	26.8
84	Clothing	8.7	>2	EC9/Port/Greece	24.9
8510	Footwear	1.8	Philippines	EC9/Port/Greece	
86	Instruments	3.5	>2	EC9/Portugal	22.9
	Other nonmanufactures	127.5	>2	EC9/Portugal	
	Other manufactures	29.5	>2	EC9/Portugal	

D. ASEAN exports to Portugal

Code	Product				
05	Vegetables	26.3	Thai/Sing	EC/Spain/Greece	10.4
2433	Lumber	0.9	Malaysia	EC/Spain	3.6
5128	Chemicals	2.6	Singapore	EC/Spain	2.9
62/2344	Rubber	13.3	>2	EC/Spain/Greece	35.7
65	Textiles	2.2	>2	EC/Spain/Greece	27.0
71	Nonelectrical machinery	3.8	Singapore	EC/Spain	5.0
72	Electrical machinery	7.3	Malaysia/Sing	EC/Spain	14.3
86	Instruments	0.8	>2	EC/Spain/Greece	15.0
	Other nonmanufactures	5.1	>2	EC/Spain/Greece	
	Other manufactures	2.0	Singapore	EC/Spain	

Sources: See data-sources appendix.
*In cases where 1988 data were incomplete, 1987 data were used.

Table 5. *Discriminatory effects of European integration on South Korea*

SITC	Description	1987 exports (US$m)	Internal competition	Average tariff (%)	Nontariff barriers on developing country exports	GSP status
A. South Korean exports to the EC						
31	Fish	35.1	Spain/Port/Greece	13.0	High	Y
5	Fruits and vegetables	4.0	Spain/Port/Greece	7.0	High	Y
Other 0	Other food	2.9	Spain/Port/Greece	10.0	High	Y
1210	Tobacco, unmanufactured	34.2	Spain/Port/Greece	30.0	High	Y
2440	Cork, raw and waste	0.3	Spain/Portugal	3.0	Low	Y
26-9/33	Other nonmanufactures	22.5	Spain/Port/Greece	7.0	Low	Y
51	Organic and inorganic chemicals	66.8	Spain/Port/Greece	12.0	Low	Y
52-3	Coal, dyes	10.4	Spain/Port/Greece	12.0	Low	Y
541	Medicinal, etc. products	15.3	Spain/Port/Greece	7.0	Low	Y
5530	Perfume, cosmetics, etc.	0.3	Spain/Port/Greece	12.0	Low	Y
5541	Soaps	0.2	Spain/Portugal	6.0	Low	Y
571	Explosives, pyrotech products	3.1	Spain	7.0	Low	Y
581	Plastic materials, etc.	35.1	Spain/Port/Greece	8.0	Low	N
599	Chemicals, n.e.s.	6.8	Spain/Port/Greece	7.0	Low	Y
611	Leather	22.0	Spain/Port/Greece	8.0	Low	Y
629	Rubber articles, n.e.s.	108.0	Spain/Port/Greece	6.0	High	Y
63	Wood and cork	21.6	Spain/Port/Greece	12.0	High	N
64	Paper, paperboard and manufactures	40.8	Spain/Port/Greece	11.0	High	Y
65	Textile yarn, fabric, etc.	302.4	Spain/Port/Greece	7.0	High	Y
662-6	Nonmetallic minerals	32.6	Spain/Port/Greece	7.0	High	Y
667	Pearls, prec. & semi-prec. stones	1.7	Spain/Port/Greece	4.0	High	Y
67-8	Iron and steel	65.9	Spain/Port/Greece	6.0	High	Y
69	Metal manufactures, n.e.s.	180.7	Spain/Port/Greece	5.0	High	Y
71	Nonelectrical machinery	447.6	Spain/Port/Greece	5.0	High	Y
72	Electrical machinery	1,199.4	Spain/Port/Greece	4.0	High	Y
73	Transport equipment	301.7	Spain/Port/Greece	7.0	High	Y
812	Plumbing, heating, lighting eq.	5.6	Spain/Port/Greece	4.0	High	N
8210	Furniture	6.2	Spain/Port/Greece	5.0	High	N
8310	Travel goods, handbags	196.8	Spain/Port/Greece	7.0	High	N
84	Clothing	1,576.2	Spain/Port/Greece	12.0	High	Y
8510	Footwear	367.4	Spain/Port/Greece	10.0	High	N
86	Instruments, watches, clocks	95.6	Spain/Port/Greece	6.0	High	Y
89	Misc. manufactured goods, n.e.s.	934.4	Spain/Port/Greece	7.0	High	Y

B. South Korean exports to Greece

03	Fish	0.3	EC9/Spain/Portugal	6.1
51/53/59	Chemicals	1.6	EC9/Spain	13.9
62/2311	Rubber	4.2	EC9/Spain	17.2
65	Textiles	9.0	EC9/Spain/Portugal	6.3
71	Nonelectrical machinery	4.5	EC9/Spain	3.6
72	Electrical machinery	5.8	EC9/Spain/Portugal	5.7
73	Transport equipment	40.4	EC9/Spain/Portugal	9.0
83/84	Clothing	1.7	EC9/Spain	33.2
8510	Footwear	4.2	EC9/Spain/Portugal	20.0
	Other nonmanufactures	0.9	EC9/Spain	
	Other manufactures	17.0	EC9/Spain	

C. South Korean exports to Spain

03	Fish	35.0	EC9/Port/Greece	7.6
05	Fruit and vegetables	0.5	EC9/Portugal	2.5
5	Chemicals	4.9	EC9/Port/Greece	9.7
62/2311	Rubber	3.7	EC9/Port/Greece	16.2
63	Wood and cork	0.5	EC9/Portugal	4.1
65	Textiles	16.8	EC9/Portugal	16.0
66	Minerals	1.1	EC9	10.7
67	Iron and steel	6.3	EC9/Greece	13.8
71	Nonelectrical machinery	48.3	EC9/Portugal	9.3
72	Electrical machinery	89.1	EC9/Portugal	12.5
8210	Furniture	0.7	EC9/Portugal	26.8
84	Clothing	8.9	EC9/Port/Greece	24.9
8510	Footwear	10.3	EC9/Port/Greece	
86	Instruments	4.4	EC9/Portugal	22.9
	Other nonmanufactures	1.5	EC9/Portugal	
	Other manufactures	54.7	EC9/Portugal	

D. South Korean exports to Portugal

03	Fish	0.9	EC/Spain	22.9
6114	Leather	0.3	EC/Spain	14.6
62/2344	Rubber	2.6	EC/Spain/Greece	35.7
65	Textiles	0.6	EC/Spain/Greece	27.0
67	Iron and steel	4.1	EC/Spain	19.7
71	Nonelectrical machinery	6.6	EC/Spain	5.0
72	Electrical machinery	23.8	EC/Spain	14.3
73	Transport equipment	2.4	EC/Spain	11.1
8510	Footwear	1.1	EC/Spain	39.9
	Other manufactures	6.4	EC/Spain	

Sources: See data-sources appendix.

products may be converted into Community-wide quotas. An example is Japanese cars.[14] The effect of such a step depends on whether the new limitation is more or less restrictive than the sum of the individual country quotas, and on whether ASEAN and/or South Korea are excluded from the limitation. An EC-wide voluntary export restraint (VER) applied only to Japanese models may work in favor of South Korean exports, and may even attract direct foreign investment to South Korea. With respect to the all-important multifiber agreement, it is too early to tell whether the limitations on textile imports will be more or less restrictive than the ones now in existence. The outcome here also depends on negotiations taking place in the now-delayed Uruguay Round. It would no longer be possible, however, to have country limitations on textile imports, so only EC-wide restrictions will exist. And that should have the effect of liberalizing imports.[15] The same point applies to the EC GSP. While the new EC quota system will not necessarily be more restrictive and could even be more liberal, the continued uncertainties are of considerable concern to developing Asia.

Third, the freeing of service transactions and of factor mobility within the Community is unlikely to have serious consequences for ASEAN or South Korea, as they are not significant exporters of services. But even in this case there are possible repercussions. For example, South Korean construction companies bid on many foreign contracts. To the extent that the EC would eliminate national preferences on government contracts, but open such public works for bids confined to Community members, that would constitute discrimination against South Korean or ASEAN construction companies. The US-Canada FTA has a similar provision, which may next be extended to Mexico, also to the detriment of Asian competitors. The effect of these provisions on manufacturing exports, however, would be minimal, because they affect mainly high-technology commodities not exported by ASEAN or South Korea.[16] On the other hand, the extremely complex and sensitive negotiations for an EC Social Contract, which would have sweeping implications for the transborder flow of labor in the EC, could lead to a more protectionist external commercial policy if adjustment costs are high.

Fourth, should Eastern Europe enter the Community, or otherwise negotiate preferential agreements with the EC, it would be harmful to Asian countries because East European countries are potentially highly competitive in some of the products exported by ASEAN and South Korea. German unification may have other

unspecified effects, especially in the capital markets. Fifth, the NIEs and ASEAN countries have experienced increased exposure to anti-dumping measures imposed — and investigated — by the EC commission, a trend that is increasing in importance and is widely seen as a vehicle for protection rather than to ensure fair competition (Robertson, 1991).

On the positive side, the Cecchini Report (1988) estimates a one-time potential increase in EC GNP of 2.5–6.5% to result from the unified market. Assuming the low end of the range to be the more realistic, this should stimulate some additional imports from Asia; but in the case of NTBs, it would simply make the restrictions more binding. Second, the fact that newly introduced products will now require one rather than 12 sets of testing and certification will help the EC as well as foreign firms. But that is more relevant to the United States and Japan than to ASEAN and South Korea.

4. EFFECTS ON DIRECT FOREIGN INVESTMENT

In the previous sections we identified the following categories likely to be severely affected by North American and European integration. (Table 6)

Apart from trade diversion there may be investment diversion. Direct foreign investment in ASEAN and South Korea has been instrumental in the economic dynamism of these countries, providing an important source of capital (especially in the manufacturing sector), stimulating exports, and providing new technologies essential to be competitive in the contemporary global marketplace. To the extent that a heavily affected industry in ASEAN or South Korea is also one in which these two regions are recipients of large direct foreign investment (DFI) flows, such investment may be moved to one of the three North American countries (e.g., Mexico) or to Europe. Table 7 displays DFI data in four countries[17] by aggregative industry groups.

Considering the trade-affected commodity categories and the sectoral distribution of DFI, investment diversion from ASEAN may occur in food, chemicals, textiles, metals and electronics, while in the case of South Korea it may occur in chemicals, machinery, electronics, and transport equipment. Some of these industries are considered key to future economic development, and a reduction in DFI could have important negative implications. For example, in South Korea, the share of foreign affiliate employment in the electric and electronic machinery industry

Table 6. *Summary of affected ASEAN and South Korean exports due to economic integration in North America and Europe*

ASEAN exports to:		South Korean exports to:	
North America	Europe	North America	Europe
Organic chemicals	Rubber manufactures	Organic chemicals	Chemicals
Chemical compounds	Veneer and plywood	Leather manufactures	Articles of rubber
Veneer	Textiles & clothing	Textiles & clothing	Textiles & clothing
Textiles & clothing	Precious stones	Iron & steel	Iron & steel
Precious stones	Metals	Metal manufactures	Metal manufactures
Iron & steel	Machinery items	Machinery items	Machinery items
Machinery items	Transport equipment	Nonmotor road vehicles	Transport equipment
Footwear	Footwear	Travel goods	Travel goods
Travel goods	Instruments	Furs	Footwear
Instruments	Fish	Footwear	Instruments
Fish	Fruits & vegetables	Instruments	Tobacco
Preserved fruits	Vegetable oils	Fish	Fish
Fresh nuts	Tobacco		
Raw sugar	Other foods		
Food preparations			
Petroleum products			

Table 7. *Direct foreign investment in 1988 (US$m)*

Industry	Indonesia	Malaysia	Thailand	South Korea
Food	231.0	267.4	48.6	13.5
Textiles	213.2	88.0	44.3	20.5
Wood products	104.3	—	—	4.3
Paper and printing	1,505.6	10.8	—	—
Rubber products	—	324.1	—	—
Chemicals	1,554.3	261.7	77.0	280.6
Metal products	190.1	180.2	77.5	13.4
Nonmetallic products	29.8	41.3	—	13.0
Machinery	—	—	—	65.0
Transport equipment	—	7.3	28.7	43.1
Electrical & electronic products	—	596.5	249.4	267.9

Sources: See data-sources appendix.

increased from 37% in 1976 to 57% in 1986, and foreign affiliate exports of Malaysia, the Philippines, and Thailand grew by more than 30% per year over 1976–86 (Plummer and Ramstetter, 1991).

An additional effect will be some reallocation of DFI away from South Korea, Singapore, and Taiwan and in favor of the four large ASEAN countries, because of "graduation" from the US GSP. As South Korea, Taiwan, and Singapore lost their GSP status in 1988, some foreign investors may wish to direct their investment to countries retaining that preferred status. A North American Free-Trade area, however, will lead to diversion of NIE-originated investment to Mexico, instead of ASEAN. As the NIEs have been rapidly increasing their manufacturing investment in ASEAN, this effect could be highly significant. An example would be a recent decision (August 1991) by South Korea-based Kia Motors to open an automobile manufacturing plant in Mexico in anticipation of the North American FTA.

Developments in Europe will likely affect investment in ASEAN and the Asian NIEs. On the positive side, the anticipated faster growth in the EC due to economic unification, should continue to stimulate DFI. On the other hand, the EC itself will become a more attractive location for investment, because the expanded market would afford opportunities to exploit economies of scale, and then could draw DFI away from Asia. Furthermore, by reason of scale economies and other factors, EC industries would become more formidable global competitions, and that may affect adversely the position of other areas, including ASEAN, in all markets. In addition, fears of a "Fortress Europe" scenario, in which the EC becomes more protectionist after 1992, would lead companies to invest in Europe in order to take advantage of increased protection or avoid future discrimination. And if "national treatment" for crossborder investments is confined to members of the EC, that may draw DFI away from Asian countries. The same holds true for the US-Canada FTA that might be extended to Mexico. Moreover, the recent political liberalization in Eastern Europe and the unification of East and West Germany, coupled with a movement away from planned toward market economies in the Eastern bloc, should draw a substantial amount of investment capital from the developed world. This would be especially true for the EC, which has already signed trade pacts with Eastern Europe, and is taking a leading responsibility in the reconstruction of the East, as is seen in the case of the fledgling European Bank for Reconstruction and Development. On balance, these developments would tend to draw DFI away from Asia, and may also cause a redirection of official development assistance away from ASEAN.

5. OPTIONS FOR ASEAN AND THE ASIAN NIEs

This paper investigated possible effects of emerging trade blocs in North America and Europe on ASEAN and South Korea using a commodity matching technique that allows us to identify the most severely impacted industries, as well as to quantify the general terms of trade effects. Trade diversion of ASEAN exports in North America and Europe, including only the effect of tariff removal is estimated at 4 and 8%, respectively, of its exports to the two regions, while for South Korea the relevant figures are 5% in both cases. The diversionary impact on ASEAN of European integration is greater than that of North America, partly because European tariff rates are higher than those of the United States. The aggregate effect would be much larger if the removal of NTBs were incorporated in the estimates. Not only is the overall impact significant, but several severely affected indus-

tries will bear most of the brunt, and often those are dynamic growth sectors. The fact that many Asian industries were found to compete with similar ones in Europe and North America, attests to the convergence of global industrial production as Asian development proceeds apace. Also certain service sectors in Asia, such as construction, may sustain trade diversion. Moreover, while expected investment diversion is difficult to quantify, there is a potential for considerable investment diversion in important areas of production. As Asia-Pacific developing countries continue to base their development strategies on international trade and investment, these trends are of concern. ASEAN and the NIEs may seek ways to minimize the adverse impact.

Thus far, the most important step taken by Asian countries was to participate actively in the GATT. A global tariff reduction negotiated under the Uruguay Round would reduce the margin of discrimination that ASEAN would face in Europe and North America. The possible failure of the Uruguay Round, however, would likely stimulate the drive toward regional blocs. Hence, although a global trading system based on the principle of nondiscrimination is the best route for Asia, other options need to be explored.

As an initial step, ASEAN could enhance its existing regional integration programs. While an ASEAN FTA was unthinkable even a few years ago, external (e.g., bilateralism and growing protectionism in the developed countries) and internal (e.g., consistent outward-oriented development strategies) forces have made such an agreement a reality. An ASEAN FTA has the added advantage of increasing its clout at the GATT and in bilateral negotiations.

Second, ASEAN and the Asian NIEs could consider possible bilateral accords among themselves and possibly with other Pacific nations, such as Japan. Economic interdependence in Asia has been growing rapidly, but so far only informal measures of region-wide cooperation are in place. A formal agreement, such as an FTA, could strengthen existing links and present new opportunities. The creation of an Asian trade grouping to match those of North America and Europe could have a detrimental effect on the multilateral trading system embodied in the GATT agreement. But in reality, an Asia-wide agreement would only formalize what seems to be a residual left by the other two trading blocs. Moreover, an Asian trade grouping could serve a constructive role in underlining the critical importance of future GATT negotiations. In fact, it can be argued that the recently proposed "East

Asian Trade Grouping" was conceived out of a frustration with EC and North American dominance at the GATT.

Finally, ASEAN and the Asian NIEs could enter into preferential agreements with North America. Any regional FTA configurations (such as an ASEAN/NIE or Pacific Rim FTA) could dedicate itself to the principle of "open regionalism," allowing a country to join if certain criteria are met. In fact, such arrangements would likely be a *quid pro quo* to Japan's joining any type of Asian trade bloc.

NOTES

1. Another regional scheme among developed countries is the Australia–New Zealand FTA, where the arrangement goes well beyond free trade in commodities to cover service transactions and factor movements. The effect of this scheme on Asia is not dealt with in this paper.

2. Because Brunei is a very small sultanate whose economy is almost entirely based on petroleum production, the analysis in this paper concentrates on the other five ASEAN countries.

3. Taiwan, another Asian NIE, is excluded from the analysis because it is not part of the UN data base.

4. For details see UNCTAD (1989).

5. In fact, using a general equilibrium model Brown (1989) shows the EC GSP to be *detrimental* to developing countries.

6. In 1989 eligibility was restored to 209 Mexican products valued at $1.3 billion, so that Mexico accounted for $2.5 billion or a full one-quarter of GSP duty-free imports into the United States.

7. Doubling the cut-off points would reduce the number of selected categories by about 10–15%.

8. These data were supplied to us through the courtesy of Mr. Sam Laird.

9. Another measure, known as the "coverage ratio," shows the percent of trade in a given category subject to NTBs. But the "frequency" measure is a better indicator of how onerous the NTBs are.

10. For a review of the economic dimension of implementing the Unified Market, or "EC 1992," see EC Commission (1988).

11. For many manufactured products this change may mean a reduction in tariffs leading to external trade creation; while for agriculture it is likely to lead to increased protection.

12. This qualitative discussion follows the framework of analysis suggested by Kreinin (1991), which gives a general overview of the effects of EC-1992 on third countries.

13. In all likelihood, national industrial subsidies would also be harmonized. As a percentage of industrial value added, these range from 3.6% in the United Kingdom and 4% in Germany, to 7.1% in Italy.

14. An agreement reached between Japan and the EC in 1991, specifies that until the year 2000, Japanese auto exports to the EC would be limited to 1.2 million units per year, and the output of Japanese cars inside the Community will not exceed 1.2 million per year. The latter figure is consistent with Japanese production plans.

15. Currently, if the import quota of EC country A has not been filled, while in country B the quota is binding, it is not possible to use the slack in A to increase imports into B.

16. Products where public procurement accounts for a large share of the market and where discrimination against imports is important are: defense equipment, aircraft and space equipment, electric power-generating machinery, medical equipment, railway equipment, ships, telephone exchanges, computers, and metal constructions. Lundberg (1990, Table 2).

17. Comparable data for the other countries were not available.

REFERENCES

Asian Development Bank, *Asian Development Outlook 1991* (Manila: Asian Development Bank, 1991).

Asian Development Bank, *Key Indicators of Developing Member Countries of ADB* (Manila: Asian Development Bank, July 1989).

Bank of Indonesia, *Annual Reports* (Jakarta: Bank of Indonesia, various years).

Bank of Thailand, "Statistical Publication," Mimeo (Bangkok: Bank of Thailand, July 1990).

Brown, Drucilla, "Trade effects of the European schemes of the generalized system of preferences," *Economic Development and Cultural Change*, Vol. 37, No. 4, 1989, pp. 757–76.

Brunei, Ministry of Finance, *Brunei Statistical Yearbook 1986* (Brunei: Ministry of Finance, 1987).

Brunei, Ministry of Finance, *Brunei Statistical Yearbook 1975/76* (Brunei: Ministry of Finance, 1977).

Cawley, Richard and Michael Davenport, "Partial

Equilibrium Calculations," in EC Commission, *Cost of Non-Europe: Basic Findings, Volume 2, Studies on the Economies of Integration* (Luxembourg: Office for Official Publications of the EC, 1988), p. 8–47.

Commission of the European Communities, "Generalized System of Preferences: Guidelines for the 1990s," *Communication from the Commission to the Council*, COM (90) 329 Final (Brussels: EC Commission, July 6, 1990).

EC Commission, *The European Economy*, No. 35 (Brussels: EC Commission, March 1988).

International Monetary Fund, *International Financial Statistics* (Washington, DC: International Monetary Fund, various issues).

Korea, *Business Korea Yearbook* (Seoul: Korean government, 1989/1990).

Kreinin, M. E., "Effect of exchange rate changes on the prices and volume of trade," *International Monetary Fund Staff Papers* (July 1977), pp. 297–329.

Kreinin, M. E., "EC-1992 and World Trade and the World Trading System," in G. N. Yannopoulos (Ed.), *1992 Europe and America* (Manchester: Manchester University Press, 1991).

Lundberg, Lars, "Nordic industry and the EEC internal market," in Lyck Lise (Ed.), *The Nordic Countries and the Internal Market of the EEC* (Coppenhagen: H. Forlag, 1990), table 1.

Malaysia, Ministry of Finance, *Economic Report* (Kuala Lumpur: Ministry of Finance, various years).

Plummer, Michael G., "The economic effects of the second enlargement of the European Community," Ph.D. dissertation (East Lansing, MI: Michigan State University, 1988), p. 89.

Plummer, Michael, and Eric Ramstetter, "Multinational affiliates and the changing division of labor in the Asia-Pacific Region," in E. Ramstetter (Ed.), *Direct Investment in Asia's Developing Economies and Structural Changes in the Asia-Pacific Region* (Boulder, CO: Westview, forthcoming).

Reinert, K. A., and C. R. Shields, "Trade substitution elasticities of a North American Free Trade Area," Office of Economics, USITC Working Paper No. 91-81-B (July 1991).

Robertson, David, "EC92 and East Asian trade," Paper presented at International Trade and Finance Association Conference (Marseilles: May 1991).

Roland-Holst, D., K. A. Reinert, and C. R. Shields, "North American Trade liberalization and the role of nontariff barriers," in USITC Report under Investigation No. 332–317, Paper No. 5 (February 1992).

Tovias, Alfred, *Foreign Economic Relations of the European Community: The Impact of Spain and Portugal* (Boulder: Lynne Rienner Publishers, 1990), pp. 7–9.

Trigueros, Ignacio, "A free trade agreement between Mexico and the United States?" in Jeffrey Schott (Ed.), *Free Trade Areas and U.S. Trade Policy* (Washington, DC: Institute for International Economics, 1989), p. 259.

UNCTAD, "GSP Scheme of the European Community," Trade and Development Board, TD/B/GSP/EEC/18 (Geneva: UNCTAD, March 1, 1990).

UNCTAD, "GSP Handbook on the Scheme of Canada," UNCTAD/TAP/247/Rev. March 2, 1990.

UNCTAD, "The General System of Preferences: Handbook, the United States of America," Mimeo (Geneva: UNCTAD, 1989).

United Nations, *Commodity Trade Statistics* (Geneva: UNCTAD, various issues).

United Nations, *Statistical Papers*, Series M., No. 34/Rev. 2 and No. 34/Rev. 3 (New York: United Nations, 1986).

US Government, "United States-Canada Free-Trade Agreement: Communication from the President of the United States," Annex 401.2, 100th Congress, Second Session, House Document 100–216 (Washington, DC: U.S. Government Printing Office, 1988).

Weintraub, Sidney, "The impact of the agreement on Mexico," in Peter Morici (Ed.), *Making Free Trade Work: The Canada-U.S. Agreement* (New York and London: Council on Foreign Relations, 1990).

World Bank, *World Development Report 1990* (New York: Oxford University Press, 1990).

APPENDIX: SOURCES OF DATA

Trade Data: United Nations, *Commodity Trade Statistics*, relevant issues, 1985–88.

Investment Data: Indonesia — Bank of Indonesia, *Annual Reports*, 1984/5, 1985/6, 1986/7, 1987/8, 1988/9; Malaysia — *Economic Report*, Ministry of Finance, 1985/6, 1986/7, 1987/8, 1988/9, 1989/90; Thailand — Bank of Thailand, July 1990; Korea — *Business Korea Yearbook*, 1989/90.

Tariff Data: (a) For the United States and Canada — US Government (1988). Concordances to match US and Canadian national tariff data with SITC classifications was done using United Nations, *Statistical Papers*, Series M., No. 34/Rev. 2 and No. 34/Rev. 3. (b) For the EC, Spain, Portugal, and Greece — Cawley, and Davenport (1988), 8.47; and Plummer (1988), p. 89.

GSP data: (a) For Canada — UNCTAD, *GSP Handbook on the Scheme of Canada*, UNCTAD/TAP/247/Rev. March 2, 1990; (b) For the United States, UNCTAD, *GSP Handbook on the Scheme of the United States of America*, UNCTAD/TAP/163/Rev. 12, GE.89-56557, revised April 1989; and (3) For the EC, UNCTAD, *GSP Scheme of the European Economic Community*, Trade and Development Board, TD/B/GSP/EEC/18, March 1, 1990; and Commission of the European Communities, "Generalized System of Preferences: Guidelines for the 1990s," *Communication from the Commission to the Council*, COM(90)329 Final, Brussels, July 6, 1990.

NTB data: UNCTAD computer files made available to the World Bank and supplied by Sam Laird.

Basic statistical data: Asian Development Bank (1991; July 1989). Brunei, Ministry of Finance (1977, 1987). International Monetary Fund (Yearbook, 1990; December 1990). World Bank (1990).

[4]

Journal of Economic Integration
9(1), March 1994, 1-28

Economic Effects of the North American Free-Trade Area on Australia and New Zealand

Mordechai E. Kreinin*
Michigan State University

Michael G. Plummer*
Brandeis University

Abstract

The paper analyzes the effects of the North American Free-Trade (NAFTA) on Australia and New Zealand. Using a commodity matching technique, it identifies the industries that would be most affected by the preferential trading arrangement. Trade diversion obtains in a wide-range of disaggregated primary and manufactured commodity areas. Total trade diversion is estimated as a terms of trade effect. The effects of integration on trade in services and foreign investment flows are also evaluated.

I. Introduction

Regional integration in Europe is proceeding apace, with the twelve EC countries having achieved a unified market in 1993. At the same time, the U.S.-Canada Free-Trade Area is going through a ten-year transitional period, and negotiations with Mexico are underway to form a North American

---

* Mordechai E. Kreinin: Department of Economics, Michigan State University, East Lansing, Michigan 48824-1038, U.S.A.; Michael G. Plummer: Department of Economics, Brandeis University, Waltham, MA 02254-9110, U.S.A. Tel: 617-736-2240, Fax: 617-736-2263; The authors are indebted to the East-West Center for financial and technical support and for providing a stimulating environment in which this research was pursued. We also wish to thank anonymous referees and the editor for helpful comments.

2   Economic Effects of the North American Free-Trade Area

Free-Trade Area (NAFTA), encompassing the three countries. Each regional grouping, while it may be favorable to overall world welfare, would affect outsiders adversely by creating trade and investment diversion.[1] In a recent paper,[2] we investigated the effects of such regional groupings on ASEAN and Korea. This paper will assess the effects of NAFTA on Australia and New Zealand, employing similar methodology.

Both Australia and New Zealand have already been affected by the integration steps taken in Europe, the Common Agriculture Policy (CAP) of the EC being a case in point. Consisting of domestic price supports, import controls *via* the variable levy, and export subsidies, the CAP converted the EC from a net importer to a net exporter of food products, denying Australia and New Zealand important markets and affecting their terms of trade adversely. Australian and New Zealand terms of trade have experienced a significant decline since the implementation of the CAP in the 1960s and the accession of the United Kingdom in the mid-1970s. Grouping the two countries together and using 1980 as the base-index year (*i.e.*, 1980=100), the terms of trade deteriorated from 122 in 1960 and 125 in 1965 to 101 in 1976 and 85 in 1986.[3] In the summer of 1991, Australian wheat exporters to third markets (such as China) were caught in the cross-fire of a grain subsidy war between the EC and the United States.

EC discrimination is not confined to farm products, as the Common

---

1. In creating a free-trade area, trade and investment diversion stem from the inherent preferential treatment accorded partner countries at the expense of third countries. Empirically, trade diversion is measured as the reduction in exports from third countries to the integrating area caused by the discrimination. It is a function of: (1) the extent to which commodity exports of, say, Australia, to an integrating country (*e.g.*, the United States) overlaps with that of a partner country (*e.g.*, Canada); (2) the degree of discrimination against outsiders in the "overlapping" or "matched" commodities; and (3) the price elasticity of import demand and elasticity of substitution between partner and non-partner exports. Investment diversion results from the redirection of domestic and foreign investment away from third countries toward the trading area. This effect would be most pronounced in industries sustaining extensive trade diversion.

2. Kreinin, Mordechai E. and Michael G. Plummer, "Effects of Economic Integration in Industrial Countries on ASEAN and the Asian NIEs," *World Development*, forthcoming 1992.

3. United Nations, *Monthly Bulletin of Statistics*, January 1984 and January 1991.

External Tariff caused some trade and, perhaps, investment diversion, and the EC 1992 program may affect adversely the export of services to Europe. Moreover, the recent (January 1994) "European Economic Area" (EEA) agreement between the EC and the European Free-Trade Association (EFTA), and the new association agreements being forged between the EC and several East European countries, could amplify these effects, especially if the agricultural sector is eventually included. Thus, the implications of NAFTA for Australia and New Zealand are super-imposed upon the discriminatory impact of European integration.

Raw materials play an important role in the exports of both Australia and New Zealand, and preferential treatment under NAFTA, which brings together two of the world's premier resource-rich economies, could potentially lead to further deterioration in terms of trade. Raw materials constitute 13 and 21 percent respectively of Australia and New Zealand's exports (1989)[4] — among the highest shares in the developed world. Australia is the third largest exporter of raw materials in the world behind the United States and Canada, and New Zealand is thirteenth.[5]

But in terms of future growth, NAFTA's effects on manufacturing and services are perhaps more important. Both countries have undergone significant restructuring since the mid-1980s, a result of policy changes designed to render their economies more efficient and competitive in the international marketplace. A new emphasis has been placed on non-traditional, "sunrise" industries, particularly in manufacturing and tradable services. These initiatives have included lower protection and extensive deregulation in such sensitive areas as banking and finance, certain aspects of the airline industry, and a range of value-added services in telecommunications (Australia).[6] Australia has even endeavored to promote its trade in services through export finance facilities under the Export Finance and Insurance Corporation. New Zealand also places great importance on service trade,

---

4. GATT, *International Trade 1989-1990*, Volume II (Geneva: GATT, 1990); p. 42.
5. Ibid.
6. GATT, *Trade Policy Review: Australia* (Geneva: GATT, March 1990). In addition, Bell South (United States) and Cable & Wireless (United Kingdom) have purchased the Australian telecommunications satellite, "AUSSAT," and have been given permission to compete in the Australian market with domestic services.

not only in the traditionally large sectors of tourism and transport and storage, but increasingly in communication and insurance, which are projected to have among the highest export growth rates over the 1991-1995 period.[7] The importance attached to trade in services is underscored by the relevant provisions in the Australia-New Zealand free-trade accord.

Thus, the implications of NAFTA for Australia and New Zealand will be relevant to a wide range of economic sectors. These are treated quantitatively (where possible) and qualitatively (where necessary) in the present paper. Section II introduces the approach employed here, estimates the trade diversion effect, and assesses possible investment diversion. Section III summarizes the results of the paper and suggests possible options for Australia and New Zealand to mitigate the derisory effects of NAFTA.

II. Assessment of Trade and Investment Diversion

In the contemporary international economy, free-trade areas tend to go beyond the establishment of duty-free status for intra-regional trade. Because tariffs have become less important relative to non-tariff barriers (NTBs), such as quotas and voluntary export restraints, special arrangements are needed to deal with NTBs. While it is not yet clear how comprehensive the NAFTA pact will be, it may mirror the U.S.-Canada Free-Trade area, perhaps with some form of *decalage* privileges for Mexico.[8] For our present purpose, we assume that the arrangement will allow for comprehensive free-trade in NAFTA, including the eventual elimination of all tariff and non-tariff barriers on merchandise trade. Agreements on other areas currently being considered, such as trade in services and factor flows, are excluded from the present quantitative analysis.

How would such a free-trade affect Australia and New Zealand? With the United States, Canada and Mexico gaining unrestricted access to each

7. New Zealand Institute of Economic Research, *Sectoral Projections* (Wellington: New Zealand Institute of Economic Research, September 1990), Tables 6 and 7.

8. *Decalage*, or "getting out of step," clauses refer to the allowance of certain contracting parties in a preferential trading area to have a longer transition process. This practice tends to be followed in the cases of trading areas that include countries at different levels of economic development.

other's markets, Australia and New Zealand will be at a relative competitive disadvantage in those export commodities that "overlap" the internal-source exports. The extent of this discrimination depends on the pre-integration levels of trade restrictions that the United States, Canada, and Mexico apply on a most-favored nation basis prior to the agreement. Hence, the values of trade in overlapping or "matched" commodities and the level of tariffs and nontariff barriers taken together would determine the extent of potential trade diversion.

A. Trade Diversion

We employ a disaggregative approach, based on the 4-digit SITC commodity categories in assessing the economic effects of NAFTA on Australia and New Zealand. For each commodity group, the exports of Australia-New Zealand to a NAFTA market (*e.g.* the United States) were matched with exports from a competing internal NAFTA source (Canada or Mexico). A minimum value cut-off point had to be imposed, in order to identify the most relevant categories. While there is no theoretical guideline to the selection of the cut-off value, we chose a low point in most cases, not only in order to be comprehensive, but also to capture growing industries that may be in the vanguard of future export growth. This is particularly important for Australia and New Zealand, each of which is undergoing vast structural changes which may lead to growth in non-traditional manufactured exports. Hence, for Australian exports and internal competition, the selected cut-off value in each commodity is $500,000. As New Zealand is a much smaller country, the minimum value for its exports and internal competition is set at $250,000. The most recent export data-set available for Australia is 1989 and for New Zealand it is 1990[9]. In order to conserve space, the tables below aggregate certain 4-digit categories into 3-digit (or even 2-digit) categories, whenever such aggregation in appropriate.[10]

---

9. In some cases, comprehensive data were not available for Australia in 1989 (New Zealand in 1990); in such instances, 1988 (1989) data were used, as indicated in the tables to follow.

10. Detailed tables for all 4-digit SITC categories are available from the second author upon request.

Australian exports to the United States that compete directly with at least one internal source (Canada or Mexico) are shown in Table 1-A. For each matched 4-digit commodity group, the table shows the value of exports, the competing internal source(s), and the average U.S. most-favored nation tariff (or range of tariffs if the category was aggregated to a higher level).[11] In addition, the extent of non-tariff barrier (NTB) protection facing industrial-country exports is estimated using data compiled from a World Bank-UNCTAD study.[12] These NTBs are ranked in relative terms as being very high, high, average, low, very low, and zero, and apply to developed countries.[13] The chosen indices, not available for Canada and Mexico, were based on frequency ratios rather than coverage ratios.[14] This information was not available for Canada and Mexico. This approach enables us to identify the commodity categories that are likely to be impacted by NAFTA. The quantitative estimates are confined to the discriminatory impact of tariffs, and not of the NTBs, and as such represent a substantial understatement.

Tariff Effects: There is a large number and considerable variety of Australian exports to the United States that could be adversely affected by NAFTA (Table 1-A). Bovine meat is the largest Australian export in the data

---

11. The average tariffs were calculated for each SITC grouping by converting the U.S. tariff code into its SITC equivalent. The same method was used in the case of the Canadian tariff. For sources used, please see the Appendix on data sources.

12. We are grateful to Mr. Sam Laird who made this information available to us.

13. In assessing the effects of U.S. NTBs, it is useful to distinguish between those applied to developed countries – which are relevant to the present analysis – and developing countries, as the frequency ratios differ.

14. Coverage ratios are problematic in that they gauge the importance of NTBs in direct proportion to import share, thereby suggesting an inherent bias. If an NTB in a certain commodity category is responsible for a small import share, the coverage ratio value would be low, when in fact it should be high. For example, the Japanese ban on rice imports would give zero weight to rice in calculating coverage ratios, thereby giving the impression that NTBs are not restrictive. Hence, if the coverage ratio is to be used, extreme care needs to be taken in treating the effects of NTBs. See, for example, Trefler, Daniel [1993], "Trade Liberalization and the Theory of Endogenous Protection: An Econometric Study of U.S. Import Policy," *Journal of Political Economy*, February, and Kreinin, Mordechai [1991], *International Economics: A Policy Approach*, Sixth Edition; pp.371-372.

Mordechai E. Kreinin and Michael G. Plummer   7

Table 1
Discriminatory Effects of North American Integration on Australia

SITC	Description	1989[a] Australian Exports (US$m)	Internal Competition	Range of Average Tariff (%)	Nontariff Barriers
A. Australian Exports to the United States					
0111	Bovine meat	632.0	Canada/Mexico	7	High
0113	Pig meat	2.3	Canada	2	High
0116	Edible offal	4.6	Canada	5	High
0138	Prepared/processed meat	5.9	Canada	5	High
0222	Milk and cream, dry	3.9	Canada	2	High
0240	Cheese and curd	11.7	Canada	15	High
0311/13	Fish	101.1	Canada/Mexico	1	High
0320	Fish, *etc.*, tinned/prepared	1.5	Canada/Mexico	7	High
0470	Meal and flour	0.6	Canada/Mexico	10	High
0481	Breakfast food	1.7	Canada/Mexico	7	High
0484	Bread	1.0	Canada/Mexico	2	High
0488	Cereal	0.6	Canada/Mexico	9	High
0517	Nuts	10.3	Canada/Mexico	0	High
0519	Fresh fruit	1.1	Canada/Mexico	10	High
0520	Dried fruit	1.0	Canada/Mexico	10	High
0532	Preserved fruit	2.5	Mexico	12	High
0539	Fruit nuts	1.9	Canada/Mexico	13	High
0542	Dry vegetables	2.4	Canada/Mexico	0	High
0546	Vegetables, simply preserved	0.8	Canada/Mexico	14	High
0615	Molasses	9.5	Canada/Mexico	0	High
0620	Sugar	0.7	Canada/Mexico	10	High
0990	Food preparations	2.0	Canada/Mexico	7	High
1110/21	Beverages and wine	18.0	Canada/Mexico	10-13	High
2218	Oil seeds/nuts	1.5	Canada/Mexico	2	High
2433	Lumber	1.4	Canada/Mexico	0	Low
2664	Waste of synthetic fibers	0.7	Canada/Mexico	2	Low
2769	Crude minerals	1.4	Canada/Mexico	1	High
2813	Iron ore	2.3	Canada	0	High
283	Copper, nickel, lead, nonfer. ores	106.6	Canada/Mexico	0-1	High
2840	Nonferrous metal scraps	0.8	Canada/Mexico	0	High
2860	Uranium, *etc.*	30.9	Canada	0	High
2919	Animal materials	1.4	Canada/Mexico	1	Low
2925	Seeds	2.3	Canada/Mexico	0	Low
2927	Cut flowers	1.4	Canada/Mexico	5	Low
3214	Coal	2.1	Canada	0	Very high
3218	Coke of coal	42.8	Canada	0	Very high
3310	Crude petroleum	225.0	Canada/Mexico	0	Very high

8   Economic Effects of the North American Free-Trade Area on Australia and New Zealand

Table 1 (continued)

SITC	Description	1989[a] Australian Exports (US$m)	Internal Competition	Range of Average Tariff (%)	Nontariff Barriers
3325	Lubricating oils, greases	4.1	Canada	6	Very high
4113	Animal oils, *etc.*	0.6	Canada	12	Very low
5143	Metal comp.	1.1	Canada/Mexico	2	Very low
5331	Coloring material	2.7	Canada/Mexico	4	Very low
5413	Antibiotics	1.6	Canada/Mexico	5	Very low
5417/19	Pharmaceuticals	9.0	Canada/Mexico	4-5	Very low
5511	Essential oils, resinoids	1.3	Canada/Mexico	2	Very low
5530	Perfume, cosmetics, *etc.*	1.7	Canada/Mexico	5	Very low
5812	Products of polymerizing, *etc.*	2.5	Canada/Mexico	4	Very low
5992	Pesticides, disinfectants	6.5	Canada/Mexico	5	Very low
5995	Starch	14.9	Canada/Mexico	4	Very low
5999	Chemical products	0.7	Canada/Mexico	5	Very low
6114	Leather, bovine, n.e.s., equine	5.9	Canada/Mexico	4	Zero
6130	Fur skins	1.0	Canada/Mexico	3	Zero
6291	Rubber tire, tubes	1.1	Canada/Mexico	3	Low
6299	Other rubber articles	1.4	Canada/Mexico	3	Low
6429	Paper articles	0.6	Canada/Mexico	4	Low
6532	Woven wool fabrics	1.0	Canada/Mexico	17	Average
6535	Woven synthetic fabrics	2.7	Canada/Mexico	16	Average
6569	Other textile products	5.7	Canada/Mexico	10	Average
6576	Carpets, etc., unknotted	0.9	Canada/Mexico	6	Average
6618	Mineral building products	4.1	Canada/Mexico	5	Low
6647	Safety glass	3.3	Canada/Mexico	3	Low
6648	Sheet glass	2.5	Canada/Mexico	4	Low
6649	Glass, n.e.s.	2.7	Canada/Mexico	3	Low
6672/73	Precious/semiprecious stones	13.4	Canada	0-9	Low
6714/15	Iron alloys	24.2	Canada/Mexico	4-6	Very high
6725/27	Iron/steel, blooms/coils	15.5	Canada/Mexico	4-5	Very high
6731	Iron/steel wire	3.4	Canada/Mexico	5	Very high
6732	Iron/steel bars	0.7	Canada/Mexico	5	Very high
6743/ 47/48	Iron and steel	83.0	Canada/Mexico	5-6	Very high
6770	Iron/steel wire, excl. w/rod	1.8	Canada/Mexico	5	Very high
6791	Iron cast	1.2	Canada/Mexico	2	Very high
6822	Copper, alloy	4.1	Canada/Mexico	1	Very low
6841/42	Aluminum alloys	26.7	Canada/Mexico	2-3	Very low
6861	Zinc alloys	60.7	Canada/Mexico	10	Very low
6871	Tin alloys	1.1	Canada/Mexico	0	Very low
6895	Base metals, n.e.s.	1.0	Canada/Mexico	4	Very low
6911	Structures parts, iron/steel	0.9	Canada/Mexico	4	Low

Mordechai E. Kreinin and Michael G. Plummer

Table 1 (continued)

SITC	Description	1989[a] Australian Exports (US$m)	Internal Competition	Range of Average Tariff (%)	Nontariff Barriers
6942	Steel/copper nuts/bolts	1.9	Canada/Mexico	5	
6952	Tools	2.4	Canada/Mexico	5	Low
6960	Cutlery	0.9	Canada/Mexico	7	Low
6971	Domestic stoves ovens, *etc.*	2.3	Canada/Mexico	5	Low
6981	Locksmiths wares	2.6	Canada/Mexico	3	Low
6988/89	Misc. base metal products	2.0	Canada/Mexico	3	Low
7113	Steam engines, turbines	1.0	Canada/Mexico	6	Low
7114/15	Aircraft engines	19.2	Canada/Mexico	1-3	Low
7116	Gas turbines, non-aircraft	7.2	Canada/Mexico	3	Low
7118	Engines, n.e.s.	2.3	Canada/Mexico	2	Low
7121/22	Cultivating/harvesting machinery	7.9	Canada/Mexico	0-1	Low
7143/49	Statistical/office machines	62.3	Canada/Mexico	2-3	Low
7151	Machine tools for metal	3.1	Canada/Mexico	4	Low
7173	Sewing machines	0.6	Canada	2	Low
718	Machinery for special industries	24.2	Canada/Mexico	2-3	Low
719	Nonelectrical machinery	47.5	Canada/Mexico	1-5	Low
7221	Electric power machinery	0.9	Canada/Mexico	1	Low
7222	Switchgear, *etc.*	5.3	Canada/Mexico	3	Low
7231	Insulated wire/cable	0.9	Canada/Mexico	3	Low
7249	Telecommunication equipment	25.6	Canada/Mexico	3	Low
7250	Domestic electrical equipment	0.9	Canada/Mexico	3	Low
7261	Electro-medical equipment	2.4	Canada/Mexico	5	Low
7262	X-ray apparatus	0.8	Canada/Mexico	3	Low
7291	Batteries, accumulators	1.4	Canada/Mexico	3	Low
7293	Transistors, valves, *etc.*	3.5	Canada/Mexico	2	Low
7294	Automotive elec. equipment	1.4	Canada/Mexico	2	Low
7295	Elec. measuring control equipment	9.0	Canada/Mexico	3	Low
7299	Other electrical machinery	6.5	Canada/Mexico	3	Low
7316	Freight cars, not powered	1.1	Canada/Mexico	14	Low
7321	Passenger motor vehicles, excl. buses	2.7	Canada/Mexico	0	Low
7328	Motor vehicle parts, n.e.s.	41.5	Canada/Mexico	1	Low
7341/49	Aircraft and parts	199.1	Canada/Mexico	1-2	Low
7353	Ships and boats	21.0	Canada/Mexico	1	Low
8210	Furniture	1.8	Canada/Mexico	4	Low
8411	Textile clothes, not knit	8.4	Canada/Mexico	13	Average
8413	Leather clothes, accessories	0.6	Canada/Mexico	7	Average
8414	Clothing, accessories, knit	6.7	Canada/Mexico	17	Very low
8415	Headgear	1.8	Canada/Mexico	6	Low
8416	Rubber clothing, including gloves	1.3	Canada/Mexico	7	Low
8420	Fur	1.7	Mexico	7	Low

10   Economic Effects of the North American Free-Trade Area on Australia and New Zealand

Table 1 (continued)

SITC	Description	1989[a] Australian Exports (US$m)	Internal Competition	Range of Average Tariff (%)	Nontariff Barriers
8510	Footwear	4.8	Canada/Mexico	17	Very low
8613-17	Medical instruments/equipment	15.4	Canada/Mexico	4-8	Low
8619	Measuring, controlling instruments	19.3	Canada/Mexico	3	Low
8624	Photo film	0.7	Canada/Mexico	3	Low
8630	Developed cinema film	1.5	Mexico	0	Low
8911	Sound recorders, phonographs, parts	1.4	Canada/Mexico	2	Low
8912	Sound recording tapes, discs	8.5	Canada/Mexico	3	Low
8921	Printed books, globes, *etc.*	4.9	Canada/Mexico	1	Low
8924	Picture postcards, *etc.*	0.5	Canada/Mexico	4	Low
8929	Printed matter, n.e.s.	3.7	Canada/Mexico	2	Low
8930	Plastic articles, n.e.s.	5.5	Canada/Mexico	4	Low
8942	Toys, indoor games	2.4	Canada/Mexico	6	Low
8944	Outdoor sporting goods	2.0	Canada/Mexico	4	Low
8960	Works of art, *etc.*	14.9	Canada/Mexico	0	Low
8971	Real jewelry, gold, silver	1.1	Canada/Mexico	7	Low
8996	Hearing aids, orthopedic aids	17.4	Canada	6	Low
8999	Other manufactured goods	2.2	Canada/Mexico	7	Low
9510	War firearms, ammunition	3.0	Canada/Mexico	4	Low

B. Australian Exports to Canada

SITC	Description	1989[a] Australian Exports (US$m)	Internal Competition	Range of Average Tariff (%)	Nontariff Barriers
0111/12/16	Fresh meat	60.9	United States	0-1	
0138	Prepared/processed meat	2.5	United States	10	
0240	Cheese and curd	0.7	United States	2	
0511	Oranges, tangerines, *etc.*	0.8	United States	0	
0519/20	Fresh and dried fruit	14.5	U.S./Mexico	10-12	
0535	Fruit or vegetable juice	0.6	United States	5	
0539/42	Fruit nuts and dry vegetables	16.0	United States	9	
1110/21	Beverages and wine	7.5	United States	5-15	
2622	Wool, degreased	2.2	United States	0	
2831	Copper ores, concentrates	1.2	United States	0	
5331	Coloring material	1.9	United States	10	
5414/17	Veg, alkaloids/derivatives, medicaments	4.3	United States	9-10	
5995	Starch	0.7	United States	13	
6114	Leather, bovine, n.e.s., equine	2.6	United States	9	
6535	Woven synthetic fabrics	0.9	U.S./Mexico	29	
6652	Household, hotel, *etc.*, glass	0.5	United States	11	
6727/34/43/48	Iron and steel	4.3	U.S./Mexico	7-8	
6952	Tools	1.4	United States	10	

Table 1 (continued)

SITC	Description	1989[a] Australian Exports (US$m)	Internal Competition	Range of Average Tariff (%)	Nontariff Barriers
6981	Locksmiths wares	0.8	United States	10	
7114/15	Aircraft/piston engines	9.9	U.S./Mexico	5-6	
7149	Office machines	1.5	U.S./Mexico	6	
7184/85	Mining machinery	2.3	United States	4-10	
7192	Pumps, centrifuges	1.2	United States	6	
7193	Mechanical handling equipment	1.4	United States	6	
7198	Other machines, nonelectrical	0.7	United States	8	
7199	Machine parts, accessories, n.e.s.	0.5	U.S./Mexico	7	
7249	Telecommunication equipment	1.6	United States	6	
7295	Elec. measuring control equipment	1.6	United States	5	
7328	Motor vehicle parts	1.7	U.S./Mexico	6	
7341/49	Aircraft parts, *etc.*	2.0	United States	0-6	
8414	Clothing, accessories, knit	0.8	U.S./Mexico	25	
8618	Meters, counters, nonelectrical	1.0	United States	6	
8619	Measuring, controlling instruments	2.0	U.S./Mexico	6	
8921	Printed books, globes, *etc.*	0.8	United States	1	
8929	Printed matter, n.e.s.	0.6	United States	5	
8930	Plastic articles, n.e.s.	1.2	United States	13	
8996	Hearing aids, orthopedic aids	0.5	United States	0	
C. Australian Exports to Mexico					
0222	Milk and cream, dry	1.1	U.S./Canada		
0410	Wheat, *etc.*, unmilled	5.1	U.S./Canada		
2218	Oil seeds/nuts	16.8	U.S./Canada		
2621	Wool greasy, fleece-washed	12.0	United States		
2834/39	Lead/nonferrous ores, concentrates	8.9[b]	United States		
3324/25	Fuel/lubricating oils, greases	7.9	United States		
7183	Food machinery, nondomestic	0.8	United States		
9310	Special transactions	6.8	U.S./Canada		

Note: a. In case where 1989 data were not available, 1988 data were used.

     b. 1987 data.

set. It faces high levels of both tariff and NTB protection,[15] and competes directly with meat exported by Canada and Mexico. By contrast, aircraft

---

15. Under the U.S. Meat Import Law, Australia and New Zealand have had to restrict their exports to the United States under a voluntary restraint agreement for a variety of meat exports.

and parts constitute a large export category, but would face little discrimination in the U.S. market by virtue of low import barriers. Categories exceeding $100 million in value that confront high tariffs and/or high to NTBs, as well as competition from internal sources, include: fish, copper, and crude petroleum. Additional exports that could be severely affected are: cheese, nuts, molasses, beverages, metals, coal, medicaments, pesticides, textile products, precision stones, manganese, iron and steel products, zinc alloy, clothing and footwear, and medical instruments. An important category for Australian exports to the United States is wool, with a value exceeding $190 million (SITC 2621/22). However, because neither Canada nor Mexico competes with Australia in the U.S. market, wool is excluded.

Table 1-B provides similar information for the Canadian market, where the United States and Mexico are the competing internal sources. Canada constitutes a much less important market for Australia than does the United States. Canadian tariff barriers tend to be higher than their U.S. counterparts, but the lack of information on Canadian NTBs precludes any general comparative statements about market "openness." The most heavily impacted commodities are: meat, dried and preserved fruit, wine, medicaments, leather, iron and steel, tools, aircraft engines, office machines, telecommunications equipment, aircraft parts, and plastics. Australian wool exports face competition from the United States in the Canadian market, but the low tariff rate implies a small effect on trade.

Matched Australian exports to the Mexican market are shown in Table 1-C. That trade is relatively small, adding up to less than $50 million. Milk, wool, nonferrous ore concentrates, n.e.s., oil seed/nuts, and food machinery are the main affected commodity groups.

New Zealand's exports to NAFTA are dealt with in Table 2, where 2-A shows its "matched" exports to the United States. The most heavily impacted industries would be: meat, milk and cheese, fish, fresh and preserved fruit and vegetables, sheep skin, alcohols, wood yarn and fabrics, carpets, iron and steel, tools, clothing, and instruments. As was the case for Australia, New Zealand wool exports to the United States are important ($33 million), but because there is no internal competition in NAFTA and since U.S. protection is low, that sector would not be severely affected. In most of the affected industries, both Canada and Mexico compete with New Zealand

Mordechai E. Kreinin and Michael G. Plummer   13

Table 2
Discriminatory Effects of North American Integration on New Zealand

SITC	Description	1990[a] New Zealand Exports (US$m)	Internal Competition	Range of Average Tariff (%)	Nontariff Barriers
A. New Zealand Exports to the United States					
0012	Sheep, lambs, goats	1.9	Canada	0	High
0015	Horses, asses, mules	2.0	Canada	2	High
0111/12 /16/18	Meat	513.5	Canada/Mexico	5-7	High
0138	Prepared/processed meat	1.6	Canada	5	High
0221/22 /23	Milk and cream	7.8	Canada	2	High
0240	Cheese and curd	36.4	Canada	15	High
0311/13	Fish	123.5	Canada/Mexico	1	High
0484	Bread	1.2	Canada/Mexico	0	High
0514	Apples, fresh	21.8	Canada	0	High
0519	Fresh fruit	54.3	Canada/Mexico	10	High
0535	Fruit or vegetable juice	3.1	Canada/Mexico	0	High
0536	Fruit, temporarily preserved	0.9	Canada/Mexico	10	High
0539	Fruit nuts	0.4	Canada/Mexico	13	High
0542	Dry vegetables	0.9	Canada/Mexico	0	High
0545	Other fresh vegetables	1.3	Canada/Mexico	14	High
0546	Vegetables, simply preserved	2.2	Canada/Mexico	12	High
0819	Food waste and feed	2.8	Canada/Mexico	10	High
1121	Wine of fresh grapes, *etc.*	0.5	Canada	10	High
1123	Beer, ale, stout, porter	6.4	Canada/Mexico	0	High
2117	Sheep skin, without wool	7.1	Canada	5	Low
2432	Lumber, shaped conifer	2.8	Canada/Mexico	2	Low
2621/ 22/23	Wool	33.1	(No internal)	0-6	Low
2911	Bones, Ivory, horns, *etc.*	4.1	Mexico	0	Low
2919	Animal materials	17.7	Canada/Mexico	1	Low
2925/26 /27/29	Plants and flowers	8.2	Canada/Mexico	0-7	Low
5122/25 /29	Organic chemicals	9.1	Canada/Mexico	6-8	Very low
5416	Glycosides, glands, sera	0.7	Canada/Mexico	3	Very low
5530	Perfume, cosmetics, *etc.*	0.3	Canada/Mexico	5	Very low
5811	Products of condensation, *etc.*	0.6	Canada/Mexico	4	Very low
5812	Products of polymerizing, *etc.*	0.9	Canada/Mexico	4	Very low
5995/96	Starch and chemicals	155.6	Canada/Mexico	4	Very low
6114	Leather, bovine, n.e.s., equine	1.3	Canada/Mexico	4	Zero
6119	Leather, n.e.s.	1.1	Canada/Mexico	4	Zero

Table 2 (continued)

SITC	Description	1990[a] New Zealand Exports (US$m)	Internal Competition	Range of Average Tariff (%)	Nontariff Barriers
6130	Fur skins	0.7	Canada/Mexico	3	Zero
6291	Rubber tire, tubes	1.3	Canada/Mexico	3	Low
6299	Other rubber articles, n.e.s.	1.4	Canada/Mexico	3	Low
6314	Improved reconstituted wood	0.4	Canada/Mexico	3	Low
6328	Other wood manufactures	0.3	Canada/Mexico	5	Low
6330	Cork manufactures	0.6	Canada	10	Low
6416	Fiberboard of wood, *etc.*	0.4	Canada/Mexico	2	Low
6419	Other paper, *etc.*	1.8	Canada/Mexico	2	Low
6512	Yarn of wood, animal hair	5.2	Canada	5	Low
6532	Woven wool fabrics	0.6	Canada/Mexico	17	Average
6576	Carpets, *etc.*, unknotted	2.3	Canada/Mexico	6	Average
6612	Cement	3.4	Canada/Mexico	0	Low
6618	Mineral building products	1.0	Canada/Mexico	5	Low
6647	Safety glass	4.9	Canada/Mexico	3	Low
6727	Iron/steel, rerolling coil	13.9	Canada/Mexico	4	Very high
6741/42 /43/48	Iron and steel	44.3	Canada/Mexico	4-6	Very high
6793	Iron/steel, rough forgings	0.5	Canada/Mexico	2	Very high
6821/22	Copper, unwrought/worked alloys	6.2	Canada/Mexico	1-4	Very low
6842	Aluminum, worked alloys	3.3	Canada/Mexico	3	Very low
6933	Wire fencing, gauze, *etc.*	0.9	Canada/Mexico	4	Low
6952	Tools	1.9	Canada/Mexico	5	Low
6960	Cutlery	0.3	Canada/Mexico	7	Low
6971	Domestic stoves, ovens, etc.	0.5	Canada/Mexico	5	Low
6972	Domestic utensils, base metal	0.7	Canada/Mexico	4	Low
6981/89	Metal wares	3.4	Canada/Mexico	3	Low
7114	Aircraft engines, including jet	3.4	Canada/Mexico	3	Low
7115	Piston engines, non-aircraft	0.9	Canada/Mexico	1	Low
7116	Gas turbines, non-aircraft	1.8	Canada/Mexico	2	Low
7121	Cultivating machinery	1.3	Canada/Mexico	0	Low
7122	Harvesting, *etc.*, machinery	0.4	Canada/Mexico	1	Low
7123	Dairy farm equipment	2.3	Canada	1	Low
7143/49	Statistical/office machines	9.0	Canada/Mexico	2-3	Low
7151	Machine tools for metal	2.3	Canada/Mexico	4	Low
7182	Printing and binding machinery	1.2	Canada/Mexico	3	Low
7184	Construction/mining machinery	0.3	Canada/Mexico	2	Low
7185	Crushing, *etc.*, glass machinery	2.2	Canada/Mexico	3	Low
7191	Heating/cooling equipment	0.6	Canada/Mexico	2	Low
7192	Pumps, centrifuges	2.4	Canada/Mexico	1	Low
7193	Mechanical handling equipment	4.2	Canada/Mexico	1	Low
7195	Powered tools	0.7	Canada/Mexico	3	Low

Table 2 (continued)

SITC	Description	1990[a] New Zealand Exports (US$m)	Internal Competition	Range of Average Tariff (%)	Nontariff Barriers
7196	Nonelectrical machinery, n.e.s.	1.7	Canada/Mexico	3	Low
7198	Other machines, nonelectrical	0.8	Canada/Mexico	5	Low
7199	Machine parts, accessories	1.8	Canada/Mexico	3	Low
7221	Electric power machinery	0.4	Canada/Mexico	1	Low
7222	Switchgear, *etc.*	0.3	Canada/Mexico	3	Low
7232	Electrical insulating equipment	0.3	Canada/Mexico	3	Low
7249	Telecommunication equipment	2.0	Canada/Mexico	3	Low
7250	Domestic electrical equipment	0.7	Canada/Mexico	3	Low
7295	Elec. measuring control equipment	0.5	Canada/Mexico	3	Low
7299	Other electrical machinery	4.0	Canada/Mexico	3	Low
7321/28	Motor vehicles	21.0	Canada/Mexico	0-1	Low
7341/49	Aircraft parts, *etc.*	18.0	Canada/Mexico	1-2	Low
7353	Ships and boats, non-war	2.5	Canada/Mexico	1	Low
8210	Furniture	2.3	Canada/Mexico	3	Low
8411	Textile clothes, not knit	0.9	Canada/Mexico	13	Low
8414	Clothing, accessories, knit	1.4	Canada/Mexico	17	Average
8420	Fur	2.7	Canada	7	Average
8510	Footwear	0.8	Canada/Mexico	17	Very low
8612	Spectacles and frames	0.5	Canada/Mexico	5	Low
8613	Optical instruments	0.3	Canada/Mexico	8	Low
8616/17 /19	Professional instruments	8.7	Canada/Mexico	3-5	Low
8921	Printed books, globes, *etc.*	1.3	Canada/Mexico	1	Low
8924/29	Picture postcards, printed matter, n.e.s.	0.7	Canada/Mexico	2-4	Low
8930	Plastic articles, n.e.s.	4.6	Canada/Mexico	3	Low
8942	Toys, indoor games	0.6	Canada/Mexico	6	Low
8960	Works of art, *etc.*	0.6	Canada/Mexico	0	Low
8971	Real jewelry, gold, silver	0.5	Canada/Mexico	7	Low
8972	Imitation jewelry	0.5	Canada/Mexico	8	Low
8996	Hearing aids, orthopedic aids	0.4	Canada	6	Low

B. New Zealand Exports to Canada

SITC	Description	1990[a] New Zealand Exports (US$m)	Internal Competition	Range of Average Tariff (%)	Nontariff Barriers
0111/12 /16/18	Meat	90.1	United States	1	
0222/23	Milk, *etc.*	4.5	United States	10-17	
0240	Cheese and curd	3.0	United States	2	
0311/13	Fish	2.0	United States	0-3	
0535	Fruit or vegetable juice	1.1	United States	5	
0539	Fruit nuts	0.5	United States	9	
0545	Other fresh vegetables	0.5	United States	15	
1121	Wine of fresh grapes, *etc.*	0.3	United States	5	

Table 2 (continued)

SITC	Description	1990[a] New Zealand Exports (US$m)	Internal Competition	Range of Average Tariff (%)	Nontariff Barriers
1123	Beer, ale, stout, porter	0.3	U.S./Mexico	3	
2117/ 2622	Sheep and wool	3.8	United States	0	
2919	Animal materials	2.9	United States	1	
2927	Cut flowers	1.0	United States	15	
5416	Glycosides, glands, sera	0.3	United States	10	
5530	Perfume, cosmetics, *etc.*	0.4	United States	10	
5995	Starch	1.7	United States	13	
6119	Leather	2.2	United States	10	
6330	Cork manufactures	0.3	United States	0	
6512	Yarn of wool, animal hair	0.8	United States	13	
6576	Carpets, *etc.*, unknotted	1.4	United States	25	
6647	Safety glass	0.3	U.S./Mexico	15	
6727	Iron/steel, rerolling coil	1.6	United States	7	
6743/48 /83	Iron and steel	6.7	United States	8-11	
6822/42	Copper, alloy, aluminum, worked alloys	2.8	U.S./Mexico	7-11	
6952	Tools	5.0	United States	10	
6989	Other base metals	0.8	United States	7	
7192	Pumps, centrifuges	0.5	United States	6	
7196	Nonelectrical machinery	0.3	United States	7	
7249	Telecommunication equipment	1.0	United States	6	
7299	Other electrical machinery	0.7	U.S./Mexico	8	
7328	Motor vehicle parts	0.5	U.S./Mexico	6	
7341/49 /53	Aircraft and ships	14.5	United States	6-17	
8414	Clothing, accessories, knit	0.3	U.S./Mexico	25	
8420	Fur	0.3	United States	20	
8617	Medical instruments	0.3	United States	2	
8921	Printed books, globes, *etc.*	0.4	United States	1	
8930	Plastic articles, n.e.s.	0.8	United States	13	
C. New Zealand Exports to Mexico					
0112	Mutton, *etc.*, fresh, chilled, frozen	5.5	United States		
0222/23 /30	Milk and cream, dry/fresh; butter	102.9	U.S./Canada		
2512	Mechanical wood pulp	0.4	United States		
2621/22	Wool	1.5	United States		
5995	Starch	6.6	United States		

Note: a. In cases where 1990 data were not available, 1989 data were used.

in the U.S. market – a counter-intuitive result given the different factor endowments of Mexico and New Zealand. With respect to New Zealand exports to Canada, Table 2-B shows that milk, fish, fruit and vegetables, cut flowers, starch, leather, carpets, iron and steel, copper and aluminum, tools, and aircraft and ships will be the most heavily affected categories. New Zealand exports to Mexico are heavily dominated by dairy products (milk, cream, and butter), but mutton, wool and starch would also be among the impacted commodities.

The following is a summary list of industries in Australia-New Zealand that are likely to be heavily impacted by the discriminatory effects of NAFTA:

Industries in Australia and New Zealand Heavily Impacted by NAFTA

Bovine meat	Medicaments
Dried and preserved fruits and vegetables	Leather
Fish	Pesticides
Cheese	Textiles and Clothing
Milk	Precious stones
Wood and yarn	Nonferrous ore concentrates
Carpets	Manganese
Oil seed/nuts	Iron and steel products
Sheepskin	Tools
Cut flowers	Zinc Alloy
Starch	Footwear
Wine	Medical Instruments
Copper	Food machinery
Petroleum	Aircraft parts/engines
Nuts	Office machines
Molasses	Telecommunications equipment
Beverages	Plastics
Metals	Instruments
Coal	Ships

Although the partial equilibrium approach adopted here is best suited for the identification of the heavily impacted industries, and the aggregated effects are best estimated by CGE models (discussed below), it is useful to use our data as well to assess the aggregate effect on trade. Because NTBs cannot be quantified accurately, the answer must concentrate on the effect of tariff discrimination. Two approaches were employed, yielding roughly similar results in terms of dollar value. The first one assumes that Australia-New Zealand exporters to the United States would attempt to maintain their share of the market and would, therefore, absorb the new degree of discrimination and reduce their export price to the extent needed to remain competitive. Since the United States is a "large" country, we assume a two-thirds pass-through of the tariff,[16] so that the reduction in the Asian export price would be equal to two-thirds of the tariff. In other words, the cost of a discriminatory North American FTA (in the U.S. market) is quantified as a deterioration in Australia-New Zealand terms of trade by two-thirds of the U.S. tariff. In the case of exports to Canada and Mexico, a full pass-through is assumed, so the terms of trade effect equals the full tariff. Measured in this manner, the negative terms of trade effect on Australia is estimated at 2.4 percent, 4.5 percent, and 12.2 percent of bilateral exports to the United States, Canada, and Mexico,[17] respectively. The respective values for New Zealand exports are 4.1 percent, 4.5 percent, and 11.9 percent.[18]

An alternative approach is to apply elasticity coefficients to the price reduction engendered by the internal tariff cut, and multiply the results by Australia-New Zealand exports. A recent study of the elasticity of substitution between U.S. imports from Mexico, Canada, and the rest of the world (Reinert and Shields [1991]) for two- and three-digit commodity groups shows the overwhelming majority of the estimates cluster around 1, thereby confirming the estimates of the previous paragraph.

NTBs: One reason why the above quantitative estimates understate the expected trade diversion is that they only relate to tariff removal within the grouping. Since U.S. tariff rates are very low, except for occasional spikes, the main diversionary impact would come from removal of NTBs. It should

---

16. For a review of the pass-through considerations, see Kreinin, Mordechai [1977], "Effect of Exchange Rate Changes on the Prices and Volumes of Trade," *IMF Staff Papers*, July, and the literature cited therein.

17. For Mexico, we used an average tariff of 12 percent.

18. These calculations exclude SITC 9 as this category represents a highly-specialized and diverse group, including zoo animals and firearms. These commodities were deemed less important for the present analysis.

be noted that the NTB estimates presented here are crude, as well as aggregative. As such, they conceal important distinctions between subproducts, and are unable to identify special bilateral relationships. For example, some of the U.S.-Canada trade disputes have been going on for years and will continue to do so. Thus, the ratification of NAFTA would not mean free trade or trade diversion for all the NTBs listed.

How would a customs union or FTA affect nonmember countries in commodities subject to import quotas? Several scenarios are possible. If the import quotas on third countries are binding and remain so after integration, then removal of the NTB in, say, the United States on imports from (say) Mexico, would cause an increase in Mexican exports to the United States. U.S. output would be displaced, thereby constituting trade creation. No trade diversion would occur. Second, if the United States decides to keep overall imports constant, it would tighten the quotas on third countries. In that case, there would be trade creation as well as trade diversion. The two effects would be equal in magnitude if the added exclusion equals the increased imports from Mexico, so as to maintain overall U.S. imports constant. On the other hand, trade creation would be larger (smaller) than diversion if the new exclusions fall short of (exceed) the added internal imports. But under this scenario, there would always be some trade diversion. Under the third scenario, the increase in internal imports would reduce demand for external imports to a point where the quotas are no longer binding. This is also a case of trade diversion. Finally, if the NTBs are in the form of VERs there could be redistribution of the quota rents. Most likely, different commodities would fall under different scenarios discussed above.

A recent study (Roland-Holst, Reinert and Shields [1992]) assesses the effect of removing all impediments to trade by assuming that all price differentials between the United States, Canada, and Mexico are due to some form of trade restrictions. If finds that the diversionary impact of NTBs plus tariffs to be *ten times* greater than that caused by the removal of tariffs alone. However, multiplying our estimates by ten would no doubt lead to gross overestimation for several main reasons: Considering the role of transport costs and product differentiation, not all price differentials can be attributed to trade restrictions; not all NTBs will be removed by NAFTA;

and the multiplication factor mentioned above is likely to vary greatly by commodity groups (as in the above paragraph) and may not be so high in the heavily impacted categories. But without assigning a specific number, it is possible to conclude that the diversionary impact is likely to be several times the estimates above for mere tariff elimination. Even a factor of 2 would bring the trade diversion to well over 10 percent (of Australia-New Zealand exports to NAFTA).

However, it should be noted that the bilateral exports (our denominator) are themselves a small portion of total exports and certainly of GDP. Thus, the terms of trade effects are small relative to the overall economy, a result consistent with estimates by CGE models.

B. Service Transactions

Next it is important to consider the effects of NAFTA on the fledgling service export sectors in Australia and New Zealand. Quantitative analysis in this area is extremely difficult, given the paucity of data and definitional problems. In addition, it is not yet certain to what extent services will be freed in NAFTA. Yet several points can be made. First, trade in services has become increasingly important for the economies of Australia and New Zealand, and as this trend is likely to continue, any segmentation of the international marketplace for services will be detrimental to their respective growth. Although recent reliable data are difficult to locate, it is estimated[19] that total exports of private services as a percentage of total exports of goods and services increased from 10 percent in 1960 to 14 percent in 1984 for Australia, and from 5 percent to 20 percent for New Zealand. Second, the services sector is of great importance in attracting foreign investment to the two countries (discussed below). In 1983, 43 percent of the stock of direct foreign investment in Australia was in services, as opposed to 26 percent in manufacturing, and for New Zealand, the respective figures for the period

---

19. Taken from Stern, Robert M. and Bernard M. Hoekman [1988], "The Service Sector in Economic Structure and in International Transactions," Chapter 2 in Castle, Leslie and Christopher Findlay (eds.), *Pacific Trade in Services* (Sydney: Allen and Unwin); p. 44.

1976-1983 were 51 percent and 33 percent.[20] Third, telecommunications services (and equipment) constitute an important area in which Australia is competitive. It is developing business ties with its Asian developing neighbors, including Vietnam, Mongolia, and the Pacific Islands, through its Overseas Telecommunications Cooperation hub in Sydney. Currently, North America, the EC, and Japan are each pursuing separate telecommunications technical standards, and Australia could actually go in any direction, despite its traditional links to the EC system through its close relationship with the United Kingdom. Hence, if NAFTA ultimately leads to exclusionary technical standards in telecommunications, the export market for these services will be limited. A multilateral solution under the auspices of the International Telecommunications Union in Geneva is far from adoption, although the United States has tabled a possible framework for telecommunications at the current Uruguay Round of GATT.[21]

C. Investment Diversion

In addition to trade diversion, Australia and New Zealand could experience diversion of direct foreign investment (DFI) flows away from their home markets and toward internal NAFTA markets. When economies form an FTA, there will be changes in DFI flows to take advantage of new opportunities resulting from a *regional* (as opposed to national) division of labor. The investment effects of the FTA are at least three fold: First, as internal prices are equalized, DFI flows will be reallocated in such a way that production will take place in the most efficient location. This effect will result in a more efficient allocation of resources and, thus, can be called "investment creation."[22] Second, because the FTA distorts the relationship between part-

---

20. Ibid.; p. 50.
21. For a detailed analysis of the effects of EC 1992 on third countries in the area of telecommunications, see: Jussawalla, Meheroo, "The Anticipated Impact of Europe's Single Market on the Telecommunications Industry in Asia," in Plummer, Michael G. and William E. James (eds.), *Europe and Asia in the 1990s*, forthcoming.
22. The concept of investment creation – as well as diversion, discussed below – stems from analysis found in Kreinin, Mordechai [1964], "On the Dynamic Effects of Customs Unions," *Journal of Political Economy*, April.

ner and non-partner country prices, the former may now have a competitive advantage over the latter. Hence, some DFI will flow into partner countries not because they are more efficient, but because they have a price advantage resulting from the FTA. As this effect suggests a less efficient allocation of resources, it can be referred to as "investment diversion." Third, to the extent that the FTA becomes more efficient due to the dynamic growth effect, new profit opportunities will emerge and DFI will follow.

In sum, investment creation should obtain in industries experiencing trade creation. Although the static investment creation effect will imply a reduction in DFI to nonpartner countries, it will be at least partly offset by the growth effects. On the other hand, investment diversion is likely to obtain in industries facing trade diversion, leading to a less efficient allocation of resources and a negative growth effect. Therefore, nonpartner countries will be mainly affected by investment diversion. The higher the preferential margin, the greater the incentive for investment to flow into partner countries. Hence, a review of commodities experiencing the greatest degree of trade diversion would reveal the most likely candidates for investment diversion.

Potential investment diversion is highly significant for Australia and New Zealand for several reasons. Inflows of DFI bring new capital and technologies essential to the modernization and advancement of the two economies, which is particularly important in enhancing structural adjustment. Relative decreases in DFI from advanced economies would have important detrimental effects on long-run economic growth. Second, as Table 3 shows, the United States is an important source of DFI for both Australia and New Zealand. Matching the sectors having the largest stock of DFI with the categories experiencing the greatest trade diversion offers a general idea of the industries where most of the investment diversion would occur. Machinery and transport equipment could be affected because of Canadian and Mexican protection that would divert some investment away from Australia and New Zealand. Much of the U.S. manufacturing DFI in Australia and New Zealand is in food products, chemicals, and fabricated metals, which would be adversely affected. It should also be noted that other important sources of DFI, especially from the Asia-Pacific region, would flow to North America to take advantage of free trade, a phenomenon

Table 3
Stock of U.S. Direct Investment Abroad by Country and Major Industry

(US$ million)

| Country | Year | All Industries | Petroleum | Total | Manufacturing | | | | | | | Wholesale Trade[a] | Finance & Insurance | Other Industries[b] |
					Food & Kindred Products	Chemicals & Allied Products	Primary Fabricated Metals	Non-Electric Machinery	Electric & Electronic Machinery	Trans-portation Equipment	Other Manufac-turing			
Australia	1977	5,823.0	971.0	2,368.0	251.0	401.0	192.0	363.0	126.0	565.0	470.0	684.0	470.0	291.0
	1980	7,662.0	1,264.0	2,911.0	330.0	511.0	299.0	524.0	167.0	449.0	631.0	1,064.0	669.0	464.0
	1985	8,772.0	1,627.0	3,044.0	389.0	1,300.0	76.0	393.0	135.0	114.0	636.0	971.0	1,162.0	1,968.0
	1986	9,340.0	1,731.0	3,375.0	396.0	1,518.0	110.0	348.0	56.0	309.0	638.0	991.0	1,299.0	1,943.0
	1987	11,363.0	3,164.0	3,491.0	435.0	1,712.0	111.0	297.0	72.0	106.0	758.0	1,104.0	1,491.0	205.0
	1988	13,186.0	3,147.0	4,557.0	498.0	2,119.0	222.0	430.0	97.0	285.0	906.0	1,290.0	1,367.0	261.0
	1989	14,495.0	3,009.0	5,771.0	1,072.0	2,256.0	311.0	511.0	133.0	528.0	960.0	1,273.0	1,115.0	313.0
New Zealand	1977	410.0	na	137.0	28.0	26.0	2.0	3.0	7.0	na	na	na	15.0	5.0
	1980	578.0	na	196.0	31.0	49.0	5.0	11.0	16.0	na	na	na	16.0	3.0
	1985	576.0	na	162.0	20.0	56.0	4.0	5.0	6.0	na	na	114.0	45.0	20.0
	1986	598.0	na	171.0	20.0	57.0	5.0	6.0	7.0	na	na	123.0	53.0	23.0
	1987	743.0	na	242.0	20.0	80.0	8.0	na	8.0	na	69.0	134.0	54.0	24.0
	1988	833.0	na	213.0	-12.0	93.0	na	14.0	1.0	na	77.0	156.0	57.0	39.0
	1989	1,167.0	na	379.0	109.0	104.0	na	16.0	10.0	na	87.0	178.0	199.0	26.0

Notes: na = Not disclosed or not available.

a. Retail trade included with wholesale trade for 1977.

b. Including banking and services.

Sources: U.S. Department of Commerce, *Survey of Current Business*, August 1982, 1986, 1987, 1988, 1989, 1990; mimeos, 11/21/86.

which is already occurring.[23]

There is an increasingly close link between trade and investment in the contemporary global economy. Nearly a third of international trade is conducted between parents and affiliates of of multinational corporations. In fact, an important advantage of DFI establishments for the development of the host economy is their tendency to be more trade-oriented than domestic firms, thereby generating greater foreign exchange and increasing links with the global economy, as well as having stronger international contacts. As DFI is diverted toward North America – and Europe – trade flows between parents and affiliates will also be redirected, thereby inhibiting to some extent new economic opportunities and relationships for Australia and New Zealand.

D. Dynamic Effects

Beyond the static reallocation effects, there are dynamic growth effects of NAFTA that would stimulate imports from Australia-New Zealand. McCleery [1992] uses a computational general equilibrium (CGE) model to estimate changes in the U.S. growth rate due to NAFTA, and concludes that growth would increase by 0.1 percent, while that of Mexico would increase by 0.9 percent per year. Canada's annual growth is estimated to rise by 0.25 percent. Other studies are consistent with these results.[24] Thus, the growth effect would compensate for some of the static trade diversion. However, with any reasonable coefficient of the income elasticity of import demand in the integrating regions (say, around 1.5), it would not offset it completely. And it would certainly not offset it in the major market, the United States. Considerable diversion is likely to remain.

---

23. This will be applicable not only to the most obvious source, Japan, but also to the Asian Newly-Industrializing Economies that are already anticipating the creation of NAFTA. For example, Kia Motors of Korea recently (August 1991) signed an agreement with Mexico to produce automobiles for export to the U.S. market in anticipation of free trade.

24. For a summary of the results of general equilibrium models used to estimate the overall effects of NAFTA on the integrating economies, see Plummer, Michael G., "ASEAN and Economic Integration in the Americas," *OECD Development Centre Technical Paper*, forthcoming.

Not only that, but there should be negative dynamic effects in Australia and New Zealand themselves. The static trade and investment diversion shrinks the size of the market relative to what it would be in the absence of the regional groupings elsewhere. Hence, unfavorable dynamic effects are superimposed upon it.

III. Conclusion: What is Oceania to do?

This paper assesses the effect of economic integration in North America on Australia and New Zealand, using a commodity matching technique which allows for both quantitative and qualitative analysis. The main objective is to identify the industries in the 2 countries that will be heavily impacted by NAFTA. It is found that a number of key primary and manufactured commodities will be adversely affected. As a subsidiary goal, we estimate the overall terms of trade effect to be small. This is consistent with the results of CGE models used to quantify the effects of NAFTA on the integrating countries. Although difficult to quantify, NTBs and other forms of protection would cause further trade diversion, perhaps doubling the tariff-induced effects. Moreover, there is potential for investment diversion away from the Australian and New Zealand economies. As Australia and New Zealand are both striving to strengthen their trade and investment ties, regionalism in North America is of concern. What options are open to Australia and New Zealand to minimize the impact of NAFTA as well as the EC?

First, a liberal international trading environment is a key to expanding international trade and investment. Lower MFN tariffs and NTBs would mitigate the discriminatory effect of preferential trading agreements. Hence, Australia and New Zealand have a considerable stake in the outcome of the Uruguay Round of GATT. They should continue to press for liberalization of agricultural trade as part of the Cairn's Group, but also for success in many other areas being negotiated in Geneva, including NTBs, subsidies, trade in services, and trade-related investment measures. Also, they should work for a successful integration of trade in services into the GATT framework, perhaps as part of the proposed General Agreement on Trade in Services (GATS).

Second, Australia and New Zealand should continue to advance their respective unilateral liberalization programs. Recent reforms have rendered their economies far more competitive, and while the adjustment process has been difficult, growth is now emerging from a solid base. For example, New Zealand is included among the top-10 rankings of the 1993 *World Competitiveness Report*. In short, one attractive option is to pursue a policy of free trade.

Third, while Australia and New Zealand have already negotiated a comprehensive free-trade agreement between themselves, called "Closer Economic Relations," bilateral trade with each other is relatively small, amounting to 5 percent and 18 percent of total Australian and New Zealand exports, respectively, in 1990. On the other hand, the share of trade with the Asia-Pacific region has been booming, growing to about two-thirds of total trade in 1990. Hence, Australia and New Zealand should endeavor to form closer economic links with their Asia-Pacific neighbors, through informal as well as formal channels. The Asia-Pacific Economic Cooperation (APEC) process, which includes all of Australia's and New Zealand's major regional trading partners, could be the focus of the these efforts. Moreover, a strong APEC could serve to counter Asian arrangements that exclude Australia and New Zealand, such as the East-Asian Economic Grouping (proposed by Malaysia in December 1990) and the East-Asian Economic Caucus (agreed to by ASEAN in January 1992).

Appendix
Sources of Data

Trade Data: United Nations, *Commodity Trade Statistics*, relevant issues, 1985-1990.

Investment Data: U.S. Department of Commerce, *Survey of Current Business*, August 1982, 1986, 1987, 1988, 1989, 1990; mimeos, 11/21/86.

Tariff Data: (1) For the United States and Canada – *United States-Canada Free-Trade Agreement: Communication from the President of the United States*, Annex 401.2 100th Congress, Second Session, House Document 100-216 (Washington, D.C.: US Government Printing Office, 1988). Concordances to match US and Canadian national tariff data with SITC classifications was done using United Nations, *Statistical*

Papers, Series M., No. 34/Rev. 2 and No. 34/Rev. 3.

NTB Data: UNCTAD computer files made available to the World Bank and supplied by Sam Laird.

Terms of Trade Data: For Oceania – United Nations, *Monthly Bulletin of Statistics*, January 1984 and January 1991.

References

United Nations, *Monthly Bulletin of Statistics*, January 1984 and January 1991.

GATT [1990a], *Trade Policy Review: Australia*, Geneva, March.

GATT [1990b], *International Trade 1989-1990, Volume II*, Geneva, 1990; p. 42.

Jussawalla, Meheroo, "The Anticipated Impact of Europe's Single Market on the Telecommunications Industry in Asia," in Plummer, Michael G. and William E. James (eds.), *Europe and Asia in the 1990s*, forthcoming.

Kreinin, Mordechai E. [1991], *International Economics: A Policy Approach*, Sixth Edition, Orlando: Harcourt Brace Jovanavich; pp. 371-372.

_____ [1977], "Effect of Exchange Rate Changes on the Prices and Volumes of Trade," *IMF Staff Papers*, July.

_____ [1964], "On the Dynamic Effects of Customs Unions," *Journal of Political Economy*, April.

Kreinin, Mordechai E. and Michael G. Plummer [1992], "Effects of Economic Integration in Industrial Countries on ASEAN and the Asian NIEs," *World Development*, Vol. 20, No. 9, September; pp. 1345-1366.

New Zealand Institute of Economic Research [1990], *Sectoral Projections*, Wellington: New Zealand Institute of Economic Research, September; Tables 6 and 7.

Plummer, Michael G. [1993], "ASEAN and Economic Integration in the Americas," *OECD Development Centre Technical Papers*, July.

Reinert, K.A. and C.R. Shields [1991], "Trade Substitution Elasticities of a North American Free-Trade Area," Office of Economics, in *USITC Working Paper* No. 91-81-B, July.

Roland-Holst, D., K. A. Reinert, and C.R. Shields [1992], "North American

Trade Liberalization and the Role of Non-tariff Barriers," in *USITC Report under Investigation No. 332-317*, Paper No. 5, February.

McCleery, Robert [1992], "An Intertemporal, Linked, Macroeconomic CGE Model of the United States and Mexico," *Economy-Wide Modelling of the Economic Implications of a FTA with Mexico and a NAFTA with Canada and Mexico*, Washington, D.C.: USITC.

Trefler, Daniel [1993], "Trade Liberalization and the Theory of Endogenous Protection: An Econometric Study of U.S. Import Policy," *Journal of Political Economy*, February.

ASEAN Economic Bulletin Vol. 15, No. 2

Ex Post Estimates of the Effects of the European Single Market Programme on the Exports of Developing Countries

Mordechai E. Kreinin and Michael G. Plummer

The Single Market Programme in Europe (EC-92) was an ambitious attempt to create a common market. While EC-92 directives appeared to be outward-looking in their orientation, developing countries feared that the programme might lead to considerable trade diversion. Usually based on estimates by the Cecchini Report, ex ante *analysis of the implications of EC-92 for the exports of developing countries generally suggested a positive effect, with strong EC-92-generated import growth swamping any diversion of developing-country exports due to the enhanced price-competitiveness effect. In this article, we revisit the question using two* ex post *approaches, that is an import-growth approach and a gravity model. According to our results, EC-92 directives appear to have had a negative effect on the exports of ASEAN and China, but not on those of the Asian NIEs. As expected, the effects were concentrated in light manufacturing and in some cases electrical machinery. The effect on ASEAN and on developing Asia in total was supported by the gravity-model approach.*

I Introduction

Conventional wisdom[1] holds that one of the factors responsible for the 1997/98 Asian financial crisis was the rise in the current account and trade deficits of the afflicted countries.[2] In turn, it is plausible that regional integration schemes in Europe and North America diverted enough exports from ASEAN and South Korea to contribute to their trade deficits. The same may be said about Mercosur in South America. Diversion of Direct Foreign Investment (DFI) originating in the industrial countries is also possible if not probable. Thus, regional integration schemes may have contributed, albeit marginally, to the economic crisis in: Thailand, Indonesia, Malaysia, the Philippines (namely, the big ASEAN four) and South Korea.

This article, a part of a larger study, explores part of the puzzle: what diversionary effect did the Unified Market Programme in Europe, known as EC-92, have on the exports of developing

71

countries in Southeast Asia and elsewhere? EC-92 consists of 284 directives issued by the EC secretariat designed to remove all restrictions on the flows of trade, capital and people within the 12 members of the Community, and provide for market unification through other means. The directives began coming into force in the later part of the 1980s. While they were all supposed to be implemented by 1993, some were delayed until the mid-1990s. Theoretically, EC-92 could have had both positive and negative effects on non-members, including Asian developing countries; hence the need for empirical assessment.

II Possible Effects of EC-92

While the Cecchini Report of the European Community claimed that the internal growth effect of the EC-92 programme would be so strong as to swamp static diversionary effects on non-member countries, this cannot be taken at face value and needs to be estimated empirically. A number of studies have postulated what might be the effects of EC-92 on third-country exports. Bleaney, Greenaway, and Hine (1995) delineate a number of possible changes stemming from the EC-92 programme that might serve to reduce non-partner country penetration of EC markets: improved competitiveness of EC firms in EC and non-EC markets; trade diversion induced by internal liberalization; market exclusion due to discriminatory harmonization of technical barriers; market exclusion due to discriminatory government procurement; market exclusion due to "reciprocity" requirements; protection induced by eliminating national quotas; and protection induced by adjustment pressures (p. 86).[3] Because these effects go well beyond the traditional price-related effects of a free-trade area or customs union, empirical trade models are not well equipped to estimate their ultimate effect on trade. Hence, generating such estimates by traditional approaches has been difficult (as discussed below).

As the development of the EC-92 programme unfolded, non-member developed countries and developing nations became concerned about the possible emergence of a "Fortress Europe". This Fortress Europe might not stem from the traditional diversionary effects of a preferential trading arrangement; rather, it was feared that the creation of a community-wide set of commercial policies and the myriad compromises that would have to be made in order to push through the EC-92 programme would lead to a more protectionist *policy environment* affecting both trade and investment. Thus, even if the EC-92 programme itself were to be mostly free of any explicit discrimination against outsiders, the associated commercial policy of the EC might become more inward looking.

The European Community went through great pains to assure its non-member trading partners that it had no intention of becoming more protectionist. The programme itself appeared to be outward-looking, and the fears of EC trading partners were generally allayed.[4] Nevertheless, except at the sectoral level, little *ex post* assessment has been made of the impact of EC-92 on policy formation in the EC.

III Previous Studies

The most influential study regarding the possible (*ex ante*) effects of the EC-92 programme was the above-mentioned Cecchini Report (1988), which estimates a one-time potential increase in EC GNP of 2.5–6.5 per cent to result from the unified market. Most macroeconomic simulations and other *ex ante* models use the Cecchini estimates as growth scenarios. However, these studies tend to focus mostly on the effects of EC-92 on member countries; far less research has been devoted to estimating the effects of the programme on non-members, with some exceptions.

For example, Kreinin and Plummer (1992) presented *ex ante* estimates of the effect of the second enlargement of the EC and of NAFTA on ASEAN and South Korea. They found considerable trade diversion from Asia (they did not estimate trade creation), but it was impossible to assess and quantify the effect of EC-92 *ex ante*, using their technique. On the other hand, their highly-disaggregated data showed considerable commodity overlap between the exports of developing Asian countries and developed countries in Europe and North America. In a report for the Asian Development Bank (Staff Paper No. 48, 1991), Verbiest and Tang use a macroeconomic simulation model to estimate the effects of the completion of the internal market in the EC on Asian developing countries. While the paper suggests that "protectionist temptations" may increase as a result of EC-92, overall a positive impact on developing Asia should be expected over the medium- to long-run, assuming the Cecchini growth estimates are in the correct range. Verbiest and Tang look to the Uruguay Round and the multi-fibre negotiations as "more important than the Single Market operation in shaping the future trading relations between Asian developing countries and the EC".

Sung-Taik Han (1992) also uses the Cecchini results to simulate the effects of EC-92 on the Asian NIEs in a macroeconomic model. The price and income effects of EC-92 suggest that the Asian NIEs will initially experience a deterioration in exports due to the negative price (cost-reduction) effects, but this effect will eventually be swamped by the positive income effect. However, his microeconomic, industry-specific approach yields significant negative effects on important industries such as electrical goods and office machinery, a result which is consistent with the Kreinin and Plummer effects discussed above.

In a general way, given the stagnation of the European economy in the 1990s, it is difficult to assign high credibility to estimates based on the Cecchini growth projections. Indeed, Plummer (1994) in an *ex post* aggregative study, found considerable trade diversion to have resulted from EC-92.[5] But his paper was based on 1991 data, before many EC-92 directives had been implemented. In contrast, the present study uses 1994 data (with results confirmed for 1996) — both in the aggregate, and with some industrial disaggregation. Another *ex post* study on the effects of EC-92 was undertaken by Sapir (1997), using data over the 1986–92 period.[6] He focused mainly on the internal effects of EC-92 on member

countries and the study is preliminary in nature as it does not include post-1992 data. Sapir finds that, at the sectoral level, EC-92 actually increased extra-EC imports in the case of sectors where public procurement was important, but penalized extra-EC imports in sectors subject to medium or high non-tariff barriers (see also Sapir 1997 for a survey of empirical models of EC-92).

Hence, apart from a few studies, the *ex post* effects of the EC-92 programme on non-partner countries have been sparse. In what follows, we apply two independent models and employ post-EC-92 data to capture the effects of EC-92. These models do not allow us to distinguish between the direct effects of the EC-92 programme and policy changes occurring at the same time, emanating both from EC-92 and other sources. For example, any negative effects attributed to the EC-92 programme may have derived from an unrelated policy change. Nevertheless, EC-92 constitutes a fundamental change in the commercial policies of the EC, that is, a watershed in the process of creating the common market for goods, services, and productive factors. As such, it might be considered at least indirectly responsible for the resulting new configuration of the EC policy structure.

IV Methodology: Control Country Approach

As a first approximation we observe what happened to EC-12 imports from various developing countries between 1990 and 1994 and between 1990 and 1996. The year 1990 is a possible base year before many EC-92 directives were fully implemented, while the two later years should reflect the effect of the Unified Market Program in all its directives (1996 is the latest year for which the necessary data are available).

But many other supply and demand factors influence the change in EC imports between the two specified years. To allow for such effects we search for a "control country" – a country that is similar to the EC in all or most respects. We expect the change in imports into the EC, without the EC-92 programme, to equal the change in the control-country imports. Thus the difference between the change in EC imports and the change in the control-country imports is attributed to the EC-92 programme.[7]

While the United States appears as an appropriate control country, its own trade may have been distorted by the formation of the free trade area with Canada, even though the lion's share of bilateral trade between the two countries took place duty-free before the agreement went into effect (making the effects on trade small). Therefore we use the United States plus Canada, *netting out their trade with each other*, as control. In other words the control region is North America (*labelled NA*) in its trade with the outside world. Similar to Europe in population, real income, degree of industrialization, and other respects, NA has been used before[8] as a control country to study European integration.

However, the control-country may require adjustments to the extent that it differs from the EC in the variables that determine imports: change in competitiveness and real income between the two years under study, that is 1990 to 1994 and 1990 to 1996. With respect to competitiveness, the differential inflation between the two regions is exactly offset by the differential exchange-rate changes. Hence no adjustment is needed. But the real growth rate in NA exceeded that of the EC by 4 per cent between 1990 and 1994 and by 6 per cent between 1990 and 1996. In making the adjustment for the differential growth we assumed an income demand elasticity of 1 for all imports, and of 2 for imports of several manufacturing categories. Indeed, estimates will be provided for aggregate imports, and (disaggregated) for six important classes of manufactures. In a later section the results will be checked against those obtained from a totally different approach: that of a gravity model.

In sum the estimating equations used in this section are:

1. For aggregate imports:

$$\{(\Delta M^{EC, j}_{t, t+1} - \Delta M^{NA, j}_{t, t+1}) + [(\Delta Y^{NA}_{t, t+1} - \Delta Y^{EC}_{t, t+1}) \times \eta_y]\} \times M^{EC, j}_{1990} = NTC^{j}_{t+1} \quad (1)$$

where M = imports; j = exporting country; Y = real GDP; and η_y = income elasticity of demand for imports.

2. For selected manufacturing categories (1–2 digit SITC)

$$\{(\Delta M^{EC, j}_{90-94, k} - \Delta M^{NA, j}_{90-94, k}) + [(\Delta Y^{NA}_{90-94} - \Delta Y^{EC}_{90-94}) \times \eta_y]\} \times M^{EC, j}_{1990} = NTC^{j, k}_{1994} \quad (2)$$

where all notation is the same as in (1), with the addition of commodity k (SITC 5, 6, 71, 72, 73, 8). Recall that NA stands for North America.

While we considered Japan as another possible control country, it diverges so much from the EC over this period in terms of changes in degree of competitiveness, as proxied by changes in the real exchange rate, that its use was considered inappropriate.[9]

V Results

Table 1 presents the estimates for aggregate imports. The results are mixed. Japan sustained significant export diversion, which was considerably larger for the 1990–94 period than for the 1990–96 period. Among the developing countries there was no negative effect on the NIEs, including specifically South Korea, a country heavily afflicted by the 1997 financial crisis. If anything they benefited from the EC growth effect. Possibly the positive effect on Korea (especially in SITC 73) occurred because of EC quantitative restrictions against Japanese cars. On the other hand, China and the ASEAN group were negatively affected. And among ASEAN, the largest diversionary effect was on Malaysia and Thailand. In Latin America, Mexico and Chile were affected negatively, but the effect on Mercosur was negligible and in particular there was no effect on Brazil. Others affected negatively were North Africa, India, Pakistan and Israel.

In total, the negative diversionary effect far exceeds the positive. The EC-92 programme thus contributed at the margin to the trade deficits of Thailand and Malaysia, but not of Korea.

TABLE 1
Net Trade Creation[1] Resulting from EC 1992: Aggregate
Level Estimates, 1990–94
(1990–96; US$ millions)

Exporters	NTC_{1994}	NTC_{1996}
Selected Developed Countries:		
Australia	1,083.72	1,144.97
Japan	–13,376.20	–3,906.21
New Zealand	–388.74	109.20
ASEAN	–5,194.87	–1,901.13
Indonesia	308.74	442.09
Malaysia	–4,801.51	–3,816.61
Philippines	–351.69	508.32
Singapore	404.70	744.28
Thailand	–1,911.55	–692.00
NIEs[2]	3,906.76	10,954.05
China	–5,151.39	–6,984.01
Mercosur[3]	–650.75	–428.26
Brazil	296.71	792.31
Argentina	–498.68	–1,132.04
Chile	–1,298.23	–1,636.82
Mexico	–1,912.84	–3,896.24
North Africa[4]	–1,208.44	–6,076.13
Other Africa[5]	–313.14	–245.71
Israel	–2,041.66	–2,862.38
India	–1,250.21	–229.28
Pakistan	–788.03	–1,073.17

NOTES
1. Negative numbers indicate trade diversion.
2. NIEs: Hong Kong, Taiwan, South Korea.
3. MERCOSUR: Brazil, Argentina, Uruguay, Paraguay.
4. NORTH AFRICA: Egypt, Algeria, Morocco, Tunisia.
5. OTHER AFRICA: Zaire, Kenya.
SOURCE: United Nations, Commodity Trade Statistics (various years);
and authors' calculations (see text for methodology).

Table 2 presents the results for six manu-facturing commodity categories. It shows that the diversionary impact on Malaysia is concentrated in electrical machinery (SITC 72) and mis-cellaneous manufactures (SITC 8), while in the case of Thailand it is in SITC 8. The NIEs lost ground in machinery (SITC 71, 72) but benefited elsewhere, while the loss of China appears everywhere but is concentrated in SITC 6 and 8 (probably labour-intensive manufactures). Brazil and Chile lost ground in SITC 6.

VI Gravity Model: an Alternative Approach

It is possible to check the *direction* of change, but not the *magnitude*, of our result by using a totally

TABLE 2
Net Trade Creation[1] Resulting from EC1992: Disaggregated Level, 1990–94
(US$ millions)

Exporters	Chemicals (SITC 5)	Basic Manufacturing (SITC 6)	Machinery (SITC 71)	Electrical (SITC 72)	Transport (SITC 73)	Misc Manufacturing (SITC 8)
Selected Developed Countries						
Australia	40.90	124.53	−35.71	−29.09	−58.53	−33.79
New Zealand	29.24	2.26	6.63	−63.21	9.23	−6.67
ASEAN	−29.99	−11.97	373.11	−2,905.27	−3.40	−2,113.40
Indonesia	11.33	−9.72	−158.61	−323.63	−92.97	−294.37
Malaysia	42.31	−228.44	−145.68	−2,029.32	−104.82	−1,155.10
Philippines	10.67	−16.11	72.59	−309.22	−20.11	−101.97
Singapore	−88.15	394.84	710.56	−186.10	99.98	106.82
Thailand	−6.14	−152.54	−105.75	−56.98	114.53	−668.77
NIEs[2]	316.10	273.08	−1,783.10	−863.06	1,034.43	1,013.67
China	−600.26	−1,202.56	−764.95	−628.07	−537.74	−5,721.18
Brazil	−100.93	−1,392.60	−36.02	−125.14	136.08	32.20
Argentina	47.42	20.04	13.23	53.02	11.05	−140.40
Chile	11.77	−651.15	−4.27	−1.85	−4.75	24.11
Mexico	−159.65	−103.23	−275.21	−14.78	−58.55	−129.63

NOTE
1. Negative numbers indicate trade diversion.
2. NIEs: Hong Kong, Taiwan, South Korea.
SOURCE: United Nations, Commodity Trade Statistics (various years); and authors' calculations (see text for methodology).

FIGURE 1
Gravity Coefficients for EC and North American Imports from ASEAN

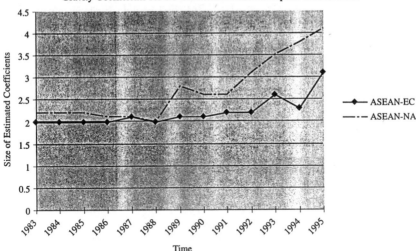

NOTES
1. Coefficients were estimated for regional binary variables in a gravity model (see text for explanation).
2. All coefficients are statistically significant at the 90 per cent level.

different approach, that of a gravity model. The model postulates that the intensity of trade between two countries depends on their respective gross domestic products (GDP), populations, and the geographical distance between them. It is a much criticized, yet widely used, approach to trade analysis. Our sample contained 5,112 bilateral trade flows each year and we estimated a gravity model for each such flow. To the above variables we added dummy variables for the ASEAN-EC trade, and for developing Asia-EC trade, where developing Asia includes ASEAN, the Asian NIEs, China, and South Asia (India, Pakistan, Bangladesh, and Sri Lanka), to find an EC-92 effect. In the overwhelming majority of cases, the estimates were robust, and the regression fit was good, with an adjusted R^2 of between 0.45 and 0.75 — very respectable for cross-sectional data and on par with other gravity models.

As mentioned earlier this approach has been subject to much criticism, not the least of which is the absence of a relative price or real exchange rate variable. Additionally, the data may reflect supply-side influences within ASEAN (or developing Asia) rather than demand effects in the EC. To overcome such concerns and to legitimize the gravity approach at least to some degree, we ran separate gravity regressions with a binary variable for ASEAN-North American trade. It is the *comparison* between the coefficient of this variable and that of the ASEAN-EC variable that would indicate any EC-92 effect on ASEAN. The same procedure was used for developing Asia.

These two coefficients for the ASEAN dummy, all of which are statistically significant at the 95 per cent level, are plotted in Figure 1. It shows that in the 1980s both coefficients tracked the same path. But at the end of the decade, when EC-92 directives began to be implemented (gradually) the two series diverge, with the NA-ASEAN dummy advancing far ahead of that of the EC-ASEAN. This confirms the negative effect of EC-92 on ASEAN exports estimated by the normalizer approach.

Figure 2 plots the same binary variables for EC-developing Asia, and for NA-developing Asia, and a similar pattern appears. It confirms the negative impact of EC-92 on Asian exports.

VII   Conclusions

EC-92 directives appear to have had a negative diversionary effect on the exports of ASEAN (especially of Malaysia and Thailand) and China, but not on those of the Asian NIEs. As expected,

the effects were concentrated in light manufacturing and in some cases electrical machinery. The effect on ASEAN and on developing Asia in total was confirmed by the gravity model approach. There remains the possibility of investment diversion which is a negative effect additive to that of trade diversion.

Finally, there is every reason to believe that the North American Free Trade Agreement (the United States, Canada and Mexico free trade area) would cause as much or more diversion of trade from Asia, because there is a great deal of commodity overlap between the exports of developing Asia and that of Mexico and Canada.[10] In a more general way our results militate against the regional approach and in favour of the

FIGURE 2
All Asia Gravity Coefficients in the EC and North America

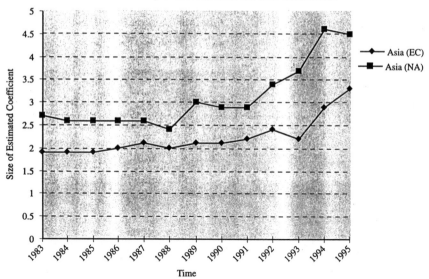

NOTES
1. Coefficients were estimated for regional binary variables in a gravity model (see text for explanation).
2. All estimated coefficients are statistically significant at the 99 per cent level.

multilateral approach to trade liberalization. Finally, in as much as regional groupings are here to stay, the best strategy for Asia or for developing countries in general is to press in the WTO for open regionalism, and for a minimum of discrimination against outsiders.

NOTES

The authors wrote this article as visitors at the Institute of Southeast Asian Studies (ISEAS). They are indebted to ISEAS for financial support, and to Prof. Chia Siow Yue, Manuel Montes, and Carolyn Gates for their generous help and substantive comments throughout the project. Ms Sangita Rao and the ISEAS staff provided excellent clerical assistance.
   1. See Manuel F. Montes, *The Currency Crisis in Southeast Asia* (Singapore: Institute of Southeast Asian Studies, 1998) and Hal Hill, "Southeast Asia's Economic Crisis: Origins, Lessons, and the Way Forward", paper delivered at the ISEAS Thirtieth Anniversary Conference, Singapore, 30 July–1 August 1998.
   2. Among the other proximate causes are the inflow (followed by outflow) of short term portfolio capital; high ratio of foreign liabilities to international reserves; a high proportion of non-performing loans of the banks; and fixed or targeted exchange rates set at unsustainable levels.
   3. M.F. Bleaney, D. Greenaway and R.C. Hine, "The Impact of the 1992 Programme on Non-EC European Countries: An Overview", in *Economic Integration in Europe and North America, edited by* M. Panic and A. Vacic (New York: United Nations, 1995).
   4. See, for example, Michael G. Plummer, "Economic Deepening and Widening in Europe: Implications for the Asia-Pacific Rim", in *Effects of European Integration on Asia, edited by* M. Toida and D. Hiratsuka (Tokyo: IDE, 1994).
   5. Plummer (1994), op. cit.
   6. Andre Sapir, "The Effects of Europe's Internal Market Program on Production and Trade Trade: A First Assessment", *Journal of Common Market Studies* (1997).
   7. M.E. Kreinin, "Effect of the EEC on Imports of Manufactures", *Economic Journal* (1972).
   8. M.E. Kreinin, "Trade Creation and Diversion of EEC Enlargement", *Kyklos* (1984).
   9. Also, it could be argued that Japan's import structure is so different from that of Europe as to make it an even less likely candidate.
   10. See Kreinin and Plummer (1992), op. cit.

Mordechai E. Kreinin is University Distinguished Professor, Department of Economics, Michigan State University. **Michael Plummer** is Associate Professor of Economics and Director, MA Programs, Graduate School of International Economics and Finance, Brandeis University.

[6]

JOURNAL
OF
ASIAN ECONOMICS

Journal of Asian Economics 10 (1999) 385–394

Motives for Japanese DFI
Survey, analysis, and implications in light of the Asian crisis

Mordechai E. Kreinin[a], Shigeyuki Abe[b], Michael G. Plummer[c],*

[a]*Distinguished University Professor, Michigan State University (USA)*
[b]*Professor of Economics, Kyoto University (Japan)*
[c]*Associate Professor of Economics, Brandeis University, Waltham, MA 02254 (USA)*

Received 1 January 1999; accepted 1 August 1999

Abstract

This paper assesses the motives for Japanese outward direct foreign investment (DFI), drawing on a comprehensive private-sector survey (Toyo Keizai) of parent companies of foreign subsidiaries. It shows that the motivations behind Japanese DFI outflows are many and varied, with "securing market share" constituting the most salient motivation. DFI as a means of avoiding trade frictions is relevant only in developed countries in five industries, including transportation equipment, machinery, and electronics. Motivations are found to differ between developed and developing host economies, as expected. © 1999 Elsevier Science Inc. All rights reserved.

JEL classification: F2

Keywords: Direct foreign investment

1. Introduction

Since the mid-1980s, global direct foreign investment (DFI) flows increased more rapidly than total world trade, which in turn grew faster than global output (United Nations 1995, p. 4). At the same time Japan emerged as a major source of such investment in the United

---

* Corresponding author.

1049-0078/99/$ – see front matter © 1999 Elsevier Science Inc. All rights reserved.
PII: S1049-0078(99)00032-9

States, Europe, and Asia.[1] The stock of Japanese DFI was valued at $464 billion in 1994, having risen five-fold since 1985 ($84 billion).[2] This compares to $621 billion for the United States and $745 billion for the 15 members of the European Union (EU). The bulk of Japanese DFI is in services (66 percent), followed by manufacturers (28 percent) and primary products (5 percent). The United States is the largest host to Japanese DFI, accounting for 42 percent of the total. It is followed by the EU (18 percent) and East Asia (16 percent).

While there has been extensive theorizing about DFI, empirical evidence concerning motivations for companies to undertake such investment is relatively scant. Japanese DFI has been analyzed to some degree in the economics and business literature. However, in the case of the former, studies tend to focus on statistical analysis of trends, profitability, and determinants, whereas the latter deals primarily with case-studies of affiliates of Japanese companies.[3] A number of monographs that appeared in the late 1980s and early 1990s considered the political economy implications of Japanese DFI. Yet, there exists no systematic examination (on a micro level) of what motivates Japanese companies to invest abroad.

This question becomes particularly important in light of the Asian crisis. Japan's big DFI "push" into Southeast Asia in the mid-late 1980s has been accredited as being a key determinant of rapid growth in the region. Moreover, the large literature analyzing the economic origins of the crisis points to the decline of DFI flows to the region relative to more foot-loose capital inflows as a salient source of financial instability. How will the crisis affect Japanese DFI flows in the medium-long term?

This paper assesses the motives for Japanese outward DFI, drawing on a comprehensive private-sector survey of parent companies of foreign subsidiaries. Some studies suggest that the same motives govern the behavior of American and European firms (Graham and Krugman 1991); however, this is clearly a testable a hypothesis and this paper takes a step in that direction by focusing explicitly on the motives for Japanese DFI abroad using a comprehensive, firm-level database of Japanese foreign affiliates. In addition, the paper speculates as to what the crisis might mean for the future of Japanese DFI flows to Asia based on the results of the survey. Finally, the paper gives some concluding remarks.

2. Motives for Japanese DFI

Tests of the theories of DFI often yielded mixed results.[4] A commonly-used framework of analysis is that of Dunning (1977), which integrates the various theories into an "eclectic approach." He suggests three necessary conditions for direct investment: (1) the firm must possess ownership advantages over other firms, namely, firm-specific assets; (2) the firm must find it beneficial to utilize these advantages directly instead of selling or leasing them ("internalization" advantages); and (3) there must be a "locational advantage" that would lead the firm to invest abroad rather than export. Such an advantage may be proximity to markets, circumvention of protective barriers, and relatively inexpensive factor costs. Economists testing the determinants of Japanese DFI focus mainly on locational advantages (Graham and Krugman 1991; Trevino and Daniels 1994; Pournarakis 1994; Gittleman and Dunning 1992; Waksugi 1994; Ozeae 1991). These and other studies dealing with the motives of Japanese DFI are based on macro data, anecdotal evidence, or case-studies. By contrast, in this study, we approach locational motivations from a firm-based, comprehensive survey.

There exists a large annual survey of Japanese corporations by Toyo Keizai soliciting their motives for investing abroad. The Research Institute of Economics and Business Administration of Kobe University developed a data bank based on this survey. In 1994, questionnaires were sent to 4482 companies of which 3332 (74 percent) responded. More importantly, responding firms that listed motives for DFI had a total of 8018 subsidiaries: 446 in Agriculture, energy and construction; 3452 in manufacturing; and 4120 in services, over half of which were in wholesale and retail trade. Finally, of the 8018 subsidiaries for which motives were given, 7121 also gave employment numbers, which form the basis for our size classification. This is the richest data set on Japanese outward DFI. We supplement the information with data gleaned from a smaller annual survey by Japan's Export-Import Bank.[5]

Data collected in the Toyo Keizai survey make it possible to classify DFI projects by host country, size of subsidiary, and type of industry. Because companies with North American and European subsidiaries expressed a similar pattern of reasons for investing abroad, they were lumped together under "developed countries," as distinguished from developing countries (mainly Asia). Of the various options, we chose to classify the size of subsidiary by numbers of workers in a three-way breakdown: small: under 50 workers; medium: between 50 and 500 workers; and large: over 500 workers. Finally, firms are classified into 10 industries. Responding firms were able to choose out of a menu of 12 possible motives presented to them, labeled in our tables: a–k and o. Unfortunately, variations in the exchange rate or expectations of such changes were not included in the questionnaire as possible motives. Since economic theory does not provide an unambiguous guide to signing of the exchange-rate effect,[6] it would have been useful to examine this relationship empirically. But lack of information made this impossible. Because each responding firm could choose more than one motive, the percent of motives can add up to more than 100 and it usually does. Finally, the qualitative nature of most variables precludes a statistical analysis; hence, the results are presented in tabular form.

Table 1 presents the 12 possible motives, coded a–k and o, against each of the 3 independent variables separately: type of host country, subsidiary size, and industry. Tables 2a and 2b report on motivations for FDI in developing countries (mainly Asia) and developed countries (North America and Europe). They offer a three-way cross-classification of responses, where only frequently-mentioned motives are listed within each cell. The codes for the motives are the same as those shown in Table 1.

The most common reason for investing abroad is to "secure local markets" (motive e). This is true for the world as a whole, and across all three variables. It also appears with the greatest frequency in all cells of Table 2 cross classification. This is clearly a marketing motive, but it might have captured other reasons as well (such as circumventing trade barriers). The annual survey (1990–96) by Japan's Export-Import bank confirms this finding. Although that survey provides no industrial breakdown and is limited to less than 600 responding companies, half the respondents in 1990 (rising to 80 percent in 1996) mentioned "preservation and expansion of market share" as a motive. This is true for DFI in all areas of the world.

Table 1
Motives for Japan's investment abroad

Motives	Destination			Subsidiary Size			Selected Industries[3]								
	World	Developed countries[1]	Dvlping countries[2]	Small (under 50 companies)	Medium (50–500)	Large (over 500 companies)	Agric.	Processed food	Textile & garments	Chemicals	Metal manfct.	Mach.	Electronics	Trans. equip	Financial services
a Use of natural resources	7%	5%	8%	6%	7%	7%	76%	40%	9%	11%	6%	2%	3%	2%	1%
b Use of (cheap) labor	17	3	30	9	28	40	32	21	58	23	32	36	49	22	0
c Favorable treatment by host government for DFI	9	2	14	3	13	25	5	4	12	11	22	18	23	20	5
d Establishing production & distribution network	33	28	39	32	43	37	33	44	65	55	43	44	48	62	3
e Securing local markets	64	66	62	73	72	63	16	53	60	75	70	71	71	72	37
f Exporting to third countries	9	5	12	9	10	15	3	10	16	11	10	15	19	8	0
g Importing back to Japan	9	4	14	7	13	11	31	20	33	8	12	15	17	13	0
h Accompanying business clients	4	4	5	4	6	4	0	0	1	5	7	5	1	18	3
i Financing & investing	6	8	3	7	2	1	0	0	0	0	1	2	0	2	43
j Acquisition & information gathering	28	37	19	43	21	12	11	19	14	19	13	12	11	15	42
k New business	14	19	9	19	11	5	13	11	4	8	9	7	11	7	19
o Trade friction	3	4	1	2	4	4	0	1	1	3	6	6	7	11	0
Number of responding companies	8018	3850	4168	3762	2673	686	75	215	299	473	376	641	406	410	702

[1] North America and W. Europe.
[2] Mainly Asia.
[3] 2355 firms are in Wholesale and Retail Trade

Table 2a
Detailed Japanese motivations by sector and size: developing countries (mainly Asia)

	Agric.	Const.	Processed food	Textile & garments	Paper & pub.	Chem.	Plastic & rubber	Porcelin & glass	Metal manuf.	Machinery	Electronics	Transport equip.	Other manuf.	Wholesale & retail trade	Fin. serv.	Real estate	Trans. serv.	Other serv.	All indus.
Small	a = 62%; b = 38; d = 43; e = 29; g = 48; k = 29	b = 24; e = 86; j = 44; o = 1	a = 76; b = 52; d = 51; e = 21; f = 12; g = 36	—	a = 30; b = 30; d = 45; e = 40; j = 35	a = 15; b = 30; d = 64; e = 77; f = 11; h = 12; j = 21; o = 5	—	—	b = 32; c = 21; d = 53; e = 65; f = 12; g = 16; j = 15; o = 7	b = 31; d = 46; e = 69; f = 17; g = 23; j = 15	b = 50; d = 67; c = 80; f = 23; g = 23; j = 23; o = 7	b = 28; c = 21; d = 55; e = 69; g = 14; h = 31; j = 14	b = 34; c = 10; d = 74; e = 66; f = 12; g = 28; o = 2	d = 35; e = 86; f = 19; g = 10; j = 41	e = 57; i = 31; j = 56	e = 50; j = 33; k = 54	d = 48; e = 55; j = 46; k = 31	e = 56; j = 44; k = 38	b = 18; d = 36; e = 72; f = 13; g = 12; j = 34; o = 1
Medium	a = 91; b = 45; c = 14; d = 32; i = 23; j = 14	b = 28; c = 18; e = 85; j = 33; o = 4	a = 43; b = 25; d = 40; e = 54; f = 17; g = 25	b = 64; c = 12; d = 68; e = 50; f = 16; g = 46	a = 37; b = 47; c = 16; d = 41; e = 34; j = 24	a = 14; b = 32; c = 17; d = 45; e = 76; f = 11; g = 11; j = 11	a = 12; b = 71; c = 28; d = 58; e = 62; f = 15; g = 20; j = 14; o = 6	b = 30; c = 30; d = 42; e = 85; f = 15; g = 15; j = 18; o = 3	b = 41; c = 29; d = 42; e = 74; g = 12; j = 12	b = 50; c = 24; d = 41; e = 71; f = 14; g = 17; o = 3	b = 67; c = 22; d = 52; e = 67; f = 24; g = 27; o = 2	b = 28; c = 25; d = 63; e = 71; g = 19; h = 16; j = 15	b = 56; c = 20; d = 44; e = 53; f = 17; g = 19	d = 32; c = 86; f = 11; h = 8; j = 29	c = 21; e = 64; i = 24; j = 64	—	d = 54; e = 51; h = 27; j = 41; k = 29	b = 35; c = 57; j = 37; k = 62	b = 40; c = 18; d = 44; e = 67; f = 12; g = 18; j = 16; o = 1
Large	—	—	—	a = 9; b = 68; c = 13; d = 58; e = 69; f = 25; g = 19	—	—	—	—	a = 23; b = 46; c = 37; d = 23; e = 54; f = 17; g = 11	b = 65; c = 37; d = 43; e = 53; f = 22; g = 15; o = 2	b = 70; c = 44; d = 33; e = 61; f = 22; g = 18	b = 37; c = 42; d = 53; e = 60; f = 12; h = 10	b = 70; c = 39; d = 35; e = 35; f = 13; g = 17; o = 4	b = 27; d = 23; e = 68; j = 33	—	—	c = 15; e = 65; j = 35	—	b = 33; c = 15; d = 40; e = 68; f = 13; g = 15; j = 22; o = 1

"—" denotes deletion of any case under 20 firms

Table 2b
Detailed Japanese motivations by sector and size: developed countries (North America & Europe)

	Agric.	Energy	Const.	Processed food	Textile & garments	Chem.	Plastic & rubber	Porcelin & glass	Metal manuf.	Machinery	Electron	Transport equip.	Other manuf.	Wholesale & retail trade	Fin. serv.	Real estate	Trans. serv.	Other serv.	All indus.
Small (under 50 companies) Under 20 firms	a = 95 k = 28	e = 80 j = 45 o = 12	—	a = 30 d = 48 f = 87 j = 35	—	d = 60 e = 72 j = 31 o = 7	d = 71 e = 92 g = 17 h = 17 o = 21	a = 14 b = 14 d = 29 e = 71 j = 29	c = 14 d = 41 e = 82 j = 18 o = 14 o = 14	d = 54 e = 79 j = 34	d = 69 e = 87 j = 36 o = 8	d = 59 e = 79 j = 42 o = 17	d = 45 e = 74 j = 26 k = 33 o = 4	d = 30 e = 88 j = 49	e = 41 l = 44 j = 50	e = 51 l = 21 j = 37 k = 38	d = 47 e = 55 j = 44	d = 27 e = 70 j = 73 k = 59	d = 30 e = 74 j = 49 o = 2
Medium (50–500)	—	—	—	a = 28 d = 39 e = 67 j = 36 o = 3	a = 13 b = 22 d = 69 e = 74 f = 30 j = 35	d = 82 e = 84 f = 16 j = 20 o = 5	b = 30 c = 17 d = 70 e = 77 l = 20 k = 17	—	d = 57 e = 880 j = 20 o = 27	d = 51 e = 83 f = 15 k = 20 o = 26	d = 54 e = 82 f = 15 j = 15 k = 33 o = 22	d = 72 e = 79 g = 13 h = 34 j = 15 o = 29	—	d = 25 e = 95 j = 33	e = 53 l = 27 j = 50 k = 69	—	d = 46 e = 45 j = 28 k = 29	e = 49 j = 49 k = 57 o = 2	d = 42 e = 81 j = 29 o = 10
Large (over 500)	—	—	—	—	—	—	—	—	—	d = 38 e = 79 j = 17 o = 21	c = 22 d = 28 e = 72 o = 17	d = 67 e = 81 f = 14 l = 14 o = 38	—	—	—	—	—	—	d = 38 e = 78 j = 17 o = 15

"—" denotes deletion of any case under 20 firms

M.E. Kreinin et al. / Journal of Asian Economics 10 (1999) 385–394 391

Similarly, "establishing production and distribution networks" (motive d) is frequently mentioned throughout in both tables, but these responses may capture the same motive as (e). Consistent with Graham and Krugman (1991), this motive does not distinguish between Japanese and U.S. DFI.

Also mentioned with great frequency is motive (j): "royalty acquisition, and information gathering." "Procurement of natural resources and materials" (a) is an important motive for setting up subsidiaries of any size in Asia in the agriculture, processed food, chemicals, metal manufacturing (large firms only), and paper and publishing. In developed host countries it is important only in energy and food.

As expected, access to cheap labor is important to medium-size and large subsidiaries located in developing countries, in agriculture and all manufacturing industries, but not in services. The frequency with which these responses are reported is similar to the one in EXIM bank surveys.

Many developing countries offer favorable treatment to incoming DFI in the form of subsidies, tax holidays, rebates, low land prices, and the like. About a quarter of responding firms that established large subsidiaries in developing countries in the following industries: rubber and plastic, porcelain and glass, metal manufacturing, machinery, electronics and transport equipment were motivated by such favorable treatment. In the EXIM survey this reason appears less important. That is not to suggest that such a policy of developing countries necessarily makes economic sense; only that it can sometimes have the desired results if properly calibrated, and directed at the right industries.

"Exporting to third markets" (f) is of some importance to firms setting up sizable subsidiaries in developing countries in the textile, machinery, and electronics industries. With respect to developed host countries, it is important in the case of small subsidiaries of processed foods; mid-sized textile, chemical, machinery, and electronics affiliates; and large transport equipment subsidiaries. Importing the output back to Japan is an important motive for firms setting up operations in developing countries in agriculture and practically all manufacturing industries. Again, the order of magnitude of these estimates jives with the responses obtained by the EXIM bank survey.

Contrary to conventional wisdom about Japanese operations abroad, "accompanying business clients" (h) is important only sporadically. In developed host countries, it appears frequently in mid-sized transport equipment subsidiaries, probably auto-parts producers. In developing host countries, it is seen in small chemical subsidiaries; transport equipment of all sizes; and medium-sized transport services. Not even the service sectors assign much importance to it. In the EXIM bank survey, the frequency of this response was low in 1990–93 but has risen rapidly since then. By 1996, it reached 16 percent of responding firms with investment in the United States, 10 percent for Japanese companies with subsidiaries in the EU, 24 percent in ASEAN[7], 14 percent in the NIEs[8] and 13 percent in China. "Financing and investing" (i) is important only for the financial services industry.

Finally, the motive "trade friction" (o) captures only government-to-government disputes as they impact upon business. A voluntary export restraint agreement (VER) would be a paramount example. On the other hand, bypassing a tariff or avoiding tariff discrimination (as in the EU or EFTA) may be included here or it may be part of the "securing local market" motive. Likewise, developing countries often have local content laws that force Japanese companies to produce there. But that, too, may come under the "securing local market" motive as the companies simply comply with requirements of the host government, without pressure from the Japanese government. In any event, this motive is concentrated in the developed host countries in five industries: transport equipment of all firm size, probably reflecting VERs on Japanese cars in the United States and Europe, plus threatened local content restrictions in the United States in the 1980's; machinery, medium and large firms, probably reflecting in part the U.S. VER on machine tools; electronics; metal manufacturing; and small porcelain and glass firms. It also appears in small construction subsidiaries. In the EXIM bank survey these motives were mentioned by 20 percent of the respondents in 1990 and the frequency diminished gradually, reaching 6–10 percent by 1996. A possible explanation of this phenomenon is that throughout the 1980's, trade pressure was an important motive for DFI. But once these investments were made, the pressure subsided, and the motive was taken over by other reasons, especially to enhance penetration of local markets.

3. Implications of the Asian Crisis for Japanese DFI

The ultimate effects of the Asian crisis on total DFI flows to the Asian region have been subject to considerable debate in the literature. Reliable DFI data will only become available several years after the crisis; hence, at this stage analysis can only be speculative. For example, Petri (1998) notes that the Asian crisis should affect DFI flows through 5 major channels, some favorable and others unfavorable.[9] First, the Asian crisis will change expectations with respect to profits in the region. Depreciating currencies will favor the production of tradeable goods at the expense of non-tradeables, so firms seeking to produce for export markets may benefit due to the price-competitiveness effect and lower relative production costs in terms of wages. Firms focusing on the domestic market will be hard hit by the recession. Second, the Asian crisis will alter the valuation of Asian investments relative to expected earnings streams. Third, policy changes that are being implemented under the auspices of the IMF could lead to more transparent corporate ownership and governance, which will lower the cost of DFI in local markets. Fourth, the Asian crisis will reduce the supply of DFI from economies like Japan and the Republic of Korea, who have become important sources of DFI to the region in recent years. Fifth, the Asian crisis will force a greater risk premium on investments in the region, as risk perceptions have increased. Petri (1998) also uses a computational general equilibrium (CGE) model to simulate the effects on DFI of the Asian crisis and estimates that, for the "Asian Crisis Economies," inward DFI stocks should fall by only 0.5 percent, but outward stocks will decline by 35 percent. Net income on DFI in the region falls by 6 percent.

Evidence from this paper on the motives for Japanese DFI abroad would suggest a decline in outward flows, at least in the short- and medium term. As Japanese foreign affiliates appear to have targeted Asia to "secure local markets," the strong economic downturn over the past 2 years does not bode well for outward flows of DFI. However, economic forecasters have generally been revising upward their estimates of economic growth in the region for all crisis-affected countries except Indonesia, and it is likely that the recession bottomed out in 1999, with possible respectable growth in 2000. Moreover, Japanese foreign affiliates in key

M.E. Kreinin et al. / Journal of Asian Economics 10 (1999) 385–394   393

sectors for Southeast Asia such as electronics do appear to be motivated at least in part by the prospect of exporting to third markets, suggesting that investments in these areas even in the short-run may not experience a decline and, in fact, could experience increases.

Nevertheless, the motives analyzed in this paper derive from the "demand side" of DFI. But supply-side considerations should be no less important, and the financial crisis in Japan itself has taken an important toll on outward flows of DFI. Thus, even a strong recovery in Asia, a more attractive investment environment, and other positive developments for inward DFI flows may have a limited effect on the overall outflows to Asia, though it could affect the distribution of Japanese DFI to Asia's advantage.

4. Conclusions

Japan has become an important source of global DFI, although as a host country it plays a limited role. The motivations behind Japanese DFI outflows are many and varied. In this study, we use an extensive data set to capture these motives at a micro-level. While securing market share constitutes a critical motivation, a number of other factors are important as well, particularly at the sectoral level. DFI as a means of avoiding trade frictions is relevant only in developed countries and in five industries, including transportation equipment, machinery, and electronics. Motivations are different for developed and developing host economies. Although the survey would have benefitted from additional choices in the questionnaire—the lack of an exchange-rate option is a particular drawback—the existing menu is sufficient in revealing motivations for Japanese DFI.

With respect to the implications of the Asian crisis on outward Japanese DFI, theory would suggest that the effect will be ambiguous. However, the results of this paper suggest that the net effect will be negative, at least in the short-run. In addition, an increase in DFI flows to the region will be critically dependent on the future course of the Japanese economy itself.

Notes

1. There are a number of studies focusing on the role of DFI in the Asian development process. See, for example, surveys in World Bank (1993) and United Nations (1995), as well as the literature cited therein.
2. DFI data in this paragraph were extracted from OECD (1996).
3. See, for example, Kreinin, Plummer and Abe (forthcoming 1998), Ramstetter (1996), Doner (1993), and Kreinin (1990).
4. For surveys, see Grey (1996) and Lizondo (1991).
5. MITI also undertakes surveys of Japanese DFI, but they are far less comprehensive and suffer from a lower response rate. For a detailed analysis and critique see Ramstetter (1996).
6. Studies using macro data yield mixed results, for example Dewenter (1995) and Goldberg and Klein (1996).
7. The Association of Southeast Asian Nations (ASEAN) includes Indonesia, the Philippines, Singapore, Thailand, Malaysia, and Brunei.

8. The Newly Industrialized Economies (NIEs) include Taiwan, South Korea, and Hong Kong.
9. This paragraph draws from Plummer (1998).

References

Dewenter, Kathryn L., "Do Exchange Rate Changes Drive Foreign Direct Investment?," *Journal of Business*, Vol. 28 (3), 1995.

Doner, Richard F., "Japanese Foreign Investment and the Creation of a Pacific Asian Region," Ch. 5 in Frankel, Jeffrey A. and Miles Kahler (eds.), *Regionalism and Rivalry: Japan and the United States in Pacific Asia* (Chicago: University of Chicago Press, 1993): 159–216.

Dunning, John H., "Trade, Location of Economic Activity and the MNE: A Search for an Eclectic Approach," in B. Ohlin, P. Hesselborn, and P. Wijkmans (eds.), *The International Allocation of Economic Activity* (London: Macmillan, 1977): 395–418.

EXIM Bank of Japan, Shigeki Tejima, *Lecture Notes on Japan's DFI*, mimeo 1997.

Gittleman, M. and J. Dunning, "Japanese Multinationals in Europe and the United States," in M. Klein and P. Welfens (eds.), *Multinationals in the New Europe and Global Trade* (London: Springer-Verlag, 1992).

Goldberg, Linda S., and Michael Klein, "FDI, Trade and Real Exchange Rate Linkages in Developing Countries," paper presented at *Managing Capital Flows and Exchange Rates: Lessons from the Pacific Rim*, Federal Reserve Bank of San Francisco, 1996.

Graham, Edward M. and Paul R. Krugman, *Foreign Direct Investment in the United States*, Second Edition (Washington, D.C.: Institute for International Economics, 1991).

Grey, H. Peter, "The Eclectic Paradigm: The Next Generation," Transnational Corporations Vol. 5, No. 2, August 1996, pp. 51–65.

JETRO, *JETRO White Paper on Foreign Direct Investment: FDI Speeds Industrial Restructuring* (Tokyo: JETRO, 1997).

Kreinin, Mordechai E., "How Closed Is Japan's Market? Additional Evidence," *World Economy* 11(4), December 1988, pp. 529–42.

Kreinin, Mordechai E., Michael G. Plummer, and Shigeyuki Abe, Export and Direct Foreign Investment Links: "A Three Country Comparison," in Kreinin, Mordechai E., Shigeyuki Abe and Michael G. Plummer (eds.), *International Economic Links* (London: Elsevier, forthcoming 1998).

Lizondo, J. Saul, "Foreign Direct Investment," in International Monetary Fund, *Determinants and Systemic Consequences of International Capital Flows* (Washington, D.C.: IMF, 1991).

OECD, *International Direct Investment Statistics Yearbook* (Paris: OECD, 1996).

Ozawa, T., "Japanese Multinationals and 1992," in B. Burgenmeier (ed.), *Multinational Firms and European Integration 1992* (London: Routledge, 1991).

Plummer, Michael G., "Trade and Investment Scenarios in light of the Asian Crisis," paper prepared for UNESCAP, September 1998.

Pournarakis, Mike, "Global Strategies of Multinationals in the Triad and the Japanese Foreign Direct Investment in the European Community," *Economia Internazionale* 47 (2–3), May–Aug. 1994, pp. 238–52.

Ramstetter, Eric D., "Estimating Economic Activities by Japanese Transnational Corporations: How to Make Sense of the Data?," *Transnational Corporations*, Vol. 5, No. 2, August 1996, pp. 107–142.

Trevino, Len J. and John D. Daniels, "An Empirical Assessment of the Preconditions of Japanese Manufacturing Foreign Direct Investment in the United States," *Weltwirtschaftliches Archiv* 130 (3), 1994, pp. 576–99.

United Nations, World Investment Report 1995: *Transnational Corporations and Competitiveness* (New York: United Nations, 1995).

Wakasugi, Ryuhei, "Is Japanese Foreign Direct Investment a Substitute for International Trade?," *Japan and the World Economy* 6 (1994), pp. 45–52.

World Bank, *East Asian Miracle* (Washington, D.C.: IBRD, 1993).

[7]
The Trade-Investment Nexus

MORDECHAI E. KREININ, MICHAEL G. PLUMMER AND SHIGEYUKI ABE

A salient feature of the emerging international economy is growing interdependence. International trade has increased as a percentage of GDP in all major (and most minor) economies, and direct foreign investment (DFI) and other financial flows have been growing exponentially. While globalization can be attributable to a number of factors, including revolutions in technology, transportation, and telecommunications, the greatest driving force may have been policy change in the direction of open international markets. The past two decades have witnessed unprecedented reductions of barriers to international exchange. While trade reform is the most frequently cited evidence, reform of DFI policies have been no less impressive. In many cases, they have even been more radical than trade reform, if only because the restrictions were initially more severe.[1]

Moreover, there is a close link between trade and DFI reform on the one hand, and trade and DFI flows on the other. In this chapter, we evaluate these relationships, which we might call the "trade-investment nexus", from several perspectives. In particular, the objective is to determine the effects of DFI on trade and *vice versa*. First, we consider some conceptual issues regarding the relationship between trade and DFI *policies*, and trade and DFI *flows*. Next, to explore the relationship between DFI and trade, we estimate the determinants of DFI by using a gravity model in which lagged trade values are used as explanatory variables. The case of developing Asia is examined as an example of how the trade-investment nexus has played a role in structural change and development.

On the Interdependence of Trade and DFI Policies: Theoretical Considerations

In analyzing policy reform, existing studies tend to place a strong emphasis on the trade sector, perhaps because readily-available

59

numerical indicators facilitate empirical inquiry, and because the GATT/WTO renders comparisons easier. Yet, policy change in developing countries *vis a vis* DFI (and other financial variables) has been impressive, though harder to quantify given the nature of investment regimes. Scarce quantitative work has been applied to the economic implications of DFI reform, let alone the specific link between trade and DFI.[2] Hence, a useful point of departure in evaluating the nature of the trade-investment nexus is to explore the relationship between trade and DFI policies.

Trade policy tends to relate closely to a country's DFI regime, though the exact relationship depends on the country's economic development strategy. In the case of an import-substitution regime, countries adopt a restrictive trade regime, limiting imports to those that are absolutely necessary (e.g. advanced capital equipment or necessary agriculture commodities). With respect to DFI policy under a protective regime, a country may wish either to ban or to promote inward investment as a means of furthering the goals of import-substitution. In the former (extreme) case, DFI is considered harmful because it allegedly undermines the ability of the country to function effectively, and so inward investment is prohibited. Alternatively, the more common choice is to allow DFI to flow into sectors in which the country has comparative disadvantage as a means of reducing imports. In the latter scenario, a country needs to compensate investors for the existing high-cost environment, through high tariffs (which are consistent with the regime anyway), fiscal incentives, monopoly rents, etc.

Few developing countries have adopted successfully the "extreme" import-substitution regimes, so market forces and economic realities dictate a loosening of DFI restrictions. However, the presence of foreign investors often results in pressures for liberalization of the import-substitution regime itself. First, while foreign investors may be satisfied with monopoly and other rents in the short run, slow growth and alienation from international production processes—of which foreign affiliates are an integral part—increasingly work to their disadvantage, to the point that they lobby for reform of the (costly) trade regime (Plummer, 1997). Thus, the sustainability of a set of trade policies becomes a function of the country's DFI policies, which in turn is intricately dependent on the trade regime.

In the case of an outward-oriented development strategy, a country uses international market forces to determine its relative efficiency. Foreign investment can be an effective means of enhancing structural adjustment in favor of a country's inherent comparative advantage; hence, an open trade regime should encourage liberal investment policies.[3] In other words, an outward-oriented development regime seeks to reduce transactions costs of doing business with the rest of the world. This requires reductions in both trade and DFI restrictions as means to lower costs.

Thus, in either regime, DFI policies support trade liberalization, and *vice versa*. Any empirical investigation into the determinants of trade or DFI policies will *per force* have to reckon with this inherent simultaneity problem. In addition, empirical investigations are burdened with another problem if trade and DFI policies are determined simultaneously as part of an overall economic strategy.

The relationship between trade and DFI *flows* (as distinguished from policies) suffers from the same type of simultaneity. Most studies maintain that causality runs from DFI to trade. The Kojima (1973) and "product life-cycle" (Vernon, 1966) models, for example, suggest specific signs for the impact of DFI on trade, depending on the investment's characteristics. More generally, however, the sign of the investment-trade relationship is not clear (Petri, 1992; Aitken *et al.*, 1994). In fact, trade and DFI might be substitutes, a possibility that finds its roots in the theoretical contribution of Mundell (1957). Our discussion of import-substitution revealed that a primary motivation for the attraction of DFI inflows is to substitute for imports. However, as has been documented extensively in the economic and business literature, such an approach ignores the complex nature of the international production process.[4] The time structure of most models of the investment-trade relationship suggests that changes in DFI at a particular time cause changes in trade at a later time. Evidence that DFI causes trade would support the trade-oriented theories based on Kojima, Vernon, and others.

But there are also reasons to expect DFI to be "determined" by past trade. DFI depends to some degree on variables that are difficult to measure, but are closely proxied by trade, and in part it is causally affected by trade. For example, the attractiveness of a host country's markets to a particular investor would be ideally measured by the host's potential demand for the investor's varieties of a product. The investor's exports of the product to the host (prior to the investment decision) provide a good proxy for this demand. In addition, prior exports to the host may also help to develop the market for the investor's products through building reputation, etc.

Another channel by which trade affects subsequent investment is through transaction costs. The difficulty of undertaking investment in the host economy would be ideally measured by transaction costs between the source and host economies (which would presumably negatively affect the rate of investment). Trade between the two economies is a useful proxy for these transaction costs. More importantly, trade may well "cause" lower transactions costs by helping the investor to accumulate information about the host economy which can be later used in establishing a subsidiary abroad.

An example of this process demonstrates how lagged trade might lead to higher levels of DFI, as well as illustrating the simultaneity problem. Ford Motor Company may choose to export to China before investing as a means of breaking into, and gathering information about, the Chinese market prior to risking a large capital outlay. It may also wish to establish its brand name. Once it enjoys an effective "beachhead" in the market and the company feels more confident about its ability to function there (i.e. uncertainty falls to a reservation level), Ford might chose to establish a plant which could sell both locally and abroad. The Chinese affiliate of Ford Motor Company, then, increases its imports from and exports to the global Ford production chain. Hence, trade precedes DFI, but DFI also precedes trade as part of a long-run marketing and investment strategy.

Capturing the Illusive Trade-Investment Nexus: An Empirical Approach

This section attempts to quantify the determinants of DFI using trade as an explanatory variable.[5] In doing so, we do not try to establish *causation* but rather *association* (WTO, 1996). Because of the simultaneity problems associated with such estimation noted above, we use lagged— rather than contemporaneous—trade values as an independent variable, as a means of trying to mitigate—though not eliminate—the problem. A five-year lag was deemed appropriate for our purposes. Consistent with other empirical models used to consider the determinants of DFI, we include the following additional explanatory variables (all of the model's variables are in log form, with the exception of the binary variables): GNP (size proxy); GNP per capita (wealth proxy; "GNCAP"); Secondary Education[6] (human capital proxy; "SECE"); Revealed Comparative Advantage[7] (competitiveness proxy at disaggregated levels; "RCA"); Distance (proxy for physical and cultural transaction costs; "DIST"); Adjacency Binary Variable (another transaction-cost proxy; "AD"); and Regional Binary Variables (Americas, "DM"; Africa, "DF"; and Asia, "DA"; all evaluated relative to Europe). If our hypothesis is correct, the estimated coefficient on lagged trade should be positive. Moreover, one would expect that DFI would be positively correlated with size, wealth, and revealed comparative advantage and negatively correlated with distance and adjacency. Estimated coefficients for secondary education would depend on the sector (e.g. positive for higher-skill-intensive sectors, negative for low-skill-intensive sectors). We use U.S. data available from the U.S. *Survey of Current Business.* Values for the dependent variable related to the stock of U.S. DFI in 40 foreign countries.

The results are presented in Table 5.1 for two periods: 1983 and

TABLE 5.1 *Determinants of U.S. DFI Abroad: Temporal Comparisons by Sector (Position; log model)*

	CONST.	TRADE 1978	TRADE (1985)	GNP	GNCAP	SECE	RCA	DIST	AD	DM	DF	DA	Aj. R²	DW
All 83	-15.5*** (9.35)	0.86* (0.37)		0.05 (0.29)	0.2 (0.27)	0.62 (0.7)		0.55 (0.83)	-0.07 (1.06)	0.51 (0.62)	-0.31 (1)	-0.56 (0.83)	0.55	2.06
All 90	-35.67* (14.06)		0.64 (0.52)	0.23 (0.41)	0.25 (0.3)	2.5* (0.99)		1.62 (1.26)	0.53 (1.55)	2.14** (1.13)	-1.8 (1.38)	-0.31 (1.21)	0.59	2.04
All Manuf. 83	-19.48*** (11.56)	1.1* (0.4)		0.1 (0.33)	-0.05 (0.32)	0.23 (0.88)	-0.37 (0.36)	0.82 (1.06)	0.75 (1.61)	-0.3 (0.92)	-2.27** (1.19)	-1.77 (1.1)	0.6	2.27
All Manuf. 90	-14.59 (9.88)		1.06* (0.33)	0.01 (0.27)	0.27 (0.22)	-0.39 (0.69)	-0.55 (0.45)	0.52 (0.88)	0.32 (1.1)	0.32 (0.86)	-1.85** (1.03)	-0.98 (0.87)	0.69	2.33
Machine 83	-25.1 (34.36)	1.85 (1.33)		0.06 (1.19)	-0.48 (1.22)	0.89 (2.99)	0.32 (0.47)	0.68 (3.1)	-0.54 (4.34)	-0.67 (2.29)	-3.72 (3.41)	-1.2 (2.53)	0.44	1.63
Machine 90	-23.73 (24.38)		2.48* (0.8)	-0.44 (0.63)	0.05 (2.11)	-2.01 (0.47)	0.04 (2.13)	1.77 (2.8)	1.54 (2.46)	-2.18 (3.18)	-5.74*** (2.04)	-2.66	0.57	1.61
Metals 83	-35.94 (47)	0.94* (0.59)		0.2 (1.13)	1.18 (0.8)	-2.61 (3.95)	-1.83*** (1.07)	2.65 (4.01)	5.12 (9.7)	1.43 (2.9)	-2.4 (4.33)	-2.24 (4.53)	0.17	3.41
Metals 90	-10.97 (12.64)		0.53 (0.5)	0.54 (0.46)	0.92* (0.42)	-1.82 (1.55)	-1.8* (0.54)	-1.26 (0.95)	-0.34 (1.89)				0.59	2.43
Elect. 83	14.1 (17.93)	0.77* (0.24)		0.02 (0.23)	0.34 (0.38)	-1.56 (1.2)	-0.27 (0.21)	-1.85 (1.47)	-0.24 (2.32)	-3.26* (1.25)	-4.15* (1.12)	0.54 (1.07)	0.8	1.24
Elect. 90	-11.2 (28.88)		0.51 (0.55)	0.28 (0.48)	0.23 (0.55)	0.12 (2.09)	0.46 (0.74)	-0.03 (2.51)	-1.17 (3.34)	2.18 (2.76)	0.31 (3.46)	0.84 (2.05)	0.23	2.34
Trans. 83	-261.93 (193.46)	-0.98 (1.97)		5.16 (3.96)	-2.97 (1.82)	23.16 (16.37)	-3.36 (3.41)	6.7 (5.91)	19.22 (17.45)				0.42	0.34
Trans. 90	-13.58 (27.47)		1.27** (0.66)	0.17 (0.93)	-0.95 (0.65)	1.7 (2.25)	0.29 (0.38)	-0.08 (1.97)	-2.37 (2.55)	1.43 (2.47)	-2.04 (2.77)	-2.26 (1.71)	0.68	2.03
Chem. 83	4.63 (10.25)	1.09* (0.46)		-0.13 (0.4)	-0.25 (0.4)	0.51 (1)	-0.18 (0.45)	-1.16*** (0.75)	-1.97 (2.14)				0.51	2.11
Chem. 90	12.25 (12.58)		1.04 (0.84)	-0.56 (0.64)	-0.05 (0.49)	0.7 (1.4)	-0.1 (0.58)	-1.01 (1.05)	-2.92 (2.07)				0.01	2.43
Other Manuf.	-11.33 (27.68)	1.26 (1.28)		-0.16 (1.07)	0.28 (1.06)	-1.39 (3.23)	-1.27 (1.11)	0.7 (2.39)	1.07 (4.87)	-0.78 (2.71)	-3.77 (3.05)	-2.91 (2.58)	0.35	3.28
Other Manuf.	-27.77** (15.12)		0.73*** (0.47)	0.27 (0.4)	0.48 (0.36)	1.02 (1.4)	-0.21 (0.5)	0.79 (1.47)	-0.32 (1.94)	2.17*** (1.37)	-1.17 (1.65)	-0.51 (1.07)	0.62	1.77

Note:
1. Dependent variable is DFI measured by position
2. All independents variable are in the log from except for dummies (i.e. AD, DM, DF, DA)
3. * 95% significance level; ** 90% significance level; *** 85% significance level
4. Variables: GNCAP = *per capita* income; SECE = secondary education enrolment rate; RCA = "revealed" comparative advantage; DIST = distance; AD = adjacency dummy; DM = Americas dummy; DF = Africa dummy; DA = Asia dummy.

1990; having 1978 and 1985, respectively, as lagged trade values. The adjusted R^2s vary but tend to be highest for the 1990 specification in the metals, transportation, and other manufactures sectors. In these cases the model explains approximately two-thirds of the variance in DFI position. Lagged trade tends to be statistically significant and of the correct sign in a majority of cases, with magnitudes of the estimated coefficients varying between 0.73 (other manufactures 1990) and 2.48 (machinery 1990) for the statistically significant variables. This would suggest that, say, a 10 percent increase in trade in other manufactures will lead to a 7.3 percent increase in DFI five years hence. These regressions show no statistically significant coefficient estimates for the size proxy, whereas parametric estimates in only a few sectors are statistically significant in the cases of the other variables.

While lagged trade is clearly an important determinant of U.S. DFI, the simultaneity bias could continue to be present even in the case of lagged trade. In order to explore this bias, Granger causality tests were run both for lagged trade on DFI and DFI on lagged trade. These tests reveal that, *in most cases, causality runs in both directions,* as was suggested in the previous section.[8] Yet it is not evident how one might go about correcting for this bias. There is no obvious instrumental variable that can be used to circumvent the problem; other approaches would require a full-fledged structural model of DFI, but would also suffer from the peculiarities of data problems in DFI regressions and model specifications. Moreover, as argued above, the trade-investment nexus is mutually reinforcing and difficult to disentangle.

Structural Transformation, Trade Liberalization, and the Role of DFI: The Case of Asia

The Asian economic development experience has often been offered as an important example of how the trade-investment nexus works to induce sustained growth in the context of an increasingly outward-oriented economic strategy. Most of the rigorous analytical work on economic growth in Asia has supported this view (e.g. Rodrik, 1995; Edwards, 1993; World Bank, 1993; and the sources therein). The majority of these studies focus on trade as the primary catalyst of development in the region. However, consistent with the above discussion of the trade-investment relationship, trade liberalization cannot be properly analyzed without also including financial (especially DFI) liberalization in identifying the roots of the regional success story.

Trade reform preceded DFI liberalization in the cases of South Korea and Taiwan (and, arguably, Japan). Even today, these countries would be considered far more open to trade than they are to DFI, though this depends to some degree on the sector. But their recent reform programs have focused on liberalizing (outward as well as inward) DFI flows.[9]

The example of the resource-rich ASEAN countries is more pertinent, as their experiences seem to have been more typical of economic reform in developing countries. First, they were forced to liberalize because of external exogenous shocks. The collapse of commodity prices, slow growth in external demand, and high global interest rates in the early-mid 1980s reduced external demand and contributed to growing debt-related and balance of payments problems.[10] Eventually, each country chose to switch to an outward-oriented development strategy. Second, liberalization was comprehensive, including both trade and investment. In addition to lowering tariffs substantially, non-tariff barriers fell even faster over the 1984/87 to 1991/93 period, from 93 percent to 7 percent in Indonesia, 8 percent to 5 percent in Malaysia, and 20 percent to 8 percent in Thailand.[11] But what is often ignored is the remarkable changes in ASEAN DFI policies over this period. In order to attract more DFI, all ASEAN countries established one-stop investment centers and worked to make investment laws as transparent as possible. Restrictive "positive lists" (which stipulated sectors where foreign investors could legally invest) were changed into short "negative lists" (sectors in which DFI would not be allowed, usually areas falling under national defence, the media, and those affecting "national sovereignty," that is, not unlike developed-country restrictions); legal equity participation was liberalized (often to 100 percent); restrictions on repatriation of profits were abolished; limitations on foreign personnel were loosened; and performance requirements were made less stringent, generally well beyond what is now the WTO-instigated minimum.

The movement towards regional economic integration in ASEAN is further evidence of the desire to integrate DFI and trade reform in the region. ASEAN's initial economic cooperation programs were established in the mid-1970s during a time of import-substitution and, predictably, these programs did not seek real economic integration. It was not until the Fourth Summit in January 1992, i.e. the first summit when all existing ASEAN countries were solidly in favor of liberalization, that the ASEAN Free-Trade Area (AFTA) was formed. Since then, AFTA commitments have increased from 10 manufactured sectors to just about all sectors; the time horizon over which AFTA would be formed was reduced from 15 years to 10 years (and there is now strong support to moving it to 7 years, i.e. by the year 2000); agreements on services and intellectual property were signed; the decision to form a region of free investment flows was agreed to at the Fifth Summit in December 1995; and a dispute settlement mechanism has been created. Trade liberalization and reductions in other border- and non-border impediments underscore the priority of ASEAN leaders to reduce transactions costs in the region as a means of bringing in DFI. AFTA has been dubbed more of an investment agreement than a trade agreement (Ariff, 1996); regional economic integration policies in ASEAN are being designed to capture potential gains through the symbiotic trade-investment relationship.

Economic growth in Asia spurred by policy reform has lead to a considerable restructuring in the exports of regional economies, which in turn have been the "engine of growth". Figures 5.1–5.3 show the changes in export structures of the Asian NIEs, ASEAN countries (excluding Singapore, which is included with the NIEs, and Vietnam, for whom data were not available), and China (for which data were available only from 1987 to 1994). Each region has undergone a considerable amount of structural transformation in its exports at the same time that it experienced exponential economic growth. In general, these changes have been in the direction of manufactures; in the cases of the NIEs and ASEAN countries, the most important exports are now in the category of electronics and machinery (SITC 7), which includes a number of sophisticated product lines. In fact, by 1994, almost one-half of all NIE exports were in this category, on par with the United States. For the ASEAN countries in 1980, these products only constituted 0.05 percent of total exports; by 1994, the share had increased to about one-third of the total.

Electronics and machinery in the ASEAN countries are characterized by extremely high foreign participation, in the form of joint ventures or wholly-owned enterprises. While data are difficult to obtain, almost all major exporting firms in these areas in Singapore and Malaysia have large foreign equity stakes, and often these exports flow back to the

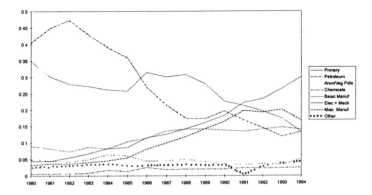

FIGURE 5.1 *Structural Change in ASEAN Exports, 1980–94 (percentage of total trade by 1-digit SITC)*

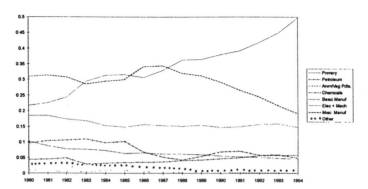

FIGURE 5.2   *Structural Change in NIE Exports, 1980–94 (percentage of total trade by 1-digit SITC)*

markets from which the DFI originates. Table 5.2 shows DFI data for most East Asian countries sourced from the U.N.'s (most recent) *World Investment Directory*. Sectoral estimates of DFI stocks in electronics are available for Hong Kong, Taiwan, Korea, Singapore, and Thailand, each classified by the OECD as a "dynamic Asian economy". In every case, electronics and electronic equipment account for the largest share of DFI among manufacturing sectors. In Hong Kong, the share comes to 46 percent of DFI. Kreinin and Plummer (1992) show that, contrary to what one might expect given differences in factor endowments, the ASEAN countries compete in a large number of product lines with Canada in the U.S. market, implying that NAFTA could actually cause a considerable amount of trade diversion. This observation is consistent with the international business literature, which places a strong emphasis on the growing international division of labor in the world economy increasingly characterized by a greater number of product lines along the production chain.

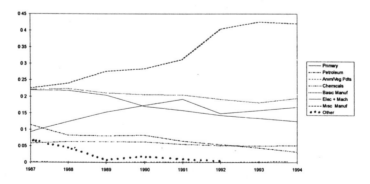

FIGURE 5.3   *Structural Change in Chinese Exports, 1987–94 (percentage of total trade by 1-digit SITC)*

TABLE 5.2 Distribution of Direct Foreign Investment in East Asia (Stock; % of total)

	Hong Kong 1989	Taiwan 1986	Singapore 1989	Korea 1988	Indonesia 1990	Malaysia 1988	Phillipines 1989	Thailand 1989	China 1988
PRIMARY	-	-	0.2%	0.9%	80.5%	28.3%	29.3%	9/2%	12.3%
Agriculture	-	-	-	0.7%	2.1%	12.9%	1.7%	1.3%	2.7%
Mining and quarrying	-	-	-	0.2%	4.2%	0.1%	3.7%	0.9%	1.4%
Oil	-	-	-	-	74.2%	15.3%	23.9%	7.0%	6.4%
SECONDARY	100.0%	88.3%	42.4%	61.5%	16.9%	41.2%	48.9%	42.8%	47.6%
Food, beverages and tobacco	7.7%	1.8%	1.4%	4.0%	1.5%	-	10.6%	3.6%	-
Textiles, leather and clothing	10.0%	8.3%	0.5%	1.4%	3.5%	-	2.4%	4.1%	-
Paper, printing and publishing	9.2%	2.2%	0.8%	0.7%	0.3%	-	0.7%	-	-
Chemical products	7.7%	17.9%	6.0%	16.8%	3.7%	-	13.3%	5.7%	-
Coal and petroleum products	-	-	-	-	-	-	-	-	-
Rubber products	-	-	-	-	-	-	-	-	-
Non-metallic products	1.2%	10.2%	0.8%	1.1%	1.5%	-	4.1%	4.5%	-
Metal products	6.3%	4.1%	2.5%	2.8%	5.9%	-	5.6%	2.1%	-
Mechanical equipment	1.4%	10.9%	2.5%	5.3%	-	-	-	-	-
Electric and electronic equipment	45.7%	28.0%	14.0%	18.9%	-	-	-	14.9%	-
Motor vehicles	-	-	-	9.9%	-	-	-	-	-
Other transport equipment	3.6%	-	1.3%	-	-	-	3.9%	-	-
Other manufacturing	5.2%	0.3%	1.3%	1.5%	0.5%	-	4.6%	6.6%	-
TERTIARY	-	11.7%	57.4%	37.6%	2.5%	30.5%	21.8%	48.0%	40.1%
Construction	-	0.1%	-	1.0%	0.4%	3.3%	0.5%	11.6%	1.6%
Wholesale and retail trade	-	0.3%	-	0.7%	1.0%	8.4%	3.5%	16.6%	3.3%
Tranport and storage	-	4.7%	-	0.6%	0.1%	-	0.3%	2.6%	1.7%
Finance, insurance and business	-	-	-	-	-	17.2%	10.4%	6.7%	0.3%
Communication	-	-	-	-	0.1%	-	0.6%	-	-
Real estate/Unallocated OE	-	-	-	7.8%	-	-	1.4%	4.2%	-
Other Services	-	6.5%	-	27.5%	0.9%	1.6%	5.1%	6.4%	29.7%
Total($US)*	3,025.10	3,973.69	26,012.40	3,700.15	3,757.50	8,317.55	1,619.12	5,533.90	20,913.00

Notes:
*Total value of DFI refers to total sectoral data (e.g., tertiary investment in Hong Kong is excluded).
Conversion to US$ (where necessary) was done using exchange rates in the Penn World Tables
Source: UN, World Investment Directory, various issues.

In sum, recent history of policy change in the East Asian region, combined with structural change in terms of exports, support the view that the trade-investment nexus is a critical feature of its regional development.

Conclusions

Between 1973 and 1995 (estimated) annual flows of DFI expanded by over 12 fold (from $25 billion to $315 billion) and the annual flows of exports grew by over 8 fold (from $575 billion to $4900 billion). In addition to discovering close theoretical justifications for the trade-investment nexus, we find strong empirical support. Given current trends in the internationalization of the world's economies, changes in technology, and new approaches to business organization in which borders have become increasingly less significant, it is likely that this relationship will be reinforced over time as the globalization of production proceeds apace. As noted in WTO (1996, p. 34):

> There can be no question that foreign direct investment and international trade generally are mutually supportive, and that together they are playing the central role in the on-going integration of the world economy. Through investment and trade, firms in each country are able to specialize in producing what they can produce most efficiently . . . This joint process is central to development strategies and, more generally, to world-wide efforts to increase wealth and raise living standards.

References

AITKEN, B., HANSON, G. H. and HARRISON, A. E. (1994) Agglomeration Economies, Foreign Investment, and Export Behavior, International Monetary Fund (Mimeo), July.

ARIFF, M. (1996) Outlooks for ASEAN and NAFTA Externalities. In NISHIJIMA, S. and SMITH, P. H. (eds) *Cooperation or Rivalry? Regional Integration in the Americas and the Pacific Rim*, pp. 209–224, Westview, Boulder.

BALASSA, B. (1965) Trade Liberalization and 'Revealed' Comparative Advantage, *Manchester School of Economic and Social Studies*, Vol. 23, pp. 99–123.

EDWARDS, S. (1993) Openness, Trade Liberalization, and Growth in Developing Countries, *Journal of Economic Literature*, Vol. 31, September, pp. 1358–1393.

HILL, H. (1996) Towards a Political Economy Explanation of Rapid Growth in Southeast Asia, *Working Papers in Trade and Development*, Working Paper No. 96/2, the Australian National University, July.

KOJIMA, K. A. (1973) Macroeconomic Approach to Foreign Direct Investment, *Hitosubashi Journal of Economics*, Vol. 14, June.

KREININ, M. E. and PLUMMER, M. G. (1992) The Effects of Economic Integration in Industrial Countries on ASEAN and the Asian NIEs, *World Development*, Vol. 20, No. 9, September.

LEE, H. and ROLAND-HOLST, D. (eds) (1997) *Economic Development and Cooperation in the Pacific Basin: Trade, Investment, and Environmental Issues*, Cambridge University Press, New York.

LEE, K. and PLUMMER, M. G. (1992) Competitive Advantages, Two-Way Foreign Investment, and Capital Accumulation in Korea, *Asian Economic Journal*, Vol. VI, No. 2, July.

MUNDELL, R. (1957) International Trade and Factor Mobility, *American Economic Review*, Vol. 67, pp. 321–336.

PETRI, P. A. (1992) Platforms in the Pacific: Trade Effects of Direct Investment in Thailand, *Journal of Asian Economics*, Vol. 3, No. 2, pp. 173–96.

PETRI, P. A. and PLUMMER, M. G. (1996) The Determinants of Direct Foreign Investment, *Brandeis University Working Paper.*

PLUMMER, M. G. (1997) DFI and Endogenous Policy Reform in Asia, prepared for the American Economic Association Meetings, New Orleans, January

RODRIK, D. (1996) Understanding Economic Policy Reform, *Journal of Economic Literature*, Vol. XXXIV, March, pp. 9–41.

United Nations, Division on Transnational Corporations and Investment (1995) *World Investment Report 1995: Transnational Corporations and Competitiveness*, United Nations, Geneva.

United Nations Conference on Trade and Development (UNCTAD) (1994) *Directory of Import Regimes, Part 1: Monitoring Import Regimes*, United Nations, New York.

VERNON, R. (1966) International Investment and International Trade in the Product Cycle, *Quarterly Journal of Economics*, Vol. 80.

World Bank (1993) *East Asian Miracle*, IBRD, Washington, DC.

World Trade Organization (WTO) (1996) Trade and Direct Foreign Investment, *Annual Report-Investment*, Press/57, 9 October, pp. 1–55.

The authors would like to thank the Research Institute for Economics and Business Administration, Kobe University, and the Japan Foundation's Center for Global Partnership for financial support in undertaking this project. They are also indebted to Mr. Jason Eis and Kaori Kiyohara for research assistance.

Notes

1. For detailed reviews of investigation regimes, see United Nations (1995) and WTO (1996).
2. Exceptions include Lee and Roland-Horst (1997) and sources surveyed in WTO (1996).
3. It is impossible to argue that an open investment regime would require an open trade regime in order to ensure the former's success in attracting DFI.
4. See, for example, WTO 1996 and its sources.
5. These regressions were undertaken as part of the "Making APEC Work" project at Brandeis University. For a more detailed evaluation of estimation results, diagnostic tests, and alternative specifications, see Petri and Plummer (1995).
6. Calculated as the secondary school enrolment rate.
7. The Revealed Comparative Advantage (RCA) index, as derived by Balassa (1965), is calculated as:
$$RCA = (X_{ij}X_j) / (X_{iw}/X_w),$$
   where: X_{ij} = exports of commodity i by country j; X_j = total exports of country j; X_{iw} = world exports of commodity i; and X_w = total world exports.
8. For a review of the problems of simultaneity bias in gravity-type regressions, see contributions in Lee and Roland-Holst (forthcoming 1997).
9. See Lee and Plummer (1992).
10. Hill (1996) gives an in-depth survey of the origins of change in ASEAN development strategies in the 1980s.
11. Non-tariff barriers are calculated on a coverage basis (UNCTAD 1994).

[8]

Export and Direct Foreign Investment Links: A Three-Country Comparison

MORDECHAI E. KREININ, MICHAEL G. PLUMMER AND SHIGEYUKI ABE

Introduction

During the 1980s and early 1990s, economic ties between East Asian countries have intensified, and closer regional trade links have made an important contribution to the region's economic growth. Significantly, deeper regional integration in East Asia has coincided with greater overall openness of their economies and an ongoing liberalization of their trade and investment regimes. Furthermore, through reform, the structure of East Asian countries' production is becoming increasingly based on comparative advantage, and their ability to absorb more sophisticated foreign technology was enhanced by rapidly-growing direct foreign investment (DFI) flows. *Prima facie* evidence would suggest that a virtuous cycle is at work in East Asia, with DFI contributing to export growth, which in turn creates pressures for further trade and investment liberalization and even greater volumes of DFI flows.

In recent years, Asian countries have experienced a sharp upsurge in international capital flows. During 1990–1993, the developing countries of Asia were the recipients of $150 billion net capital inflows, more than double the amount they had received in the previous 4 years.[1] The composition of capital flows into Asia has changed drastically in recent years. DFI flows, together with bond and equity financing, have largely replaced the formerly dominant form of capital flows into developing countries—commercial bank loans. DFI flows into several East Asian countries have risen in the 1986–1989 period, and then have surged dramatically in the 1990s (especially to China).

During 1986–1992, the sources of East Asian DFI flows have been

47

primarily intraregional: half of all DFI flows in the region originated in other East Asian countries (predominantly Hong Kong, Singapore, Korea, and Taiwan); less than a fifth originated in Japan and only one-tenth came from the United States and Western Europe.[2] The sectoral composition of DFI has also been changing. In earlier periods, investment from advanced industrial countries were channeled primarily into natural resource-based industries and related sectors, while in more recent years the NIEs have been investing primarily in manufacturing, especially in electrical machinery, electronics, non-ferrous metals, and chemicals.

As of the mid-1980s, export-oriented Japanese multinational corporations (MNCs) began to shift their production base (and in some cases even their product development location) offshore, in search of lower production costs. The steep appreciation of the yen since the mid-1980s, together with real and perceived protectionist sentiment in North America and Western Europe (directed primarily against Japanese exporters), provided a powerful incentive for Japanese MNCs to globalize their operations. Japanese DFI in Asia has been increasingly channeled into export-oriented activities. Relatively low cost Asian labor, together with their relatively advanced level of technology, were no doubt factors in inducing Japanese MNCs to relocate certain parts of their operations—production, R&D, and sales—to East Asia.

Japanese and other foreign investors in Asia have become increasingly export oriented. In 1992, the ratio of exports to total sales of Japanese affiliates in manufacturing was 45 percent in Asia compared with only 23 percent in Latin America. Currently, parts and equipment imports of Japanese affiliates in Asia from Japan constitute a significant share of their total imports (about 38 percent of the total in 1992), and although local procurement already constitutes a large share (50 percent) of their total purchases, they are expected to rise even more in the future.[3]

The DFI-trade link in Asia has often been described in terms of the "flying geese" metaphor. Accordingly, Japan is the lead country ("goose") because of its most-advanced technology. The lead country's firms combine their technological advantage with the relatively lower factor (labor) costs in the host countries, making the follower countries' (the East Asian NIEs) production more competitive in world markets and allowing for an additional source of Asian export growth. Hence, Japan leads in this scheme, followed by the NIES, who are in turn followed by other ASEAN countries and, later, China.[4]

As of 1990, Japan has accounted for 52 percent of the DFI stock of Korea, 31 percent of Singapore, 37 percent of Thailand, and 27 percent of Taiwan.[5] While the NIEs have been a significant source of foreign capital flows to other East Asian countries, they have not been major recipients of foreign capital inflows from other East Asian developing countries, relying instead on traditional sources. The NIEs were the source of 58 percent of the DFI stock in China (in 1987), 35 percent in Malaysia (1987), and 20 percent in Thailand (1988). Thus, foreign investment flows in East Asian have followed a stepwise pattern, meaning that there have been *unidirectional* flows of investment from relatively advanced countries into the less developed countries of East Asia.[6]

This paper is part of a larger study exploring the emerging patterns of trade and investment.[7] It attempts to quantify the proximate causes of DFI into East Asia from three source countries: Japan, the United States (as traditional, major sources), and South Korea (as a new source). In doing so, we are able to shed light on the nature of trade-investment links in the region, as well as the overall determinants of trade and investment. The paper also yields several practical results that can serve as guideposts for future empirical work in this field. Specifically, the paper shows that disaggregation by sectors imparts considerable precision to the empirical specification of investment relationships, while differences between source countries reveal additional interesting insights.

On the Interdependence of Trade and DFI Policies: Theoretical Considerations

In analyzing policy reform, existing studies tend to place a strong emphasis on the trade sector, perhaps because readily-available numerical indicators facilitate empirical inquiry, and because features of the General Agreement on Tariffs and Trade (GATT)/World Trade Organization (WTO) (e.g. data collection and standardization with respect to trade flows and policies) render comparisons easier. Yet, policy change in developing countries vis à vis DFI (and other financial variables) has been impressive, though harder to quantify given the nature of investment regimes. Scarce quantitative work has been applied to the economic implications of DFI reform, let along the specific link between trade and DFI.[8] Hence, a useful point of departure in evaluating the nature of the trade-investment nexus is to explore the relationship between trade and DFI policies.

Trade policy tends to relate closely to a country's DFI regime, though the exact relationship depends on the country's economic development strategy. In the case of an import-substitution policy, countries adopt a restrictive trade regime, limiting imports to those that are absolutely necessary (e.g. advanced capital equipment or necessary agriculture commodities). With respect to DFI policy under such a regime, a country may wish either to ban or to promote inward investment as a means of furthering the goals of import-substitution. In the former (extreme) case, DFI is considered harmful because it allegedly undermines the ability of the country to function and/or plan effectively, and so inward investment is prohibited. Alternatively, the more common choice is to allow DFI to flow into sectors in which the country presumably has comparative disadvantage as a means of reducing imports. In the latter scenario, a country needs to compensate investors for the existing high-cost environment, through high tariffs (which are consistent with the regime anyway), fiscal incentives, monopoly rents, etc.

Few developing countries have adopted successfully "extreme" import-substitution, so market forces and economic realities dictate a loosening of DFI restrictions. However, the presence of foreign investors often results in pressures to liberalize the import-substitution regime itself. First, while foreign investors may be satisfied with monopoly and other rents in the short run, slow growth and alienation from international production processes—of which foreign affiliates are an integral part—increasingly work to their disadvantage, to the point that they lobby for reform of the (costly) trade regime (Plummer, 1997). Thus, the sustainability of a set of trade policies becomes a function of the country's DFI policies, which in turn is intricately dependent on the trade regime.

In the case of an outward-oriented development strategy, a country uses international market forces to determine its relative efficiency. Foreign investment can be an effective means of enhancing structural adjustment in favor of a country's inherent comparative advantage; hence, an open trade regime should encourage liberal investment policies.[9] In other words, an outward-oriented development regime seeks to reduce transactions costs of doing business with the rest of the world. This requires reductions in both trade and DFI restrictions as means of lowering costs.

Thus, in either regime, DFI policies support trade liberalization, and vice versa. Any empirical investigation into the determinants of trade or DFI policies will *per force* have to reckon with this inherent simultaneity problem. In addition, empirical investigations are burdened with another problem if trade and DFI policies are determined simultaneously as part of an overall economic strategy.

The relationship between trade and DFI *flows* (as distinguished from policies) suffers from the same type of simultaneity. Most studies maintain that causality runs from DFI to trade, with other variables associated with the determinants of DFI per se.[10]

Various theories of the determinants of DFI are encompassed in Dunning's "eclectic approach". Dunning highlights three key requirements for direct investment: (i) the firm must possess "ownership advantages" over other firms; (ii) the firm must find it beneficial to utilize these advantages directly instead of selling or leasing them ("internalization" advantages); and (iii) the firm must find it profitable to combine these advantages with at least one factor input abroad so that local production dominates exporting ("locational" advantages). Locational advantages include proximity to markets, specialized suppliers, evasion of protective barriers, and factor endowment advantages.[11] Trade and DFI policies, therefore, will affect the decision of a firm to invest in a country through the various effects on locational advantages of the host country.[12]

With respect to trade-investment links, the Kojima (1978) and "product life-cycle" (Vernon, 1966) models suggest specific signs for the impact of DFI on trade, depending on the investment's character-istics. More generally, however, the sign of the investment-trade relationship is not clear (Aitken et al., 1994; Petri, 1992). In fact, trade and DFI might be substitutes, a possibility that finds its roots in the theoretical contribution of Mundell (1957). Our discussion of import-substitution revealed that a primary motivation for the attraction of DFI inflows is to substitute for imports. However, as has been documented extensively in the economic and business literature, such an approach ignores the complex nature of the international production process.[13] Evidence that DFI causes trade would support the trade-oriented theories based on Kojima, Vernon, and others.

But there are also reasons to expect DFI to be "determined" by past trade. DFI depends to some degree on variables that are difficult to measure, but are closely proxied by trade, and in part it is causally affected by trade. For example, the attractiveness of a host country's markets to a particular investor would be ideally measured by the host's potential demand for the investor's varieties of a product. The investor's exports of the product to the host (prior to the investment decision) provide a good proxy for this demand. In addition, prior exports to the host may also help to develop the market for the investor's products through building reputation, etc.

.Another channel by which trade affects subsequent investment is through transaction costs. The difficulty of undertaking investment in the host economy would be ideally measured by transaction costs between the source and host economies (which would affect negatively the rate of investment), which is one aspect of locational advantages. Trade between the two economies is a useful proxy for these transaction costs. Conversely, trade may well "cause" lower transactions costs by helping the investor to accumulate information about the host economy, which can later be used in establishing a subsidiary abroad.

An example of this process demonstrates how lagged trade might lead to higher levels of DFI, as well as illustrating the simultaneity problem. Ford Motor Company may choose to export to China before investing as a means of breaking into, and gathering information about, the Chinese market prior to risking a large capital outlay. It may also wish to establish its brand name. Once it enjoys an effective "beach-head" in the market and the company feels more confident about its ability to function there (i.e. uncertainty falls to a reservation level), Ford might chose to establish a plant that could sell both locally and abroad. The Chinese affiliate of Ford Motor Company, then, increases its imports from and exports to the global Ford production chain. Hence, trade precedes DFI, but DFI also precedes trade as part of a long-run marketing and investment strategy.

Capturing the Illusive Trade-Investment Nexus: an Empirical Approach

DFI theory suggests a wide variety of potential determinants to be examined in empirical analysis. In this section, we use trade and DFI (stock and flow) data from several sources for the United States, Korea, and Japan in order to capture the trade-investment nexus in a cross-country comparison.[14] We have chosen these countries for the following reasons: first, it was thought that a comparison between the two largest traditional (developed-country) sources of DFI would yield interesting insights into any differences/similarities between U.S. and Japanese firms. Second, adding Korea, which just joined the OECD and is an important new source of DFI allows for a "flying-geese"-type comparison of trade and DFI flows. And third, these were three countries for which data were available.

Based on the previous discussion, our general hypothesis is that exports (lagged, contemporaneous, or "front-loaded") are a critical determinant of DFI, and, at the same time, the simultaneity of the trade-investment decision-making of MNCs would suggest that DFI (lagged, contemporaneous, "front-loaded") is an essential determinant of exports. In all cases, we test this relationship by using first DFI and then exports as dependent variables. We estimate these relationships in the context of a simple model used with considerable success in the literature.[15]

The models estimated include standard variables suggested by theory, such as distance (in the Korean and U.S. cases), general measures of market supply potential (GDP), and potential market demand (population), as well as trade and investment. Because of these variables, the model resembles the familiar gravity models of the empirical trade literature, which Anderson (1979) describes as ". . .the most successful empirical trade device of the last twenty-five

years". Although sometimes criticized for their weak theoretical foundations in the trade context, gravity models also provide a natural
framework for the analysis of DFI flows.

Our model specifications are of the following forms.[16]

DFI = f\{GDP, POP, DIST, Asdum, EXP $(t, -1, t + 1)$\}
Exports = f\{GDP, POP, DIST, Asdum, DFI $(t, t-1, t+1)$\},

where: *GDP = host-country gross domestic product, a proxy for
market potential (supply side); *Pop = host-country population, a
proxy for potential market demand; *DIST = distance between the
investor and host countries, a proxy for transactions costs; *ASDUM
= a regional dummy variable for the ASEAN countries (in the case of
the United States and Korea) or Asia (in the case of Japan); and
*Exports = contemporaneous, lagged, and "forward-loaded" U.S.,
Korean, and Japanese bilateral exports, a proxy for transactions costs
and for market receptivity for the source country's products.

There are several features of the study that distinguish it from previous
efforts to estimate DFI determinants. First is the cross-country comparison
and country mix. Each observation relates to the stock of investment of
the source country in a host country (DFI is measured in U.S.$ millions
and Exports in U.S.$ thousands in all cases). The number of host
countries differs in each data set because of the differences in DFI
location and data limitations. Second, the study estimates separate
investment equations for a number of disaggregated commodity
categories, where the product breakdown differs between source
countries, again depending on data availability. DFI theory suggests that
the determinants of DFI will vary with industry characteristics because
these affect the nature of ownership and location advantages.

Since the empirical estimates involve investments in a single industry
from a single investing country, they cannot test the validity of
determinants based on "ownership advantages". Nor can they test
"internalization" effects that are specific to the technology of a
particular industry. Thus, the DFI explanatory variables in this study
all fall within the broad category of "locational" advantages in the
Dunning terminology—factors that vary with the destination of foreign
investment flows.

There is an important *caveat* concerning the data set, since DFI data
are notorious in the literature. In addition to paucity of published
data, DFI flows and stocks have been criticized as unreliable because
of definitional problems, the "mixture" of approval and actual data,
and numerous questions regarding corporate finance.[17] Nevertheless,
the Japanese, Korean, and U.S. data are consistent within themselves,
and while they differ in terms of sectoral breakdown, years available
for analysis, and definitions, regressions were run separately such that

there was no mixing of numerical apples and oranges. Hence, these preliminary results need to be evaluated in light of their general comparability, rather than as exact replications.

Results

The results are presented in Tables 1–7. We are able to produce a three-country comparison for all manufactures (Table 1), but at the disaggregated level only two countries were matched for any given industry.[18] Labor-intensive manufactures (Table 2) includes estimates for Japan and Korea, while in other commodity categories Tables 3–7 compare the United States and Japan.

Several general results obtain. First, while the adjusted R^2s are fairly high and tend to justify the choice of functional forms, they vary considerably, depending on the sector and country. The R^2s in the U.S. and Japanese regressions tend to be higher than those for Korea. Thus, the ability of the common specifications for each sector and country to explain the variance in the dependent variable differs.

Second, and perhaps most importantly, *the only consistently statistically-significant coefficients relate to the trade-investment nexus, giving strong support to our hypotheses.* In the vast majority of cases, the estimated coefficients of trade in the DFI equations, *and* DFI in the trade equations, are statistically significant, usually at the 95 percent to 99 percent level and carry a positive sign. The orders of magnitude of these coefficients are also generally plausible.

Third, the lag (or lead) structure of the trade (DFI) explanatory variables in the DFI (trade) equations makes little or no difference in the vast majority of cases. This is why we report only the con-temporaneous specifications. We had thought that by lagging these variables several years, we might reduce the simultaneity bias that is inherent in estimating trade-investment links. After experimenting with several lag structures, both forward and backward, we found that this makes little difference. Hence, to the extent that simultaneity is a problem, lags are not the answer. Yet, it is not clear how one might go about correcting for this bias. There is no obvious instrumental variable that can be used to circumvent the problem; other approaches would require a full-fledged structural model of DFI, but would also suffer from the peculiarities of data problems in DFI regressions and model specifications. Moreover, the trade-investment nexus is mutually reinforcing and difficult to disentangle. In fact, the theory developed above suggested that there is in effect no way around the simultaneity problem, as trade and investment decisions are made jointly by firms. In order to test for this statistically, we ran Granger Causality tests in Japan and the United States (the two-points of observations for Korea

TABLE 1. *All Manufactures*

DFI (dependent variable)	U.S.			Japan			Korea	
	DFI 1983	DFI 1990	Pooled^c	Log DFI 1983	DFI 1990	Pooled^c	DFI 1992	Pooled^c
Constant	1002	1960.	2253**	-65688	-504801***	-317298***	-1681*	-1033*
GDP	0.003*	0.002***	0.002**	-5.61	130.3*	76.3	-0.14	-1.2
Pop	-0.42	-0.01	-0.06	-14.6	137.6	-30.3	4.92***	7.9**
Distance	-0.09	-0.16	-0.19	14.8**	89.3***	48.1***	0.36	1.7***
Asdum^b	-0.41	-458	-71	-363	-364327*	-168555	2084***	985
Exp (contemporaneous)^a	0.001***	0.001***	0.0005***	20.9***	65.2***	59.1***	0.001***	0.001
Adj. R^2	0.74	0.77	0.77	0.76	0.88	0.79	0.19	0.06
N	33	35	68	24	25	49	67	155

Exp (dependent variable)	U.S.			Japan			Korea	
	EXP 1983	EXP 1990	Pool^c	Log EXP 1983	EXP 1990	Pool^c	EXP 1992	Pool^c
Constant	1007	2479	755	2933	7543***	5101***	735***	391***
GDP	2.77	0.51	1.05	0.88	-1.59	-0.71	253***	209***
Pop	-379	605	111	2.28	-0.8	2.34	-738***	-407***
Distance	-111	-290	-158	-0.5*	-1.17***	-0.57*	-79.2	-44***
Asdum	1717	381	261	-313.7	4743	1836	-435***	-244***
DFI (contemporaneous)^a	985***	1417***	1316***	0.037***	0.014***	0.014***	46.9***	0.97
Adj. R^2	0.71	0.74	0.75	0.75	0.87	0.78	0.28	0.25
N	33	35	68	24	24	24	80	167

Notes: ^a Lag structure of exports and DFI makes no difference on the results of the regressions.

^b In Japan regressions and Asia dummy was used rather than an ASEAN dummy.

^c In pooled observations the time variable was insignificant.

^d Other years for Japan show similar results.

*Significance at the 85 percent level; **significance at the 90 percent level; ***significance at the 95 percent level.

TABLE 2. Labor Intensive

DFI (dependent variable)	Japan (food)			Korea	
	DFI 83	DFI 90	Pool[b]	DFI 92	Pool[b]
Constant	-3732*	-24058	-13595	-1707	-1768
GDP	1.03	16.35	10.95*	0.46	-0.1
Pop	3.47	61.65	21.37	5.16***	6.63***
Distance	0.48	6.07	2.94	0.43	0.348
Asdum	1850*	3476***			
Timedum	1503***				
ASFAN	-236	-39056	-19978		
Exp (contem)[a]	94.2***	367***	275***	0.01*	0.02***
Adj. R^2	0.64	0.15	0.16	0.19	0.13
N	24	25	49	37	83

Exp (dependent variable)	Japan (food)			Korea	
	EXP 83	EXP 86–94	Pool[b]	EXP 92	Pool[b]
Constant	39.98**	86.3***	64.5***	69123***	486452**
GDP	-0.006	-0.005	-0.0016	2.35*	158***
Pop	-0.02	-0.047	-0.02	-718***	-592***
Distance	-0.0037	-0.009	-0.005	-9.6	-59.4**
Asdum	419436	392541***			
Timedum	105444				
ASFAN	-3.4	13.4	-0.66		
DFI (contem)[a]	0.0074***	0.00065***	0.00066***	43.3*	33.4***
Adj. R^2	0.62	0.09	0.11	0.19	0.2
N	24	25	49	37	83

Notes: [a]Lag structure of exports and DFI makes no difference on the results of the regressions.
[b]In pooled observations the time variable was insignificant.
*Significance at the 85 percent level; **significance at the 90 percent level; ***significance at the 95 percent level.

TABLE 3. *Chemicals*

DFI (dependent var)	U.S.			Japan		
	DFI 83	DFI 90	Pool[b]	DFI 83	DFI 90	Pool[b]
Constant	707	718	777***	-13580	-152935*	-97134**
GDP	-0.00*	-0.00	-0.00	-5.8	14.2	6.2
Pop	0.42	-0.35	-0.06	-11.7	102.5	30.5
Distance	-0.062**	-0.05	-0.06*	2.6	24.4*	14.1**
ASEAN	94	-130	17	32895*	-70575	-18196
Exp (contem)[b]	0.00***	0.001***	0.001***	48.9*	206***	187.4***
Adj. R^2	0.55	0.33	0.43	0.0006	0.25	0.29
N	30	30	60	24	25	49

Exp (dependent var)	U.S.			Japan		
	EXP 83	EXP 90	Pool[b]	EXP 83	EXP 90	Pool[b]
Constant	666	702*	306	263**	705***	493***
GDP	1.68***	1.2***	1.27***	0.026	0.003	0.017
Pop	-352	297	39	0.39	0.038	0.199
Distance	-5.91	-68	-34	-0.016	-0.065*	-0.042**
ASEAN	152	488	297	-91.8	105.3	9.25
DFI (contem)[a]	353***	413***	408***	0.002*	0.002***	0.002***
Adj. R^2	0.75	0.58	0.64	0.007	0.23	0.3
N	30	30	60	24	25	49

Notes: [a]Lag structure of exports and DFI makes no difference on the results of the regressions.
[b]In pooled observations the time variable was insignificant.
*Significance at the 85 percent level, **significance at the 90 percent level; ***significance at the 95 percent level.

TABLE 4. Electronics

DFI (dependent var)	U.S.			Japan		
	DFI 83	DFI 90	Pool[b]	DFI 83	DFI 90	Pool[b]
Constant	130	-177	79	-27698***	-264502**	-160077***
GDP	0	0.0001	0.0001	6.6*	61.5	39.3
Pop	0.18	-0.37	-0.2	6.9	59.6	16.7
Distance	-0.02*	0.03	0	2.1*	45***	22.6**
ASEAN	-214	-21122***	-227591	-120757		
Exp (contem)[a]	0.0003***	0.0001***	0.0002***	52.3***	137***	127***
Adj. R^2	0.75	0.66	0.66	0.94	0.68	0.66
N	27	27	54	24	25	49

Exp (dependent var)	U.S.			Japan		
	EXP 83	EXP 90	Pool[b]	EXP 83	EXP 90	Pool[b]
Constant	200...	244...	109...***	525***	1750***	1133***
GDP	0.94***	0.51	0.72**	-0.115	-0.27	-0.14
Pop	-580	1017	171	-0.079	0.098	0.31
Distance	4	-278***	-124***	-0.036	-0.21*	-0.1
ASEAN	105...	178...**	864...*	186**	1220	618
DFI(contem)[a]	1991***	3103***	2689***	0.018***	0.005***	0.005***
Adj. R^2	0.78	0.72	0.7	0.93	0.64	0.64
N	27	27	54	24	25	49

Notes: [a]Lag structure of exports and DFI makes no difference on the results of the regressions.
[b]In pooled observations the time variable was insignificant.
*Significance at the 85 percent level; **significance at the 90 percent level; ***significance at the 95 percent level.

TABLE 5. Machinery

DFI (dependent var)	U.S.			Japan		
	DFI 83	DFI 90	Pool[b]	DFI 83	DFI 90	Pool[b]
Constant	313	556	616**	-4499	-39741**	-26703***
GDP	0.002**	0.003***	0.001***	0.67	1.15	0.75
Pop	-0.46	-1.14	-0.4	0.49	48.4	18
Distance	-0.03	-0.05	-0.05*	1.12	41.4	2.3
ASEAN	[3]	[3]	[3]	7842	11857	10801
Exp (contem)[a]	0.0003***	0.0002*	0.0002***	4.79***	30.2***	28.9***
Adj. R^2	0.57	0.67	0.16	0.88	0.84	
N	23	23	46	24	25	49

Exp (dependent var)	U.S.			Japan		
	EXP 83	EXP 90	Pool[b]	EXP 83	EXP 90	Pool[b]
Constant	115...	212...***	174...***	503	1309**	911***
GDP	-1.25	-0.09	-0.47	0.05	0.02	0.041
Pop	-41.8	14.4	-32.6	0.78	-1.2	-0.26
Distance	-83.7	-159*	-151***	-0.02	-0.109	-0.06
ASEAN	[3]	[3]	[3]	-454	-424	-389
DFI (contem)[a]	739***	633*	891***	0.045***	0.03***	0.029***
Adj. R^2	0.31	0.36	0.35	0.04	0.87	0.84
N	23	23	46	24	25	49

Notes: [a]Lag structure of exports and DFI makes no difference on the results of the regressions.
[b]In pooled observations the time variable was insignificant.
*Significance at the 85 percent level; **significance at the 90 percent level; ***significance at the 95 percent level.

TABLE 6. Metals

DFI (dependent var)	U.S.			Japan		
	DFI 83	DFI 90	Pool[b]	DFI 83	DFI 90	Pool[b]
Constant	235**	277	298*	-32109	-36050	-34733**
GDP	2.17	-0.00001	0	-1.2	-0.8	1.2
Pop	0.07	-0.03	0.02	12.4	-31.9	-43.7
Distance	-0.01*	-0.02	-0.02**	9.6***	5.6	7.5***
ASEAN	-55.2	-103	-85	-27579	-32243	-30830
Exp (contemp)[a]	0.001***	0.001***	0.0004***	11.58	74***	51.9***
Adj. R^2	0.6	0.59	0.62	0.1	0.64	0.41
N	27	26	53	24	25	49

Exp (dependent var)	U.S.			Japan		
	EXP 83	EXP 90	Pool[b]	EXP 83	EXP 90	Pool[b]
Constant	-52574	190...	-215...	459	530**	576***
GDP	-0.001	0.28	0.28**	0.07	0.07	0.085
Pop	-7.3	75.4	-35	2.44***	0.65	1.39***
Distance	-6.8	-27	-9	-0.04	-0.058	-0.07**
ASEAN	86927	120...	929...	107	307	250
DFI (contem)	779.4***	1227***	1157***	0.003	0.01***	0.008***
Adj. R^2	0.72	0.61	0.63	0.17	0.66	0.46
N	27	26	53	24	25	49

Notes: [a]Lag structure of exports and DFI makes little difference on the results of the regressions.
[b]In pooled observations the time variable was insignificant.
*Significance at the 85 percent level; **significance at the 90 percent level; ***significance at the 95 percent level.

TABLE 7. Transport Equipment[a]

DFI (dependent var)	U.S.			Japan		
	DFI 83	DFI 90	Pool[b]	DFI 83	DFI 90	Pool[b]
Constant	437	685	594**	9207	-39136	-16086
GDP	0.001***	0.0003*	0.0005***	-4.9	32.7**	18.2**
Pop	-0.27	0.24	0.05	-6.2	16	4.5
Distance	-0.04	-0.07*	-0.05**	-0.6	14.7***	6.8**
ASEAN	9421	-85984***	-38798			
Exp (contem)[c]	0.0002***	0.0003***	0.0003***	12.4***	14.8***	15.04***
Adj. R^2	0.6	0.84	0.79	0.6	0.61	0.55
N	20	21	41	24	25	49

Exp (dependent var)	U.S.			Japan		
	EXP 83	EXP 90	Pool[b]	EXP 83	EXP 90	Pool[b]
Constant	837	-318	-102	-502	1580	612
GDP	-1.49	-0.5	-0.6	0.4	-0.92	-0.32
Pop	448	-732	-290	1.08	0.85	1.23
Distance	-73.6	57	-1.7	0.09	-0.42	-0.12
ASEAN	-831	2580	722			
DFI(contem)[c]	1994***	2412***	2279***	0.055***	0.04***	0.034***
Adj. R^2	0.48	0.81	0.75	0.61	0.47	0.49
N	20	21	41	24	25	49

Notes: [a]This is a composite industry that includes commercial aircraft with exports but not with DFI.

[b]In pooled observations the time variable was insignificant.

[c]Lag structure of exports and DFI makes no difference on the results of the regressions.

*Significance at the 85 percent level; **significance at the 90 percent level; ***significance at the 95 percent level.

precluded such a test), and found that, for many sectors, trade "granger causes" investment while investment "granger causes" trade.[19]

Fourth, other estimated coefficients usually tell an ambiguous story. In most equations, either GDP or POP is statistically significant, but rarely are they both so. Distance is statistically significant in most regressions, but not as frequently as in other gravity-based models that exclude the trade-investment relationship. This might suggest that (in these latter models) distance may be picking up part of what should be ascribed to trade (in the case of a DFI equation) or DFI (in the case of a trade equation). Finally, the ASEAN binary variable is statistically significant fairly frequently only in the case of Japan, except for specific cases with the other two countries, e.g. for Korea (all manufactures, labor-intensive industries) and the United States (electronics).

Fifth, in the "pooled" regressions, a time binary variable was included in an attempt to capture any differences that might exist between years in each data set. It was statistically insignificant in virtually all cases, implying that the estimates are not time-sensitive.

At the sectoral levels, Table 1 allows for a three-country comparison of all manufactures. Adjusted R^2s are generally highest in the case of the United States (at between 71 and 77 percent), followed by Japan and Korea in that order. In almost all cases, exports (DFI) are highly significant in the DFI (export) equations, and in *the case of the United States, these are often the only statistically significant coefficients.* For example, in the case of DFI 1983 for the United States, we estimate that a U.S.$ 1000 increase in exports is associated with a (0.001 U.S.$1 million) U.S.$1000 increase in U.S. DFI, and we estimate the same approximate order of magnitude for a 5-year lag. The ASEAN binary variable is statistically significant in some Korean regressions, but interestingly, the estimated coefficients are negative. This implies that Korean investment in the rest of the world (especially the United States) is higher than in ASEAN, holding all other variables constant. The only exception is the ASEAN binary variable where in the case of labor-intensive products it is positive and statistically significant (Table 2). Hence, Korea invests in ASEAN less than one would expect overall, as the large investment projects that Korea has in advanced areas appear to be sufficient to swamp other "biases". On the other hand, with respect to labor-intensive products, Korea has an obvious bias in favor of ASEAN.

In the more disaggregated sectors, the overall importance of a positive export–DFI link appears at all levels. While each sector has its own special idiosyncrasies, the model does a fairly good job of explaining the variance in each dependent variable, with either GDP or Population being statistically significant along with distance (in some cases). The regional dummy variable, where present, was generally statistically insignificant with the exception of U.S. investment in electronics. There the United States has a clear "bias" in favor of investment in ASEAN for the 1990 and the pooled data series. In effect, this is consistent with the story that foreign investors are taking advantage of an international division of labor in ASEAN according to their host-country comparative advantages: Korea in labor-intensive sectors, the United States in more capital- and skill-intensive sectors.[20]

We attempted a similar analysis using annual DFI *flows* (instead of stocks) and annual *changes* in exports. The results yielded the same general conclusions. In the case of all manufactures, in pooled cross-section and time series regressions (335 observations), the two variables were *positively* related and significant at the 95 percent level: a $1 increase in exports raises DFI by $0.16; and a $1 increase in DFI leads to a $0.59 rise in exports.

Conclusions

Between 1973–1995 (estimated) annual flows of DFI expanded by over 12-fold (from $25 billion to $315 billion) and the annual flows of exports grew by over 8-fold (from $575 billion to $4,900 billion).[21] We find strong empirical support to the presumption of a positive trade-investment nexus. Given the current trends in the internationalization of the world's economies, changes in technology, and new approaches to business organization in which borders have become increasingly less significant, it is likely that this relationship will be reinforced over time as the globalization of production proceeds apace. If these results hold, then DFI should be included in the estimation of trade equations, which would otherwise be mis-specified.

Notes

* The authors would like to thank Professors Shujiro Urata and Keun Lee for their generous help in providing data. Mr. Jason Eis and Kaori Kiyohara provided excellent research assistance.

1. UNCTC (1995).
2. World Bank (1994).
3. MITI (1994).
4. The computer industry offers and excellent case study of this process in East Asian. In the 1980s, U.S. and Japanese computer firms looked at the Asian NIEs as a low-cost production base. Growing technological levels in East Asia have increased their respective production capabilities so that certain computer components were no longer imported. For example, Singapore over the past 20 years has moved from making lower-end computer products to higher-end hard-drive disks. Subsequently, lower technology disk-drive production has switched to Malaysia and Thailand. This process has resulted in rapid growth and regional integration, which earlier industrial development strategies never could attain.

Intraregional trade in computers is growing much faster than external trade and it now accounts for 25 percent of the NIEs' total trade in computers. East Asian exports consist primarily of PCs, disk drives, subassemblies, parts, and peripherals (World Bank 1994, pp. 30–32).

5. These figures, as well as other included in this paragraph, were taken from Kreinin *et al.* (1997).

6. Kreinin *et al.* (1997).

7. This study expands and complements an on-going research on trade and investment links at Brandeis University (see Petri and Plummer, 1996).

8. Exceptions include Lee and Roland-Horst (1997) and sources surveyed in WTO (1996).

9. It is also possible to argue that an open investment regime would require an open trade regime in order to ensure the former's success in attracting DFI.

10. This subsection is borrowed from Petri and Plummer (1996).

11. Ramstetter (1993).

12. In fact, it is impossible to focus only on changes in host-country trade and investment policies in estimating effects on the locational advantages of a country. This is because changes in the policy environment of *other* countries are also critical in the "DFI Beauty Contest" (Petri, 1997).

13. See, for example, WTO (1996) and its sources.

14. DFI data for the United States come from the Department of Commerce, *Survey of Current Business*, various issues; for Korea, from the Bank of Korea, *Overseas Direct Investment Statistics Yearbook*, 1992 and 1995; and for Japan, from the database organized by S. Urata. Trade data were gleaned from the United Nations, *Commodity Trade Statistics*, various issues; and other data for independent variables were taken from various IMF and World Bank sources.

15. See, for example, empirical work in Lee *et al.* (1997).

16. It would have been useful to include variables for "openness" of the host country and physical infrastructure. This was attempted using a trade openness variable (trade as a percentage of GNP) for the former and telephone lines per capita (as such and adjusted for urban population) for the latter. However, none of these proxies were statistically significant in any of the regressions and, as they are considered fairly poor proxies anyway, they were dropped from the reported regressions.

17. See, for example Ramstetter (1996), and the sources therein, for an extensive critique of DFI data.

18. The Japan data allow for estimation at all levels. However, for labor-intensive goods, the U.S. data set is too small (mainly because of disclosure problems and a fairly weak presence of U.S. DFI in this category, rendering too few observations). The Korean data base had a very limited set of projects and, hence, regression results suffered fatally from too few degrees of freedom.

19. For a review of the problems of simultaneity bias in gravity-type regressions, see contributions in Lee and Roland-Holst (1997).

20. However, this is not to say that the United States is necessarily producing products at a much higher level of sophistication in ASEAN, as it is not clear where "high" in the production chain U.S. DFI in ASEAN falls. A much more disaggregated data set than exists would be required to say anything definitive about this.

21. WTO (1996).

References

AITKEN, B., HANSON, G. H. and HARRISON, A. E. (1994) *Agglomeration Economies, Foreign Investment, and Export Behavior*, International Monetary Fund, mimeo, July.

ANDERSON, K. (1997) Social Policy Dimensions of Economic Integration: Environmental and Labor Standards. In ITO, T. and KRUEGER, A. O. (eds) *Regionalism versus Multilateral Trade Agreement*, University of Chicago Press, Chicago, pp. 57–84.

DUNNING, J. H. (1981) *International Production and the Multinational Enterprise.* Allen and Unwin, London.

KOJIMA, K. (1978) Japanese Direct Foreign Investment: A Model of Multinational Business Operations, Tuttle, Tokyo.

KREININ, M., LOWINGER, T. and LAI, A. (1997) *Determinants of Inter-Asian Direct Investment Flows*, mimeo.

LEE, H. and ROLAND-HOLST, D. (eds) (1997) *Economic Development and Cooperation in the Pacific Basin: Trade, Investment, and Environmental Issues*, Cambridge University Press, New York.

LEE, H., ROLAND-HOLST, D. and VAN DER MENSBRUGGHE, D. (1997) *APEC Trade Liberalization and Structural Adjustments: Policy Assessments*, APEC Discussion Paper Series No. 11, APEC Study Center, Nagoya University, March.

MITI, *White Paper on International Trade*, Tokyo, Japan, 1994.

MUNDELL, R. (1957) International Trade and Factor Mobility, *American Economic Review*, Vol. 47(3), pp. 321–336.

PETRI, P. A. (1992) Platforms in the Pacific: Trade Effects of Direct Investment in Thailand, *Journal of Asian Economics*, Vol. 3, No. 2, pp. 173–196.

PETRI, P. A. (1997) Foreign Direct Investment in A CGE Framework, DFI Beauty Contest, Spring 1997, mimeo.

PETRI, P. A. and PLUMMER, M. G. (1996) The Determinants of Direct Foreign Investment, *Brandeis University Working Paper*.

PLUMMER, M. G. (1997) *DFI and Endogenous Policy Formation in Asia*, Presented at the Brandeis-Keio Workshop. Making APEC Work: Economic Challenges and Policy Alternatives, March 13–14, Tokyo.

RAMSTETTER, E. D. (1993) *Foreign Direct Investment and Exports of Manufacturers from Developing Countries: Part I: Economic Policies*, mimeo prepared for the UNCTAD Secretariat.

RAMSTETTER, E. D. (1996) Trends in production in Foreign Multinational Firms in Asian Economies: A Note on an Economic Myth Related to Poor Measurement, *Kansai University Review of Economics and Business*, Vol. 24, Nos 1–2, March.

UNITED NATIONS, DIVISION ON TRANSNATIONAL CORPORATIONS AND INVESTMENT (1995) *World Investment Report 1995: Transnational Corporations and Competitiveness*, United Nations, Geneva.

VERNON, R. (1966) International Investment and International Trade in the Product Cycle, *Quarterly Journal of Economics*, Vol. 80.

WORLD BANK (1994) *Building on the Uruguay Round: East Asian Leadership in Liberalization*, Office of the Vice President for East Asia and the Pacific Region, April, p. 26.

WORLD TRADE ORGANIZATION (WTO) (1996) Trade and Direct Foreign Investment, *Annua Report-Investment*, Press/57, 9 October, pp. 1–55.

[9]

Determinants of Inter-Asian Direct Investment Flows

MORDECHAI E. KREININ, THOMAS C. LOWINGER AND ANIL K. LAL

Introduction

During the 1980s and the early 1990s economic ties between East Asian countries have intensified, and their closer regional trade links have made an important contribution to the region's economic growth. Significantly, greater regional integration in East Asia has coincided with greater overall openness of their economies and an ongoing liberalization of their trade and investment regimes. Furthermore, the structures of East Asian countries' production have become increasingly based on their comparative advantage and their ability to absorb sophisticated foreign technology was enhanced by rapidly growing FDI flows. There appears to be a virtuous cycle at work in East Asia, with FDI contributing to export growth, which, in turn, is creating pressures for further trade and investment liberalization, and leading to an even greater volume of FDI flows. This chapter examines empirically the factors responsible for direct investment flows within East Asia.

East Asian Trade and Economic Interdependence

The rate of growth of East Asian trade in the 1980s and the early 1990s has been nothing short of spectacular. Between 1980 and 1993 East Asian exports quadrupled (from $124 billion to $505 billion) and the region's share of world exports more than doubled from 6.3 to 13.6 percent. Correspondingly, intra-area trade also increased dramatically.

194

To date, East Asian countries have not formed a formal trading bloc and there is no sign that Japan and the NIEs are interested in promoting or joining an East Asian FTA.[1] But 'private-sector integration' has proceeded apace through trade and investment. It has been argued that East Asia may constitute a 'natural' trading bloc, wherein a relatively high degree of integration can occur because of the existence of so called 'natural' of geographic proximities among East Asian countries.[2] Arguably, economic integration in East Asia could have proceeded spontaneously, without the benefits of a formal agreement or common institutions. Indeed, recent studies have shown that East Asia's intra-regional trade, as a share of total trade, has increased from about 33 percent in 1980 to 41 percent in 1990. Kreinin and Plummer (1994) define a 'natural' trading bloc as one that would preserve country's comparative advantage ranking should it choose to enter a regional trading bloc. Based on that definition, they conclude that a free trading area that includes Japan, Korea, and the East Asian developing countries would be economically efficient.[3]

Moreover, the greater intensity of East Asian direct investment flows (discussed in the following section), together with the persistence of their trade and overall market reforms, would be expected to act as a catalyst for greater economic integration in the region.

Recently, Frankel and Wei (1995) estimated a gravity model of trade and detected the existence of a powerful East Asian trade bias.[4] However, until the 1970s the relative importance of East Asian intra-regional trade had in fact been declining as the region forged ever closer ties with the U.S. and with other industrialized counties outside the region. But in the 1980s the rapid growth of the East Asian regional market began to outweigh the expansion of extra-regional markets, and intra-regional trade in East Asia was on the rise again. Significantly, greater regional integration in East Asia has coincided with a greater overall openness of their economies toward the rest of the world.

FDI Flows in East Asia

In recent years Asian countries have experienced a sharp upsurge in international capital flows. During 1990–93, the developing countries of Asia were the recipient of $150 billion in net capital inflows, more than double the amount they had received in the previous four years. The composition of capital flows into Asia has changed drastically in recent years. FDI, together with bond and equity financing, has largely replaced the formerly dominant form of capital flows into developing countries—commercial bank loans. In Asia a significant part of the increase in overall foreign capital inflow can be attributed to the rapid growth of FDI. FDI flows into several East Asian countries have risen in the 1986–89 period, and then have surged dramatically in the early 1990s.

During 1986–92, the sources of East Asian FDI flows have been primarily intra-regional: about one-half of all FDI flows in the region originated from other East Asian countries (predominantly in Hong Kong, Singapore, Korea, and Taiwan); less than a fifth originated from Japan and only one-tenth came from the U.S. and Western Europe (World Bank, 1994, p. 26). The sectoral composition of FDI has also been changing. In earlier years, direct investments from advanced industrial countries were channeled primarily into natural resource based industries and related sectors, while in more recent years the NIEs have been investing primarily in manufacturing, especially in electrical machinery, electronics, nonferrous metals and chemicals.

Starting in the mid-1980s, export oriented Japanese multinational enterprises (MNEs) began to shift their production base (and in some cases even their product development location) offshore, in search of lower production costs. The steep appreciation of the yen since the mid-1980s, together with visible protectionist sentiment in North America and Western Europe (directed primarily against Japanese exports), provided a powerful incentive for Japanese MNEs to globalize their operations. Japanese FDI in Asia has been increasingly channeled into export oriented activities. The relatively low cost of Asian labor, together with the relatively advanced level of production in the region, have induced Japanese MNEs to relocate certain parts of their operations—production, R&D, and sales—to East Asia.

Japanese and other foreign investors in Asia have become increasingly export oriented. In 1992, the ratio of exports to total sales of Japanese affiliates in manufacturing was 45 percent in Asia compared to only 23 percent in Latin America. Currently, parts and equipment imports of Japanese affiliates in Asia form Japan constitute a significant share of their total imports (about 38 percent of the total in 1992), and although local procurement already constitutes a large share (50 percent) of their total purchases, it is expected to rise even more in the future (MITI, 1994). The FDI-trade link in Asia has often been described in terms of the 'flying geese' metaphor, wherein Japan is the lead ('goose') country because of its advanced technology. The lead country's firms combine their technological advantage with the relatively lower factor (labor) costs in the host countries, which in turn make the follower countries' (initially the East Asian NIEs) production more competitive in world markets, which then allows exports from their Asian base to grow even more rapidly. Japan, the lead country in this scheme, is usually followed by the NIEs, which in turn are followed by Malaysia, Thailand, and later on China.[5]

The Pattern and Structure of FDI Flows in East Asia

In the span of a few decades, several East Asian countries (e.g. Japan, South Korea, Hong Kong, Singapore, and Taiwan) have transformed themselves from largely backward and poor countries, into relatively prosperous and technologically sophisticated economies. Initially, this group of countries, (except Japan) has been the recipient of most foreign direct investment flows into Asia. But, beginning in the late 1970s there has been a huge surge in foreign direct investment flows in other East Asian countries—China, Malaysia, Indonesia, Philippines, Thailand, and more recently Vietnam. The experience of East Asian countries suggests the existence of a strong connection between FDI and improved access to foreign markets. Initially, foreign-owned firms established subsidiaries in East Asia in order to exploit the local markets. However, more recent experience suggests that multinationals are adopting global strategies intended to link their subsidiaries in Asia through global assembly and marketing networks into 'borderless factories' (export-oriented FDI).

To analyze the reasons behind the increase in FDI flows in East Asia, we have classified the East Asian countries as follows: (1) Japan; (2) the Newly Industrialized Economies (NIEs)—Hong Kong, Korea, Singapore, Korea, and Taiwan; and (3) 'others'—China, Indonesia, Malaysia, Philippines, Thailand, and Vietnam. Japan has been the recipient of only small amounts of foreign capital inflows form other countries in East Asia, while it has been a major source of the foreign capital flowing into other countries in the region. For example, Japan has accounted for 52 percent of the FDI stock of Korea, 31 percent of Singapore's, 37 percent of Thailand's, and 27 percent of Taiwan's (Table 9.1). While the NIEs have become a significant source of foreign capital flows into 'other' East Asian countries, they have not been major recipients of foreign capital flows from 'other' East Asian countries. The NIEs were the source of 58 percent of the FDI stock of China (in 1987), 35 percent of Malaysia's (1987), and 20 percent of Thailand's (1988). Thus the direction of foreign investment flows in East Asia followed a stepwise pattern, meaning that there has been *unidirectional* investment flow from relatively advanced countries into the less developed countries of the region.

What factors are then responsible for the flow of foreign direct investment into the NIEs and 'other' East Asian economies? Using multiple regression analysis, we have to estimated the effects of relative market size, relative labor costs, exchange rates and the degree of openness, on foreign direct investment flows in East Asia.

In addition, we sought to test Findlay's (1978) theory that technological know-how among countries spreads much like a

TABLE 9.1 *Stock of FDI in East Asian Countries (percent of total)*

Host country (year)	EU	USA	Japan	Source NIEs	Others	Total
Japan (1990)	18.3	46.5	–	2.8	32.4	100.0
Hong Kong* (1989)	14.7	32.4	29.9	2.2	21.9	100.0
Korea (1988)	9.4	27.7	52.0	3.8	7.0	100.0
Singapore* (1989)	28.7	33.2	30.7	NA	NA	100.0
Taiwan (1988)	13.4	32.1	26.8	14.8	12.9	100.0
China (1987)	8.3	15.8	7.2	58.2	10.6	100.0
Indonesia (1988)	12.1	5.8	18.4	10.8	52.8	100.0
Malaysia (1987)	24.0	6.1	20.1	35.1	14.7	100.0
Philippines (1989)	11.2	55.7	14.5	9.5	9.2	100.0
Thailand (1988)	12.4	24.2	36.7	20.1	6.6	100.0
Vietnam (1989)	57.3	0.2	14.4	7.1	21.0	100.0

* refers to manufacturing only.
Source: United Nations (1992).

contagious disease, i.e. it disperses more rapidly and more extensively the greater the contact among people and businesses. As noted by Findlay (1978, p. 5), 'Contact with firms with a higher level of efficiency enables the relatively backward ones to improve not only by copying or imitating but also by inducing them to 'try harder'. In Findlay's model, international trade can be an important conduit through which people in one country come in contact with people in another, and through which they can learn about a foreign country's products and innovations. His model postulates that the rate of international technology transfer is higher, the greater is the technology gap between the advanced country (e.g. Japan) and a relatively backward country (such as a NIE). However a *minimum* level of technology in the host country is needed for the relatively backward country to be able to absorb the technology received from the more advanced country. Furthermore, the rate at which new technology can be transferred to a recipient country through FDI, may depend on a number of other factors (e.g. the educational level of the domestic labor force) that must be specified in the empirical estimation.

This study attempts to quantify the approximate causes of Japan's direct investment in eight East Asian countries, and to test whether the motivations behind Japanese direct investment were different for the NIE host countries that for the other East Asian host countries. Second, it attempts to quantify factors responsible for FDI flows from Japan and the NIEs into 'other' East Asian countries and to determine whether there is a difference between the Japanese and the NIEs' behavior as FDI source countries. Finally, we inquire whether the relative differences between the source and host countries, in terms of certain postulated economic characteristics, can explain the flow of investment into the countries. Accordingly, the following specification was estimated:

$$FDI(t)=f(PC(t),OPEN(t),ER(t),RWR(t),PEMP(t),POP(t),IGDP(t)) \, 1(1)$$

Where:

FDI(t) is the FDI flow from a source country into a host country, at time 't'.

PC(t) is the per capita GDP of the host country divided by that of the source country, at time 't'. (relative per-capita GDP)

GDP (t) is the GDP of the host country divided by that of the source country, at time 't'.

OPEN(t) is the overall degree of openness of the host country's economy (the proportion of total trade to GDP) relative to that of the source country, at time 't'.

ER(t) is the host country's exchange rate in domestic currency units, relative to that of the source country's currency at time 't'.

RWR(t) is the monthly industrial wage rate in the host country relative to that of the source country, at time 't'.

PEMP(t) is the proportion of host country population employed in its industrial sector, at time 't'.

POP(t) is the population of the host country relative to the population of the source country, at time 't'.

IGDP(t) is the proportion of total investment in GDP of the host country, relative to that of the source country, at time 't'.

Consistent data on FDI flows or stocks are difficult to obtain. In this study we have used United Nations (1992) data to examine FDI flows in East Asia. Since continuous time series data were not available for Thailand and Vietnam, those two countries were dropped from the analysis. The foreign investment data used for estimation purposed were obtained from the respective government agencies of East Asian countries. The data on explanatory economic variables were taken form the Penn World tables of the National Bureau of Economic Research (NBER) and have been updated whenever necessary. The data cover the period form 1984 to 1992, and the variables were expressed in current U.S. dollars, or have been converted to U.S. dollars using the current exchange rates.

Ordinary least squares were used to estimate the relationship given in Equation (1), and since all variables were expressed in log linear form, the estimated coefficients refer to the relevant elasticities. The

Durbin-Watson statistic was used to test for first order serial correlation, and the White test statistic was used to test for heteroscadasticity. The Chow test allowed us to test for structural breaks in the sample and adjustments were made to overcome the small sample problem. Table 9.2 reports the results of the first set of regressions, that tested the factors responsible for Japanese investment flows into eight East Asian countries—four NIEs and the four 'other' East Asian countries. The regression results suggest that the closer an East Asian country is to Japan in terms of its population, openness, and its relative wage rates in manufacturing, the larger is the investment flow from Japan in to that country. Also, the greater is the Japanese currency's appreciation relative to the currency of an East Asian country, the larger is the Japanese foreign investment flow into that country. This may have been the principal reason why Japanese investment flows into the NIEs have been significantly larger than that of other East Asian countries. We have also attempted to test whether the regressions explaining FDI in the NIEs differ from those destined into other East Asian countries. The Chow F test for structural break confirmed the null hypothesis that the regressions for these two sub-groups were not significantly different.

Finally, Table 9.3 reports the results of tests for FDI flows from Japan and the NIEs into 'other' East Asian countries. The Chow F test for structural break confirmed the null hypothesis that there is no

TABLE 9.2 *Estimated Equation for Japanese Foreign Investment in East Asian Countries (NIEs and Others)*

Variable	Coefficient
Intercept	−18.45
	{−4.86}
POP(t)	1.34
	{3.93}
OPEN(t)	2.94
	{8.24}
ER(t)	0.2
	{2.59}
RWR(t)	0.75
	{2.31}
R2	0.73
Adjusted R2	0.71
Durbin-Watson	1.86

Notes: The figures in parentheses indicate t-values.
The above coefficients are significant at 5% level of significance.

TABLE 9.3 *Estimated Equation for Japanese and NIEs Foreign Investment in Other East Asian Counties*

Variable	Coefficient
Intercept	−93.64
	{−4.02}
POP(t)	2.97
	{3.37}
GDP(t)	−3.39
	{−4.12}
OPEN(t)	2.64
	{3.30}
PEMP(t)	22.62
	{2.82}
RWR(t)	1.47
	{5.07}
R2	0.72
Adjusted R2	0.69
Durbin-Watson	1.78

Notes: The figures in parenthesis indicate t-values.
The above coefficients are significant at 5% level of significance.

significant difference in the regressions between the Japanese and the NIEs' FDI flows into 'other' East Asian countries. Once again, the smaller the difference between 'other' East Asian host countries and the East Asian source countries (Japan or the NIEs) in population, openness, and the wage rates, the greater are the FDI flows. On the other hand, the larger the difference in their GDPs, the greater is the foreign investment inflow into 'other' East Asian countries. Finally, the greater the ratio of employment in the industrial sector relative to the population of the host country, the larger is the inflow of foreign direct investment from the source countries. In general, these estimates accord with prior expectations and are generally consistent with received theory explaining direct investment flows.

Conclusions

This chapter has examined the pattern and structure of FDI flows in East Asia. FDI flows in the region have followed a consistent and unidirectional pattern, first flowing from Japan into the NIEs and subsequently flowing from Japan and the NIEs into 'other' less-developed East Asian economies. The regression results suggest that the closer an East Asian country is to Japan, in terms of its population, openness and the relative wages in its manufacturing sector, the greater will be the volume of investment flow from Japan into that East Asian country. Furthermore, an appreciation of the Yen relative to the host country's currency apparently resulted in greater flows of Japanese direct investment into East Asian countries. Similar results also hold for the NIE's direct investment flows into 'other' Asian countries.

References

BHAGWATI, J. (1992) Regionalism vs Multilateralsim, *The World Economy*, September, Vol. 15, No. 5, 535–556.

DAS, S. (1987) Externalities and Technological Transfer Through Multinational Corporations, *Journal of International Economics*, Vol. 22, 171–182.

FINDLAY, R. (1978) Relative Backwardness, Direct Foreign Investment, and the Transfer of Technology: A Simple Dynamic Model, *Quarterly Journal of Economics*, February, Vol. 62, No. 1, 1–16.

International Monetary Fund (1994) *International Trade Policies: The Uruguay Round and Beyond*, Vol II, Washington, DC.

FRANKEL, J. and WEI, S. (1995) The New Regionalism and Asia: Impact and Options. Paper presented at the Conference on the Emerging Global Trading Environment and Developing Asia, Asian Development Bank, Manila, May 29–31.

KREININ, M. E. and PLUMMER, M. G. (1994) Natural Economic Blocs: An Alternative Formulation, *The International Trade Journal*, Summer, Vol. 8, No. 2, 193–205.

KRUGMAN, P. (1993) Regionalism vs Multilateralism: Analytical Notes. In DE MELO, J. and PANAGARIYA, A. (eds) *New Dimensions in Regional Integration*, Cambridge University Press, New York.

MARTIN, W., PETRI, P. A. and YANAGISHIMA, K. (1994) Charting the Pacific: An Empirical Assessment of Integration Initiatives, *The International Trade Journal*, Winter, Vol. 8, No. 4, 447–482.

Ministry of International Trade and Finance (1994) *White Paper on International Trade.* Tokyo, Japan.

SUMMERS, L. (1991) Regionalism and the World Trading System, *Policy Implications of Trade and Currency Zones*, Federal Reserve Bank of Kansas City Symposium, Jackson Hole, Wyoming, August, 295–302.

United Nations Centre on Transnational Corporations (1992) *World Investment Directory 1992*, United Nations, New York.

World Bank (1994) Building on the Uruguay Round: East Asian Leadership in Liberalization. Discussion Paper, Office of the Vice President East Asia and the Pacific Region, Washington DC, April 22, 1–59.

Notes

1. Several countries in the region did form such a bloc. In particular, the Association of Southeast Asian Nations (ASEAN) was established in February 1977. It includes Indonesia, Malaysia, Philippines, Singapore, Thailand, and Brunei, with Vietnam

joining recently. In January, 1992, ASEAN member countries agreed to implement a common Effective Preferential Tariff Scheme (CEPT) with the aim of moving toward an ASEAN free trade area (AFTA). The stated objective of AFTA was to increase member countries' manufacturing competitiveness by attracting more FDI and thereby expanding their production base. See, IMF (1994, p. 125).

2. For arguments in support of the 'natural' trading bloc hypothesis see Krugman (1993) and Summers (1991). Among those that professed skepticism, see for example, Bhagwati (1992).

3. Despite the current relatively high share of intra-regional trade in East Asian total trade, East Asia has not regained the share of intra-regional in total trade that existed before World War II. Its trade share is significantly lower than those that prevail today in Western Europe. See, Martin, Petri and Yanagishima (1994, pp. 450–451).

4. The two most important factors that explain bilateral trade flows (exports plus imports) in the gravity model are: geographic distances between countries and their economic size (measured by their GDPs). By using an East-Asian regional 'dummy' variable in their panel regressions, Frankel and Wei (1995, p. 20) came to the startling conclusion that ' . . . two East Asian countries made 700% more than two random economies in the world.'

5. The computer industry offers an excellent case study of this process in East Asia. In the 1980s, U.S. and Japanese computer firms looked at the Asian NIEs as a low cost production base. Over time, growing technological sophistication in East Asia has increased the region's productive capability so that certain computer components are no longer imported. Singapore, for example, over the past 20 years has moved from making lower-end computer products to higher-end disk drives. Subsequently, lower technology disk drive production has switched to Malaysia and Thailand. This process has resulted in rapid growth and a greater regional integration that earlier industrial development strategies did not attain. Intra-regional trade in computers is growing much faster than external trade and it now accounts for 25 percent of the NIEs total trade in computers. East Asian exports consist primarily of PCs, disk drives, subassemblies, parts, and peripherals. See World Bank, 1994, pp. 30–32.

PART III

ECONOMIC INTEGRATION IN ASIA

[10]

"NATURAL" ECONOMIC BLOCS: AN ALTERNATIVE FORMULATION

Mordechai E. Kreinin and Michael G. Plummer

This article offers an alternative to what has become a conventional definition of "natural" regional grouping. Instead of focusing on the total value of intraregional trade or its share in the region's total trade, it focuses on the pattern of trade prior to integration. It formulates a method for assessing the degree to which joining a regional bloc would distort the ranking of a country's industries by comparative advantage. A "natural" grouping is one that would largely preserve the comparative advantage of the constituent countries. It occurs if each of the constituent countries' exports to the world as a whole has a commodity mix similar to its exports to the integrating region.

*   *   *   *   *

I. INTRODUCTION

With the advent of the Unified market in Europe and NAFTA[1] in North America, there has been increasing interest in regional eco-

Mordechai E. Kreinin is Professor Economics at Michigan State University.

Michael G. Plummer is Assistant Professor of Economics at Brandeis University.

We thank Deepthie Wickramasinghe and Yeben Liu for research assistance, and Vivian Kiyonaga and Cynthia Nakachi for clerical help.

[1]NAFTA is a free trade agreement between the United States, Canada, and Mexico.

ISSN: 0885-3908. THE INTERNATIONAL TRADE JOURNAL, Volume VIII, No. 2, Summer 1994 193

nomic integration. While the possibility of a tripolar would is being assessed, the Asian Pacific region shows little or no enthusiasm for an all-encompassing free trade area (FTA). Rather, small groupings, such as ASEAN[2] or ASEAN and the NIEs,[3] are more likely to emerge. Similarly, Latin America and Africa each contain several small economic blocs.

Following in the Viner–Meade tradition, the welfare effect of a preferential trading arrangement is assessed in terms of the static trade creation/trade diversion dichotomy. While in the case of large regions, such as the European Community (EC) and NAFTA, interest attaches to their impact on global welfare, and in the case of small groupings, such as ASEAN, interest centers on the effect on the integrating region itself, for the effect on world welfare is negligible.[4]

Because measuring trade creation and diversion, especially ex ante, is an arduous process, economists developed general economic criteria for assessing whether a regional grouping is likely to result in net trade creation. For example, the larger the economic area encompassed by a bloc, and the greater the share of intrabloc trade in their total trade prior to integration, the more likely it is to be trade creating—the extreme case being an FTA that encompasses the entire world. Similar conditions relate to the cost–price structure and the tariff levels and structures of individual members before and after the

---

[2] The Association of Southeast Asian Nations (ASEAN) is composed of six member states: Brunei Darussalam, Indonesia, Malaysia, the Philippines, Singapore, and Thailand. Brunei is excluded from the analysis due to paucity of data, and Singapore is included with the NIEs group. Hence, ASEAN is made up of the four resource-rich, large countries (ASEAN-4).

[3] The Asian Newly Industrialized Economies consist of South Korea, Taiwan, Hong Kong, and Singapore. However, Taiwan is excluded from the analysis (except in Table I) because it is not part of the UN database. Hence only three NIEs or ANIEs, are included.

[4] For analyses of the economic effects and implications of enhanced economic integration in ASEAN, including the recently established ASEAN Free Trade Area (AFTA), see Imada et al. (1992) and Naya and Plummer (1991).

formation of a regional grouping. Partly because of its simplicity, the most widely used rule of thumb is the share of intraregional trade in the bloc's total trade prior to integration. Following Krugman,[5] the case of a large share of intrabloc trade has been dubbed a "natural" FTA. While there is no theoretical guidance to determine how large is "large," a 50% minimum has been used as a rough rule of thumb. However, even the three members of NAFTA (the United States, Canada, and Mexico), where the share of intra bloc trade in total trade is only one third, has sometimes been referred to as a "natural" grouping. Jeffrey Frankel employs the same approach but takes the analysis a step further by adjusting intraregional trade for growth and also by using and estimating a gravity model.[6]

II. AN ALTERNATIVE FORMULATION

What Krugman, Frankel, and others have in common is reliance on some modified measure of trade volume or value. Indeed, an examination of the share of intrabloc in total bloc trade has become commonplace in assessing regional groupings. But suppose an FTA meets the criteria of 50% intratrade: it still leaves unmeasured the degree of distortion introduced by the FTA to the remaining 50% of trade. Conversely, suppose ASEAN and the Asian NIEs combined exchange among themselves only one quarter of their total trade, so that they fall considerably short of the 50% rule of thumb, yet the degree to which the remaining three quarters of their trade is distorted is very small. Could the fact that the distortion is minimal not offset the shortfall from 50%? What is needed is an alternative measure that would assess the degree of distortion caused by regional integration. Rather than focus on some measure of trade volume or value, the alternative approach proposed here focuses on the *pattern* of trade.

---

[5]Paul Krugman (1991a, 1991b).
[6]See Jeffrey A. Frankel (1992) and the literature cited therein.

In particular, this approach develops a method for assessing the degree to which the ranking of a country's industries by comparative advantage would be preserved if it joins a given trade bloc, and the degree to which that ranking would be distorted by such a move. It measures the extent to which the product mix of the country's export to the world at large corresponds to that of its exports to the bloc that it contemplates joining. To accomplish this we use a proxy for comparative advantage (known as revealed comparative advantage or RCA) to rank a country's 600 four-digit Standard International Trade Classification (SITC) industries relative to the world as a whole. We then recalculate the country's RCA with respect to the regional grouping of which it would be a member and again rank the RCAs from the highest on down. Finally a rank correlation coefficient is calculated between the two ranked commodity lists. While the approach can be applied to any country and group of countries, we use to to assess the distortionary effects of integration among East Asian countries. The methodology is explained below with reference to East Asia.

RCA—A Proxy for Comparative Advantage

In the absence of a comprehensive cost–price dataset for individual industries, we analyze a country's competitive structure by using RCA indices. The index assumes that ranking industries by their export performance represents their ranking by the country's comparative advantage.[7] It is defined as the share of commodity i in country j's total exports relative to the commodity share in total world

---

[7]This index was developed by Balassa (1965). A number of the assumptions underlying this approach have been questioned, but the measures are used frequently as a facile and informative index (see, for example, Kreinin, 1966; Bowen, 1983; and Yeats, 1985). This index is preferable to export–import ratios since data on relative export performance are not distorted by differences in the degree of tariff protection as long as all exporters are subject to the same tariff. As Years (1985) points out, however, voluntary exports restraints, MFN tariffs, and the Multi-Fiber Agreement all have discriminatory effects. But in the case of the ASEAN countries, these differences are negligible.

exports:

$$\text{RCA} = (X_{ij}/X_j)/(X_{iw}/X_w)$$

where

X_{ij} = exports of commodity i by country j

X_j = total exports of country j

X_{iw} = world exports of commodity i

X_w = total world exports

This formula was calculated for each four-digit SITC (over 600 industries) for each of the ASEAN-4 countries, the three Asian NIEs, and Japan.

An RCA of 1 means that the share of i in the country's total exports equals the share of i in total world exports. With an RCA ratio greater than unity commodity i is more important in country j exports than it is in total world trade, implying that the country has a comparative advantage in the product. The converse holds for a ratio smaller than unity. The higher the index for a given commodity, the higher it is assumed to be in the ranking of goods by comparative advantage. The 600 SITC industries were therefore ranked by their RCAs from the highest on down.

While the RCA index may be distorted by various trade policies (such as export subsidies), these are not significant in the case of developing Asia. Moreover, we also computed a dynamic variant of the index that would not be subject to the problem unless the policies change over time. In that measure, each of the four magnitudes in the above formula is the *change* between two periods, such as between 1981 and 1990. Under this variant a country is said to have a comparative advantage in commodity i if its share in the country's total exports *grew faster* than the growth in the share of the commodity in total world trade over the same period. The entire analysis was carried out with the dynamic as well as the static indices. But since the results are very similar, only the static version is discussed and reported here.

Another possible problem is that the 600 four-digit commodity classification may not be refined enough to capture all trade in differentiated products. While a more detailed product breakdown may be useful in this context, the problem is less important for developing than for developed countries.

Regional Blocs

We next carry each country's RCA calculation with respect to the bloc it might join (rather than the world as a whole). In the case of East Asia two alternative blocs are considered:

Bloc 1:   ASEAN-4 and the three Asian NIEs
Bloc 2[8]: ASEAN-4, the Asian NIEs, and Japan

RCAs were calculated for each country with respect to the two alternative blocs and the 600 industries ranked as before.

As a final step, a Spearman rank correlation coefficient is computed for each country between the RCA ranking relative to the entire world, on the one hand, and the RCA ranking relative to each of the two alternative blocs, defined above as bloc 1 and bloc 2, on the other. The Spearman is a nonparametric estimate showing how the rankings of two series are correlated with each other. The estimates range from -1 to $+1$: perfect rank correlation would be utility in absolute value, while complete lack of each correlation is zero. For our purposes, a high rank correlation means that the ranking of a country's industries by comparative advantage (relative to the world as a whole) would be

---

[8]A more comprehensive Asian Pacific region that includes the above eight countries plus Australia and New Zealand was also considered. But the results were similar to those of "Bloc 2" and so they are not reported here.

largely preserved if the country is included in an FTA with a country composition of bloc 1 or bloc 2. A low coefficient would suggest that the ranking of the country's industries would be distorted by regional integration.[9] These correlations were computed for the dynamic concept as well, but the results were very similar to those of the RCAs and hence are not reported here.

As in the case of the "share of intratrade" approach, there is no theoretical guidance to determine how large a coefficient should be considered high. But if one follows the same rule of thumb as in the traditional approach, the critical value would be around 0.5.

III. RESULTS FOR EAST ASIA

Table I displays the direction of trade of the East Asian countries and of two country groups (ASEAN-4 and the four Asian NIEs). Under the conventional criterion of the share of intratrade in total trade, neither a bloc consisting of ASEAN and the Asian NIEs (bloc 1) nor a broader group that includes Japan (bloc 2) would be economically efficient. The preintegration intratrade shares in these two cases are about 22% and 32% respectively (Table I).

Table II presents the results of the alternative approach developed here, also for a preintegration period. The first column shows the Spearman coefficients between total world and a narrowly defined FTA (bloc 1). Separate estimates are given for "all commodities" and for manufactures (SITC 5–8).[10] The year varies somewhat between countries depending on the availability of data. But for each country the same year was used to calculate the commodity ranking with

---

[9] This approach is consistent with the argument in Deardorff and Stern (1991).

[10] We also computed the rank correlation coefficients for each one-digit SITC. These tables are available from the second author on request.

Table I
Export Matrix, 1990 (Percentage of Total Exports)

From/to	World (US$m)	East Asia	ASEAN + ANIEs	ANIEs	ASEAN-4	Japan	United States	EC12
World	3,339,600	16.2	9.9	7.3	2.6	6.3	14.9	40.6
East Asia	636,306	32.5	24.4	17.0	7.4	8.1	28.7	16.5
ASEAN + ANIEs	348,628	36.7	22.0	14.8	7.2	14.7	25.4	15.4
Asian NIEs	262,568	32.1	20.6	12.4	8.2	11.5	27.4	15.3
Hong Kong	82,144	19.4	13.7	9.7	4.0	5.7	24.1	17.0
Korea	60,457	35.7	14.8	10.3	4.5	20.9	31.7	12.9
Singapore	52,753	42.0	33.2	12.3	20.9	8.8	21.3	14.4
Taiwan	67,214	37.0	24.6	17.8	6.8	12.4	32.4	16.0
ASEAN-4	86,060	50.6	26.2	22.0	4.2	24.4	19.3	15.9
Indonesia	25,675	63.3	20.8	18.5	2.3	42.5	13.1	11.8
Malaysia	29,409	54.2	38.9	32.9	6.0	15.3	17.0	14.9
Philippines	8,171	36.4	16.5	12.3	4.2	19.9	38.0	17.8
Thailand	22,805	36.7	19.3	15.3	4.0	17.4	22.7	20.9
Japan	287,678	27.4	27.4	19.7	7.7	—	31.7	17.8

Sources: International Monetary Fund, *Direction of Trade Statistics*, Yearbook 1991; Republic of China, Minstry of Finance, Department of Statistics, *Monthly Statistics of Exports and Imports*; *Taiwan Area, The Republic of China*, No. 257 (January 1991).

respect to the world as a whole and to bloc 1. All countries except Singapore have coefficients well in excess of 0.5, and most are above 0.7, with Indonesia and the Philippines have the highest values. The second column shows the rank correlation coefficients between the product ranking based on the world as a whole and one that refers to a regional group consisting of ASEAN, the NIEs, and Japan (bloc 2). The coefficients are higher than in the second column, and in three of the ASEAN countries they are above 0.9. None of the ASEAN member states has an estimate below 0.7. Singapore's coefficients increase notably in bloc 2 from bloc 1, and Japan's coefficients are also high. While not reported here, the same rank correlation coefficients were calculated for 1981 as well. In the case of ASEAN they were somewhat higher than those for the most recent year, while in the case of Hong Kong and Singapore they were lower. All estimates are significant at the 1% level of probability (t test).

A "natural" FTA is defined as one in which the Spearman correlation coefficients are high for all member countries. What the above results suggest is that even a narrowly defined FTA (bloc 1) would be economically efficient in a sense of causing minimal distortion to the ranking of industries by comparative advantage in each of the member countries. Indeed the estimates reported in the table (both columns)

Table II

Spearman Rank Correlation Coefficients for Japan, ASEAN, and the NIEs between (a) RCAs Relative to Total World and to Various Asian Groupings in 1988, 1989, 1990, and (b) RCAs in 1981 and the Most Recent Year for Total World

	Bloc 1	Bloc 2	World 81
Japan			
All commodities			
World 90	—	0.79	0.89
SITC 5–8			
World 90	—	0.68	0.85
ASEAN			
Malaysia			
All commodities			
World 88	0.71	0.87	0.70
SITC 5–8			
World 88	0.72	0.86	0.65
Indonesia			
All commodities			
World 89	0.81	0.90	0.51
SITC 5–8			
World 89	0.85	0.92	0.45
Thailand			
All commodities			
World 90	0.77	0.89	0.66
SITC 5–8			
World 90	0.77	0.90	0.63
Philippines			
All commodities			
World 88	0.82	0.92	0.71
SITC 5–8			
World 88	0.81	0.91	0.67

(*table continues on next page*)

Table II
Spearman Rank Correlation Coefficients for Japan, ASEAN,
and the NIEs between (a) RCAs Relative to Total World and to
Various Asian Groupings in 1988, 1989, 1990, and (b) RCAs in
1981 and the Most Recent Year for Total World (*Continued*)

	Bloc 1	Bloc 2	World 81
	Asian NIEs		
Korea			
All commodities			
World 90	0.61	0.76	0.61
SITC 5–8			
World 90	0.57	0.68	0.53
Hong Kong			
All commodities			
World 90	0.72	0.81	0.77
SITC 5–8			
World 90	0.76	0.84	0.80
Singapore			
All commodities			
World 89	0.44	0.71	0.65
SITC 5–8			
World 89	0.44	0.70	0.57

would likely be higher had Taiwan been included in both blocs. Its
certainly belongs in any of the regional grouping suggested here, but it
is not part of the UN dataset. Surely bloc 2, which includes both Japan
and developing East Asia, would be economically efficient. These
results depart from those obtained by the traditional approach.

IV. CHANGES IN THE COMPETITIVE STRUCTURE OF THE EAST ASIAN ECONOMIES

East Asia is considered the most rapidly growing region in the
world. In the process of growth and industrialization, the competitive
structure of these countries is changing as they move to produce
increasingly sophisticated products. And these developments can be
identified by alterations in the ranking of industries by RCAs over time.

While the detailed rankings (e.g., the top 20 or 30 ranked industries for each country and for each year) are not presented here,[11] column 3 of Table II offers summary statistics that captures the degree of change in each country. It rank-correlates the RCAs relative to total world in 1981 with the latest year for which data are available (1988, 1989, or 1990, depending on the country). The lower the coefficient, the greater the structural change that has taken place.

Least changed was Japan, with coefficients of 0.89 and 0.85 for all commodities and manufactures, respectively. This is consistent with expectations, as that country was already fully developed in 1981. Greatest change occurred in Indonesia, followed by Korea and Singapore. The remaining countries experienced moderate change. Because Malaysia and Thailand are sometimes referred to as second-tier NIEs , and since Thailand had data for 1990, we rank-correlated the RCAs in manufactures of Thailand in 1990 with those of Korea 1981. This is an attempt to determine whether Thailand attained by 1990 a competitive structure similar to the one reached by Korea 9 years earlier. But the Spearman coefficient was only 0.44. Evidently, Thailand has some way to progress before reaching the position of a full-fledged NIE.

V. CONCLUSION

Countries form and/or join customs unions or FTAs for a variety of economic or political reasons. On the economic side these reasons include a desire to realize economies of scale in production and distribution, to improve the investment climate, to enjoy possible dynamic benefits from integration, and to lock in sensible macroeconomic policies (as in the case of Mexico in NAFTA or Spain in the EC). Because it is not possible to assess in advance the impact of these benefits or the degree to which they would be realized, it is useful to

---

[11] Such tables are available from the second author on request.

determine, ahead of integration, whether an economic bloc would be welfare enhancing in a static sense. The term "natural economic bloc" was devised as a short-cut or a hard-and-fast rule to make such a determination. Traditionally it relies on the share of intrabloc trade in the bloc's total trade prior to integration, or some variant of that measure. As a rule of thumb, it is sometimes suggested that if the share exceeds one half, the region can be regarded as a natural bloc.

In contrast to a measure that focuses on the *volumes* or *value* of trade, the alternative approach proposed here focuses on the *pattern* of trade. In terms of economic efficiency it is beneficial for a country to join a regional bloc if such a step would not greatly distort its comparative advantage. This article develops a method for assessing the extent to which comparative advantage would be preserved if and when a country integrates with others. If such preservation occurs in all members of a proposed FTA, then the grouping can be labeled a natural bloc. On that definition a bloc consisting of ASEAN and the Asian NIEs, and certainly one consisting of the above countries plus Japan, is a natural economic grouping. This is at variance with an assessment based on the traditional criterion.

REFERENCES

Balassa, Bela. 1965. "Trade Liberalization and 'Revealed' Comparative Advantage," *Manchester School of Economic and Social Studies*, Vol. 23, pp. 99–123.

Bowen, Harry P. 1983. "On the Theoretical Interpretation of Indices of Trade Intensity and Revealed Comparative Advantage," *Weltwirtschaftliches Archiv*, Vol 119, pp. 464–72.

Deardorff, Alan, and Robert Stern. 1991. "Multilateral Negotiations and Preferential Trading Arrangements," Prepared for Conference on Analytical and Negotiating Issues in the Global Trading System, University of Michigan, October 31–November 1.

Frankel, Jeffrey A. 1992. "Is Japan Creating a Yen Block in East Asia and the Pacific," NBER Working Paper No. 4050, April.

Imada, Pearl, Seiji Naya, and Manuel Montes. 1992. *A free Trade Area: Implications for ASEAN*. Singapore: ISEAS.

International Monetary Fund, *Direction of Trade Statistics, Yearbook 1991*.

Kreinin, Mordechai E. 1966. "On the Restrictive Effect of the Tariff," *The Manchester School*, January.

Krugman, Paul. 1991a. "Is Bilateralism Bad?" in Helpman, E., and Razim, A., Eds., *International Trade and Policy*. Cambridge: MIT Press.

Krugman, Paul. 1991b. "The Move Towards Free Trade Zones," in *Symposium on the Policy Implications of Trade and Currency Zone*, sponsored by the Federal Reserve Bank of Kansas City, Jackson Hole, Wyoming, August.

Republic of China, Ministry of Finance, Department of Statistics, *Monthly Statistics of Exports and Imports, Taiwan Area, The Republic of China*, No. 257 (January 1991).

Naya, Seiji, and Michael G. Plummer. 1991. "ASEAN Economic Cooperation in the New International Economic Environment," *ASEAN Economic Bulletin*, Vol. 7, No. 3 (March), pp. 261–276.

United Nations, *Commodity Trade Statistics*, various issues 1981–1991.

Yeats, A. J. 1985. "On the Appropriate Interpretation of the Revealed Comparative Advantage Index: Implications of a Methodology Based on Industry Sector Analysis," *Weltwirtschaftliches Archiv*, Vol. 121, pp. 61–73.

INTERNATIONAL ECONOMIC JOURNAL

1

Volume 8, Number 2, Summer 1994

STRUCTURAL CHANGE AND REGIONAL INTEGRATION IN EAST ASIA

MORDECHAI E. KREININ

Michigan State University

MICHAEL G. PLUMMER*

Brandeis University

This paper develops a measure of structural change of a country's exports, and applies it to East Asian countries. The results suggest that: (1) sizeable changes in the structural patterns of developing East Asian trade have occurred over the past decade; (2) the manufacturing sector has been restructured at a faster pace than primary commodities; (3) in general, intra-regional trade has been changing more rapidly than global trade; and (4) ASEAN development consists largely of upgrading industrial structure as against expansion of traditional exports. [F15, O12]

1. INTRODUCTION

While the East Asian economies (ASEAN and the Asian NIEs)[1] are extremely diverse in terms of culture, history, socio-political orientation, and economic structure, they have achieved high levels of growth due to a stable macroeconomic environment and outward-oriented economic policy reforms. Since the mid-1980s, the ASEAN countries have been particularly bold in implementing wide-ranging changes in financial, trade, and investment policies, reaping substantial dividends from these programs in a very short time span.

A major result of the policy changes has been an increased "internationalization" of the developing economies of East Asia, with a greater dependence on international transactions. The share of exports in GDP in the NIEs has grown from a range of 14-93 percent (depending on the country) in 1970 to a range of 32-134 percent in 1990; for ASEAN, the respective shares have grown from 13-46 percent to 26-74 percent.[2] Moreover, intra-regional trade and investment as a percentage of total trade and investment have also grown. In addition, the composition of these exports has been changing rapidly, with the NIEs exporting increasingly-sophisticated manufactures

---

*The authors are indebted to the East-West Center for financial and technical support and for providing a stimulating environment in which this research was pursued. We also wish to thank anonymous referees and the editor for helpful comments.

[1] The Asian NIEs include Taiwan, Singapore, Hong Kong, and South Korea; ASEAN has as member-states Indonesia, Malaysia, the Philippines, Thailand, Singapore and Brunei Darussalam. Because of lack of data, Taiwan and Brunei are excluded from both groups in most of the statistical analysis.

[2] James, et al. (1993).

and the ASEAN-4 countries exporting more basic manufactures as opposed to primary products.

Table 1 shows the direction of exports of the ASEAN-4 and the Asian NIEs for manufactures in 1981 and 1990. In 1981 ASEAN primary commodity exports were double that of manufacturing; by 1990, manufacturing exports had grown to exceed primary products by 60 percent. This attests to the rapid industrialization of the four countries. While intra-ASEAN trade is a minor component of ASEAN trade, combined with the NIEs they constitute a market for nearly one-fourth of ASEAN manufacturing exports, and East Asia (ASEAN-4, NIEs-3, and Japan) accounts for over 40 percent of the total. East Asia is a destination for one-third of manufactured exports of the NIEs and ASEAN combined and for nearly one half of primary commodities.[3]

Table 1. Directions of East Asian Manufacturing Exports, 1981 and 1990

SITC 5-8 US$ millions

			Percent of exports destined to:				
	Year	World	ASEAN-4 (%)	NIEs (%)	East Asia (%)	United States (%)	EC-12 (%)
ASEAN-4	1981	8,021	3.1	21.7	35.3	25.1	23.8
	1990	30,518	3.7	21.1	40.5	26.0	19.1
Malaysia	1981	3,240	2.7	21.9	36.0	27.5	23.8
	1990	9,639	3.8	29.4	40.3	32.1	17.0
Thailand	1981	2,214	4.1	18.2	31.0	22.8	26.4
	1990	8,761	3.1	16.3	42.1	26.5	21.2
Philippines	1981	1,450	2.4	12.5	25.3	37.7	19.3
	1990	2,604	4.8	14.2	31.7	34.9	18.2
Indonesia	1981	1,115	3.3	39.9	54.6	6.4	24.9
	1990	9,514	3.9	19.0	41.5	16.8	19.4
Asian NIEs	1981	49,721	8.8	6.0	23.5	27.3	15.9
	1990	175,525	7.7	6.8	23.8	28.0	16.7
Singapore	1981	10,410	22.3	5.8	38.5	21.5	12.9
	1990	38,311	19.6	7.1	32.4	27.7	17.7
Korea	1981	19,242	3.2	7.0	23.4	28.4	13.7
	1990	61,014	5.1	8.5	30.5	31.4	14.2
Hong Kong	1981	20,069	7.2	5.0	15.9	29.1	19.7
	1990	76,200	3.9	5.1	14.2	25.5	18.2
East Asia[a]	1981	204,560	7.3	9.3	19.1	26.3	14.3
	1990	483,440	7.5	11.8	23.6	30.2	18.1

Source: United Nations, *Commodity Trade Statistics*, various years.

[a]East Asia includes ASEAN-4, NIEs-3, and Japan

[3]Direction of Trade in primary products is available from the second author upon request.

This paper analyses structural and compositional change in the trade of developing East Asia. Section 2 develops a measure of structural change of a country's exports, and then compares the structural change of each country's global trade with the structural change of its trade with the region. Section 3 examines the changes in comparative advantage of individual industries in the region. Some final remarks are given in a concluding section.

2. STRUCTURAL CHANGE IN THE PATTERNS OF EAST ASIAN TRADE

As a country moves up the economic development ladder, the composition of its exports is altered to reflect changes in the ranking of its industries by comparative advantage. A rapidly-changing ranking of industries implies an inherent dynamism in a country's economy. Moreover, this change in the ranking of industries can be compared with the degree of change that has occurred in the country's trade with the Asian region, to determine whether intra-regional trade is evolving faster than trade with the world as a whole.

Below, we evaluate the temporal changes in the ranking of industries by comparative advantage in East Asia over the 1981-1990 period, both for global and regional trade. Using indices of revealed comparative advantage (RCA) as proxies, we first correlate the 1980 and 1990 rankings of disaggregated (4-digit SITC) industries of East Asian trade with the world, in order to assess the degree to which comparative advantage has changed over time. Next, the same procedure is applied to intra-bloc trade, with several definitions of possible East Asian groupings. Finally, we compare the degree to which intra-bloc comparative advantage has changed relative to global comparative advantage.

RCA as a Proxy for Comparative Advantage

In the absence of a comprehensive cost-price data set for individual industries, we analyze a country's competitive structure by using RCA indices. The index assumes that ranking industries by their export performance represents their ranking by the country's comparative advantage.[4] It is defined as the share of commodity i in country j's total exports relative to the commodity's share in total world exports:

$$RCA = (X_{ij}/X_j)/(X_{iw}/X_w), \tag{1}$$

[4]This index was developed by Balassa (1965). A number of the assumptions underlying this approach have been questioned, but the measures are used frequently as an informative index-- see, for example, Kreinin (1966), Bowen (1983) and Yeats (1985). This index is preferable to export-import ratios since data on relative export performance are not distorted by differences in the degree of tariff protection as long as all exporters are subject to the same tariff. As Yeats (1985) points out, however, voluntary export restraints and non-tariff barriers have discriminatory effects. But in the case of the ASEAN countries, these differences are negligible.

4   M. E. KREININ AND M. G. PLUMMER

where X_{ij} = exports of commodity i by country j; X_j = total exports of country j; X_{iw} = world exports of commodity i, and X_w = total world exports. This formula was calculated for each 4-digit SITC (over 600 industries) for each of the ASEAN-4 countries, the three Asian NIEs, and for Japan.

An RCA of 1 means that the share of i in the country's total exports equals the share of i in total world exports. With an RCA ratio greater than unity commodity i is more important in country j exports than it is in total world trade, implying that the country has a comparative advantage in the product. The converse holds for a ratio smaller than unity. The higher the index for a given commodity, the higher it is assumed to be in the ranking of goods by comparative advantage. The 600 4-digit SITC industries were therefore ranked by their RCAs from the highest on down.

A dynamic variant of this index is also useful. In it, each of the four magnitudes in the above formula is the *change* between two periods, such as between 1981 and 1990. Under this variant a country is said to have a comparative advantage in commodity i if its share in the country's total exports *grew* faster than the growth in the share of the commodity in total world trade over the same period. That index was also calculated, and labelled RT. Both the RCAs and RTs were computed and ranked for each country for the year 1981 and 1990 (or the latest year, which was 1989 for all ASEAN-4 countries save Thailand).

Alternative Regional Blocs

We next define three possible regional blocs in East Asia:

Bloc 1: ASEAN-4
Bloc 2: ASEAN-4, and the three Asian NIEs
Bloc 3:[5] ASEAN-4, the Asian NIEs, and Japan
Bloc 4: The world as a whole

RCAs (and RTs) for both years were calculated for each country with respect to each of the alternative blocs, and the 600 industries ranked as before. To measure the degree of structural change, a Spearman Rank Correlation Coefficient was computed for each country between the RCA rankings in 1981 and the latest year for which data are available. A separate calculation was made for the country's exports to the world as a whole, and to each of the relevant regional blocs defined above. The Spearman Rank Correlation Coefficient is a non-parametric estimate, showing how the ranking of two series are correlated with each other. The estimates range from -1 to $+1$: perfect rank correlation would be unity in absolute value, while complete lack of correlation would be zero. For our purposes, *a high rank correlation means that over time the ranking of a country's industries by comparative advantage in the specified*

---

[5]A more comprehensive Asia-Pacific region which includes the above eight countries plus Australia and New Zealand was also considered. But the results were similar to those of "Bloc 3," and so they are not reported here.

bloc has changed little. A low coefficient means that the ranking has changed considerably, suggesting rapid structural change. These correlations were computed for the dynamic concept (RT) as well, but the results were very similar to those of the RCAs and hence are not reported here.[6] However, the RT measure will be used in Section 3.

Overall Degree of Change

In the process of growth and industrialization, the competitive structure of East Asian economies changes, as they move to produce increasingly sophisticated products. These developments can be measured by alterations in the ranking of industries by RCAs over time. Column 1 of Table 2 offers summary statistics that capture the degree of change in each country. It rank-correlates the RCAs relative to the world in 1981 with 1990. The lower the coefficient, the greater the structural change that has taken place.

As expected, Japan experienced least change, with coefficients of 0.89 and 0.85 for all commodities and manufactures, respectively. Greatest change occurred in Indonesia, followed by Korea and Singapore. The remaining countries experienced moderate change.

Regional Structural Changes

Similar methodology was applied to each country's exports to the 3 alternative regions. The results are given in columns 2, 3, and 4 of Table 2, for trade with Bloc 1 (ASEAN-4), Bloc 2 (ASEAN-4 and the NIEs) and Bloc 3 (ASEAN-4, the NIEs and Japan), respectively. While only two commodity categories are shown (i.e., all commodities and manufactures), estimates at the 1-digit SITC level are also available from the second author upon request. Taking the ASEAN-4 countries first, we note that substantial changes in regional trading patterns occur for all bloc definitions. In each case and each country, the structure of manufactured exports has changed more rapidly than for all commodities, implying that the manufactured sector has been restructured more rapidly than other sectors. Within the ASEAN-4 group, manu-factured exports have changed considerably, with correlation coefficients falling in the 0.49 to 0.53 range. With respect to trade with the two broader regional blocs, Indonesia's manufactured exports have changed the most, with coefficients of 0.34 and 0.39 for trade with Blocs 2 and 3, respectively. This result is consistent with the economic reform program of Indonesia, which was more extensive than in any other ASEAN country.

While structural adjustment in regional trade of the NIEs tended to be less than in the case of ASEAN-4, substantial change did occur. The degree of change within the Bloc 2 configuration was generally the same for all NIEs (in the range of 0.49 to 0.53

---

[6]An adaptation of this methodology to formal regional groupings has been used in Kreinin and Plummer (1994).

for both commodity groupings), but structural change in trading patterns with Bloc 3 was clearly greatest in the case of Korea. Once again, Japanese trade was subject to the least change.

Table 2. Structural Change in East Asian Trade Patterns:
Spearman Rank Correlation Coefficients between 1981 and 1990;
RCA Rankings for Overall Trade and Regional Trade

	Change Relative to				Revealed Structural Change Coefficients		
	World	Bloc 1	Bloc2	Bloc3	Bloc1	Bloc2	Bloc3
ASENA-4							
Indonesia: All	0.51	0.57	0.41	0.46	0.89	1.24	1.11
SITC 5-8	0.45	0.53	0.34	0.39	0.85	1.32	1.15
Malaysia: All	0.70	0.51	0.56	0.60	1.37	1.25	1.17
SITC 5-8	0.65	0.49	0.48	0.57	1.33	1.35	1.14
Thailand: All	0.71	0.56	0.54	0.60	1.28	1.31	1.18
SITC 5-8	0.67	0.50	0.48	0.55	1.34	1.40	1.22
Asian NIEs							
South Korea: All	0.61		0.53	0.46		1.15	1.33
SITC 5-8	0.53		0.50	0.50		1.06	1.06
Hong Kong: All	0.77		0.54	0.63		1.43	1.22
SITC 5-8	0.80		0.53	0.66		1.51	1.21
Singapore: All	0.65		0.51	0.57		1.27	1.14
SITC 5-8	0.57		0.49	0.52		1.16	1.10
Japan: All	0.89			0.78			1.14
SITC 5-8	0.85			0.73			1.16

Notes: 1. Bloc 1 = ASEAN-4; Bloc 2 = ASEAN-4 + NIEs; Bloc 3 = ASEAN + NIEs + Japan
2. See text for explanation of RCA and RSCC calculations.
3. Latest year data are for 1989 for all ASEAN-4 countries save Thailand.

Comparison of the first column in table 2 (labelled "World") with the subsequent three columns, reveals whether the restructuring of intra-regional trade was faster or slower than the restructuring of a country's trade with the world as a whole. In all instances (except for Indonesia with respect to Bloc 1), the coefficients pertaining to trade with any of the three blocs are smaller than their counterparts pertaining to trade with the world as a whole. This is true for ASEAN, the Asian NIEs, and Japan. And in many cases the difference is substantial.

Hence, it appears that Asian countries are restructuring their intra-regional trade at a faster pace than their global trade. Two factors may account for this result: First, economic development in East Asia has taken place at a faster pace than in the world as a whole, implying that changes in economic complementarity have been greater within the region. Second, East Asian countries have been liberalizing their respective commercial policies far more rapidly than has the rest of world, allowing for greater expansion and diversification of trade.[7]

While the previous section evaluated trends in the pattern of trade of East Asian economies, it did not examine the changing composition of the most dynamic industries in ASEAN and the Asian NIEs. The next section addresses this issue by comparing the actual composition of the most dynamic 4-digit SITC industries over time.

3. THE CHANGING COMPETITIVE STRUCTURE OF EAST ASIA

The ASEAN-4

Table 3a presents the top 20 RCA industries for the ASEAN-4 covering manufactured goods (SITC 5-8), where only commodity groups with a minimum export of $20 million are included. The first column refers to 1981 and the second to the latest available year for each country (1988, 1989 or 1990). The third column shows the top 20 RT (ratio of RCA's between the end year and 1981), using a low $5 million cutoff for the end year. The low cutoff is designed to capture incipient industries. The RT numbers do not follow from the first two columns; rather they are calculated independently for all commodity groups. In contrast to the first two columns, the RTs highlight the dynamic changes occurring in these rapidly-growing economies. Only the top 20 RTs are included. There are numerous other industries in which ASEAN has a comparative advantage, but did not make the cutoff value for inclusion in the table.

In the primary materials category, the list of which is available from the second author upon request, there are no surprises. ASEAN comparative advantage in 1989 was concentrated in several food items (rice, sugar, flour, cocoa, copra, fish, fruits, energy/oil and natural gas), and various oils. There is great similarity between the 1981 and 1989 lists. However, several new commodities, including pulpwood, bauxite, and new oil products, appear on the RT list.

RCAs in manufacturing are lower than those in primary products, signaling the fact that the ASEAN countries are still in the early stage of industrialization. This is further highlighted by the fact that the industries included on the list are either material-based and/or labor intensive (SITC 6 and 8). The only exception is steel products which is presumably a capital-intensive industry. No items of the SITC 72 made the list, and indeed very few of them (radio receivers and transistors) have RCAs above 1. This is contrary to expectations, given the often-cited reports about ASEAN being an assembly venue for electrical equipment. By the last 1980's, they

---

[7]More ambitious ASEAN economic integration programs in the 1980s might be offered as a third possible explanation for greater change within the region. However, these programs have had an extremely limited impact on trade. For a discussion, see Naya and Plummer (1991).

8   M. E. KREININ AND M. G. PLUMMER

Table 3. Changing Competitive Structure of ASEAN and the NIEs:
Industries by International Competitive Standing:
Based on 1981 and 1989/1990 RCAs and 1989/1990/81 RCAs

Static (minimum exports of $20 million)						Dynamic (minimum exports of $5 million)		
1981			1990			Ratio 1990/1981		
SITC		RCA	SITC		RCA	SITC		RT
a. ASEAN: Top 20 (SITC 5-8)								
6871	Tin alloys	25.6	6792	Steel cast	31.2	6727	Iron/steel coil	2,735.7
6312	Plywood	6.6	6784	Steel conduit	23.1	6841	Aluminum alloys	264.4
6673	Precious stones	5.3	6871	Tin alloys	20.1	5214	Ald. compounds	208.2
8416	Rubber gloves	4.9	6312	Plywood	19.4	6743	Iron/steel uncoat.	199.6
8991	Carved woods	4.7	6514	Cotton	16.0	6782	Iron/steel tube	182.5
6327	Wood manuf.	4.4	8416	Rubber gloves	14.9	7197	Ball bearings	162.7
6311	Veneer sheets	4.2	6578	Mats	11.8	6514	Cotton yarn	159.7
6519	Textile fiber	3.9	6327	Wood Manuf.	9.5	6861	Zinc alloys	125.5
8992	Brooms	3.4	6129	Leather manuf.	9.4	7114	Aircraft engines	114.6
7293	Transistors	3.1	6673	Precious stones	8.0	6941	Steel/copper nails	103.1
6536	Woven fabrics	3.0	6561	Textile bags	7.5	6113	Calf leather	99.8
6578	Mats	2.5	6713	Iron/steel powder	7.1	5611	Chemical fertilizer	59.7
6556	Cordage	1.9	6521	Grey woven cotton	6.2	6644	Glass surface	53.4
6561	Textile bags	1.9	8992	Brooms	5.2	6747	Timmed plates	44.2
6831	Unwrought nickel	1.9	8991	Carved goods	5.0	6674	Synthetic stones	43.8
6521	Grey woven cotton	1.6	6519	Textile fibers	4.5	5619	Fertilizer	43.4
6555	Elastic fabrics	1.4	6555	Elastic fabrics	4.5	6412	Print paper	43.1
6557	Hat bodies	1.4	6311	Veneer sheets	4.4	6822	Copper alloys	38.7
6518	Wood simply wrkd.	1.3	6812	Platinum metals	4.4	7149	Office machines	38.5
6328	Other wood	1.3	6612	Cement	4.3	7359	Ships and boats	37.4
b. NIEs: Top 25 (SITC 5-8)								
6578	Mats	17.9	6750	Iron/steel hoops	13.7	6714	Manganese	377.4
8413	Leather clothes	10.7	6982	Base metal safes	13.5	6750	Iron.steel hoops	52.5
8310	Travel goods	9.0	6555	Elastic fabric	13.1	7327	Truck chasis	33.4
8942	Tops	8.9	6984	Iron.steel anchors	12.7	6113	Calf leather	23.0
5214	Coal	8.7	8994	Umbrellas	7.6	6982	Base metal safes	16.2
6531	Silk fabrics	8.6	8413	Leather clothes	6.9	6515	Flax ramie	15.9
8999	Other manuf., nes	8.5	8310	Travel goods	6.7	7194	Domestic appliances	13.4
8411	Textile clothes	8.3	7242	Radio Receivers	6.5	7143	Statistical machines	13.1
8994	Umbrellas	8.3	8972	Imitation jewelry	6.4	5126	Inorganic esters	9.5
8641	Watches	8.1	7316	Freight cars	6.1	6538	Glass fiber	8.5
6511	Silk	7.7	8942	Toys	6.0	6851	Lead alloys	8.3
8420	Fur clothes	7.3	6515	Flax ramie	5.7	7111	Steam boilers	6.7
7242	Radio receivers	7.2	6562	Made-up canvas	4.8	5819	Plastic materials	5.7
6312	Plywood	7.2	8999	Other manuf., nes	4.7	6119	Leather	5.5
8972	Imitation jewelry	7.1	7315	Passenger cars	4.5	6821	Copper alloys	5.2

STRUCTURAL CHANGE AND REGIONAL INTEGRATION   9

Table 3. Changing Competitive Structure of ASEAN and the NIEs:
Industries by International Competitive Standing:
Based on 1981 and 1989/1990 RCAs and 1989/1990/81 RCAs

Static (minimum exports of $20 million)					Dynamic (minimum exports of $5 million)		
1981		1990			Ratio 1990/1981		
SITC	RCA	SITC		RCA	SITC		RT
b. NIEs: Top 25 (SITC 5-8)							
8414	Clothing access.	7.1	6979	Base metals	4.4	8919	Musical instr parts	5.2
8991	Carved goods	6.5	5713	Pyro tech	4.4	5128	Organic compounds	4.9
8415	Headgear	6.0	8641	Watches	4.4	6715	Other ferrous alloys	4.8
6521	Grey woven cotton	5.8	6531	Silk fabric	4.3	6321	Boxes, cases, crates	4.7
7316	Freight cars	5.7	6871	Tin alloys	4.3	7113	Steam engines	4.2
8992	Brooms	5.6	8420	Fur clothes	4.3	7141	Typewriters	4.0
6562	Canvas	5.4	8951	Office supplies	4.2	6781	Cast iron	3.9
6556	Cordage	5.3	6537	Knit fabric	4.1	7333	Nonmtr vehicles, nes	3.9
6934	Expanded metal	5.2	8414	Clothing access.	3.8	6421	Paper container	3.7
6972	Base metal	5.1	8411	Textile cloth	3.8	6861	Zinc alloy	3.6

did not acquire a comparative advantage in these items, although individual countries (for which the RCA tables are available from the second author upon request), *such as Thailand and Malaysia, did register RCAs greater than* 1 *in several of these categories.* Malaysia has RCAs greater than 1 for TV receivers, radio broadcast equipment, and transistors, while Thailand has RCAs greater than 1 in T. V. receivers, electric insulating wire, domestic electrical equipment, and transistors, and the Philippines--in transistors.

Moreover the dynamic version of the RCAs (third column of the table) includes several machinery items (SITC 71) as well as ships and boats, and several chemicals (SITC 5). Beyond these, there is a concentration in material-based products (SITC 6). But there are industries that failed to make the top 20 cutoff, and yet have high RTs, signaling rapid growth. There is a high concentration of these in the SITC 71 (machinery) and 72 (electronics), 82-85 (furniture, textiles, footwear), 897 (jewelry items), and a few chemicals (SITC 5).

Given the nature of the RCA calculations, it is possible for up-scale ASEAN manufactured exports to be booming, and yet for the RCAs to remain low. For example, Thai exports of telecommunication equipment grew from $2 million to almost $300 million during 1981-1990, but the RCA comes to only 0.7. On the other hand, the dynamic calculations do reflect the growth in many SITC 5 and 7 industries, as shown in Table 3.

The individual-country lists reveal some important insights. Many natural-resource based products, in which ASEAN countries have a comparative advantage (e.g. rubber and timber products for Malaysia and Indonesia), are declining in importance as more processing takes place domestically (e.g., veneer or furniture), and as resources are shifted to more advanced industries. The same holds true for mineral-based products, such as aluminum, iron, steel, and so on. To some degree this change is policy driven, as when the exports of certain raw materials such as rattan are banned, forcing producers to process the material at home. Second, Indonesia experienced a large change in the composition of its primary products exports in the 1980s, and a large increase in textile exports. Third, there were substantial changes in the top 20 ranked manufacturing industries between 1981 and 1990. Moreover, over the four year period 1987-1990,[8] Thailand moved to produce several advanced products including office machines, radio and TV receivers, certain electrical equipment, freight cars, and sound recordings, at the expense of certain labor-intensive industries, such as textiles.

The NIEs

Table 3b presents the RCAs for the three NIEs combined in 1981 and 1990. It shows the 25 top manufacturing industries (SITC 5-8) ranked in terms of the RCAs, both for the static and dynamic (RT) versions. In 1981 high RCAs were observed mainly in textiles and clothing and certain other labor-intensive commodities. By 1990, these goods declined in importance and higher-technology products emerged, including cars, TV receivers, and certain instruments. The advent of various machinery items (SITC 71), certain chemicals, and mineral-based manufactures, is shown in the dynamic list. Country RCAs for Korea, Singapore, and Hong Kong in 1981 and 1990 are available from the second author upon request. Within the primary commodities, Korea has only strong comparative advantage in fish and certain vegetables. In the "dynamic" list, the interesting development is the appearance of natural gas and motor spirits on the list.[9]

Within the manufacturing sector in 1981, there was a large concentration of high RCAs in textiles and clothing (SITC 65 and 84), and other labor-intensive products. There were but few capital intensive items, such as metals and ships on the list. By 1990, while many textile and metal items remained on the list, several were replaced by higher-tech products such as telecommunication equipments, freight cars, and automotive electronics. Although Korean exports of road motor vehicles boomed over the period, rising from $70 million to $1.8 billion, Korea did not acquire a comparative advantage in that industry (RCA = 0.3). Contrary to expectations, a strong movement into the area of machinery and transport equipment (SITC 7) is not evident in the static RCAs. On the other hand, the dynamic concept of comparative advantage does capture this change, where 13 of the top 30 industries were in SITC 7,

---

[8]For Thailand we calculated and ranked RCAs for 1987 in addition to 1981 and 1990.

[9]Once again, rankings of primary commodities for the NIEs are available from the second author upon request.

and 3 in chemicals (SITC 5). Only half the industries are in the textiles, clothing and materials categories, compared to 90 percent in the static tabulations.

Regarding changes in comparative advantage of the two (resource-poor) city-states, Hong Kong and Singapore, weak RCAs are observed for primary commodities except in certain processing areas, with more consistency over time for Hong Kong than Singapore. In manufactures, Hong Kong also exhibits fewer changes in comparative advantage, with continuing high values for textiles and clothing and some movement into certain machinery items (SITC 72). On the other hand, Singapore has been shedding its textile and clothing exports in favor of diverse SITC 7 commodities. Singapore appears to be the most industrialized of the NIEs.

4. CONCLUSION

This paper considers the degree to which structural change and regionalization are taking place in East Asian economies. The methodology developed in the first part compares the 1981 ranking of comparative advantage industries in East Asian economies, using RCAs calculated at the 4-digit SITC level, to that of 1990 (or the latest year), for global trade and for trade with these alternative trade bloc configurations. Spearman Rank Correlation Coefficients are derived to assess the degree to which structural change has occurred. The results suggest that: (1) sizeable changes in the structural patterns of developing East Asian trade with the world are in evidence for all countries; (2) the manufacturing sector has been restructured at a faster pace than primary commodities; and (3) in general, intra-regional trade has been changing more rapidly than global trade.

In its second part, the paper considers in some detail the changing competitive structure of the developing East Asian countries. it highlights the upgrading of these economies as they move from strictly labor intensive and material based exports to more sophisticated and diverse products. An evaluation of dynamic changes in comparative advantage reveal a rapid movement toward the production of more sophisticated products in East Asia.

In the East Asian development literature,[10] It has been argued that, while growth is clearly taking place in ASEAN, it is based on traditional manufactures. Our analysis suggests that this is not the case; on the contrary, considerable upgrading is occurring. And while it is impossible to assess the degree to which this drive is due to the influx of direct foreign investment (DFI), the relatively small share of DFI in total capital formation in most East Asian economies implies that much of this upgrading can be attributable to an indigenous process.

[10]For example, see Yoshihara (1988), for a standard argument regarding "growth without development" in Southeast Asia.

REFERENCES

Balassa, Bela, "Trade Liberalization and 'Revealed' Comparative Advantage," *Manchester School of Economic and Social Studies*, March 1965, 99-123.

Bowen, Harry P., "On the Theoretical Interpretation of Indices of Trade Intensity and Revealed Comparative Advantage," *Weltwirtschaftliches Archiv*, 1983, 464-472.

James, William E., Kreinin Mordechai E., and Plummer, Michael G., *Competitiveness, Growth, and Interdependence in the PECC Region*, Osaka: JAPANPECC, 1993.

Kreinin, Modechai E., "On the Restrictive Effect of the Tariff," *Manchester School of Economic and Social Studies*, January 1966, 15-21.

Kreinin, Mordechai E., and Plummer, Michael G., "'Natural' Economic Blocs: An Alternative Formulation," *International Trade Journal*, Volume VIII, Number 2, Summer 1994.

Naya, Seiji and Plummer, Michael G., "ASEAN Economic Cooperation in the New International Economic Environment," *ASEAN Economic Buletin*, March 1991, 261-276.

Yeats, Alexander J., "On the Appropriate Interpretation of the Revealed Comparative Advantage Index: Implications of a Methodology Based on Industry Sector Analysis," *Weltwirtschaftliches Archiv*, 1985, 61-73.

Yoshihara, Kunio, *The Rise of Ersatz Capitalism in Southeast Asia*, Singapore: Oxford University Press, 1988.

Mailing Address: Professor Mordechai E. Kreinin, Department of Economics, Michigan State University, East Lansing, Michigan 48824-1038, U. S. A.
Mailing Address: Professor Michael G. Plummer, Lemberg Program, Department of Economics, Brandeis University, Waltham, MA 02254-9110, U. S. A.

[12]

REGIONAL ECONOMIC INTEGRATION AND DYNAMIC POLICY REFORM: THE "SPECIAL" CASE OF DEVELOPING ASIA

*Michael G. Plummer**

While many studies have considered the importance of economic reform in developing countries and the economic effects of regional economic integration, few have related the two in a systematic way. This paper considers the implications of regional economic integration as part of the outward-oriented development strategy in Asian developing countries. It first reviews the special characteristics of developing countries which make regional economic integration an especially attractive option, as part of a liberal economic development strategy. It is argued that existing studies strongly underestimate the usefulness of regional economic integration for development by ignoring its most important dimensions: rather than relating to the traditional (static) welfare results of economic integration, the salutary effects of regional economic integration obtain through reinforcement of policy reform, as well as "dynamic" benefits inherent in regional economic integration at many levels. Hence, regional economic integration is not only a "building bloc" of unilateral liberalization but also a catalyst in the economic development process. The paper demonstrates how this "open regionalism" is being played out in the Association of South East Asian Nations (ASEAN) and the Asia-Pacific Economic Cooperation Forum (APEC).

I. RATIONALE AND ORGANIZATION

Few would dispute that the tremendous economic performance of a number of Asian countries can be traced to effective policy reform (for example, James, Naya and Meier 1991, Edwards 1993, World Bank 1993, Rodrik 1996). Arguably, the policy-induced East Asian economic success story has led to the adoption of outward-oriented reforms in other developing regions, such as Latin America and South Asia (for example, Edwards 1993; Rodrik 1996). There remains, nevertheless, a considerable debate in economics literature regarding the importance of reform in development strategies, the determinants of economic reform programmes and factors related to the sequencing of these reforms (Dollar 1992, World Bank 1993, Rodrik 1995, Sachs and Warner, 1995, and the literature cited therein). There has emerged a general consensus that: (a) outward-

*   Brandeis University and Kobe University, Research Institute for Economics and Business Administration, Kobe, Japan.

1

Asia-Pacific Development Journal   Vol. 4, No. 1, June 1997

looking development strategies are necessary though not sufficient conditions for sustained economic growth and development; (b) stable macroeconomic variables through sage policy management are essential in providing a solid basis for growth and in harnessing the dynamics of outward orientation; and (c) policies geared toward micro-restructuring need to accompany financial/macroeconomic reforms in the long-run.[1] Much less consensus, however, is found in the evaluation of such specific issues as industrial policy or, more generally, the role of the State in certain areas of the economy, for example, reform of volatile financial areas such as short-term capital flows[2], exchange-rate management and the relationship between political structure and economic reform (World Bank, 1993). Nevertheless, the general debate has moved decidedly in favour of the effectiveness of a liberal trade sector, open policies vis-à-vis foreign direct investment (FDI), development of internationally consistent "deep integration" policies, effective provision of infrastructure (physical and human capital), and the overriding importance of prudent monetary and fiscal policies.

Although the body of research on economic reform is impressive, one area that the economics literature has tended to neglect has been the relationship between economic reform and regional economic integration. Ever since the mid-1980s, when the United States of America began to pursue regional economic integration accords aggressively and the European Union made its major push to create a single market, the literature has been flooded with theoretical and empirical studies regarding the economic effects and general desirability of various preferential trading agreements, and even their implications for the world trading system. However, to the extent that this literature focused on the developing world at all, it was mainly aimed at the economic effects of integration agreements on these countries (for example, Kreinin and Plummer 1992, Anderson and Snape 1994, Plummer 1994, Cuyvers 1996, Ariff 1996), descriptions and taxonomies of such arrangements (see, for example, World Trade Organization 1995, Pomfret 1997) or applications to developing-country groupings but with the use of theoretical and empirical models designed essentially for a developed-country context (for example, Brown, Deardorf and Stern 1995, DeRosa 1995, Adams and Park 1995). The recent strain in the literature focusing on "natural" economic blocs, which provides a key role for geography and evidence from pre-integration trading patterns (Krugman 1991, Frankel 1992, Kreinin and Plummer 1994), circumvents the traditional need for standard neoclassical assumptions and parametric estimation. This is an advantage for developing countries in which such estimation is often difficult but it comes at the cost of weak conclusions with respect to the effects on static resource allocation.[3] Moreover, the core academic debate over

---

[1]   Of course, there are scholars who disagree with this consensus (for example, Taylor, 1991), but they tend to be a small minority in mainstream economics and seem to be decreasing in number over time.

[2]   Much of this literature developed after the Mexican peso crisis in December 1994. See, for example, World Bank (1995) and the literature cited therein for a surprisingly pessimistic view of openness toward liquid international capital flows.

[3]   "Weak" is used here in the context of implicit analysis applied to the economic effects of regional groupings. For example, Krugman (1991) notes that the greater intra-regional trade as a percentage of total

Asia-Pacific Development Journal   Vol. 4, No. 1, June 1997

regional economic groupings as "building blocs vs. stumbling blocs" (Lawrence, 1991) has largely skipped over the important relationship between regional economic integration and domestic economic policy formation, particularly in developing countries.[4]

This void in the literature is particularly problematic for developing Asia, which has been strengthening existing regional economic integration accords and/or pursuing incremental schemes at the same time that it has been engaging in the pervasive policy reform noted above. If the regional economic integration movement were implicitly a threat to these economic reform programmes, officials would presumably be following contradictory policy stances. On the other hand, if formal regional economic integration agreements strengthen economic reform, such accords should be embraced, especially if they are also able to generate dynamic benefits (which, as argued in this paper, tend to be more important in the case of developing countries). In this case, the logical next step would be to delineate areas in which regional economic integration accords would best suit the needs of developing countries.

The purpose of this paper is to address more fully the relationship between economic reform and regional economic integration in the East Asian context. It could best be described as an integrated survey of the applied and theoretical literature and an attempt to identify and expound the emerging role of regional economic integration as an essential feature of economic reform in developing Asia. In doing so, it provides strong support for the notion that existing and emerging regional groupings in Asia are outward-oriented and complementary (perhaps even essential) to the goals of unilateral and multilateral liberalization and domestic economic reform.

The paper is organized as follows: first, using the existing theoretical and empirical literature applied to regional economic integration accords, it details why regional economic integration involving developing countries differs qualitatively from that between developed countries (section II). Second, it focuses more fully on the relationship between regional economic integration and policy reform in developing countries (section III). Extending from the literature on endogenous policy reform, it makes the case that the relationship is strongly positive, but also a function of the choice of the liberalization agenda. In section IV, the paper uses the explicit cases of the ASEAN Free Trade Area (AFTA) and APEC as evidence of this positive relationship. Some concluding comments on the importance of using regional economic integration as an effective agent in strengthening and maximizing the effects of reform in East Asia are given in section V.

---

trade, the more "natural" is the bloc and, hence, the greater the potential for net trade creation. Frankel (1992) uses a gravity model to detect "biases" toward intraregional trade, and Kreinin and Plummer (1994) use non-parametric estimates of the consistency of trade patterns as a proxy for a "natural" bloc. None of these models estimates trade creation and trade diversion directly, and while they do circumvent the need for difficult parametric estimation (for example, import elasticities of demand, cross-elasticities and supply elasticities), this is done at a cost. See Pomfret (1997) for a more detailed critique of the "natural economic bloc" literature.

[4]   One exception is Petri and Plummer (1996), which develops a series of propositions supporting the view that regional economic integration tends to reinforce openness.

II. WHY DEVELOPING COUNTRIES ARE, INDEED, SPECIAL

At least superficially, most economists would find the statement that "developing countries are special" to be so uncontroversial as to lack any need for defence. After all, development economics is an established field within the economics profession; most economics departments dedicate part of their curriculum to the study of development economics as a "special" area; there is a myriad of economic development journals; and many "traditional" economists have applied their sophisticated tools to developing countries as well as to developed areas.

Yet, there is an interesting ambivalence in the literature with respect to the notion that developing countries are "special" requiring special analysis. Stating that "developing countries are different" today is often evaluated in the context of the 1950s and 1960s, when such expressions were common among pundits and policy makers supporting import-substitution, a "new international economic order," and "special and differential treatment". Theodore Schultz was a highly influential figure during this period who argued that, indeed, economic analysis applied to developed countries could also be applied in a developing-country context, with certain adjustments. Schultz's potent arguments are convincing: many neoclassical prescriptions applied to East Asian countries testify to his wisdom, as do the policy failures of his intellectual adversaries. Nevertheless, developing countries are different and require special treatment in economic modelling.

By noting that developing countries are different, we do not suppose that policies designed for developed countries will not be effective in developing countries. Obviously, they have been; good economics is good economics. What we intend to draw attention to here is that the very characteristics of developing countries require modular adjustments in order to capture the peculiarities of developing countries. The (often implicit) support for this notion is in evidence in the very existence and activities of the World Bank, the International Monetary Fund, development assistance programmes and hundreds of other international and national organizations. Still, in much of the trade literature, there is often a strong analytical position that developing countries are no different. A number of these differences are outlined below and presented in the context of policy reform and the regional economic integration analysis which is to follow.[5] For convenience, these items are grouped according to their relationship to the financial sector or the real sector or to political-economy considerations, with the understanding that the dichotomy between the real and financial sectors is often artificial.[6]

---

[5] As such, the review is not intended to be comprehensive but rather specific to regional economic integration.

[6] For a discussion of the links between trade and financial variables, see Yamazawa and Asano (1996), Lee and Roland-Holst (1997), and Petri (1992).

Financial sector constraints

First, developing countries are poorer and tend to have a wider gap in the distribution of income. This has a variety of implications for economic reform, as it highlights the role of the government in redistributing income (see Rodrik, 1996 and its sources) and in providing certain social safety nets, as well as in taxation. It puts an important constraint on changes that should be made in fiscal policies, and often other financial areas such as exchange rate management.[7]

Second, financial systems in developing countries tend to be less developed, and the price mechanism does not work as well. This makes modelling of the real and financial sectors in developing countries more difficult. Moreover, data obtained in developing countries and assumptions regarding market clearing that are so essential, especially to general equilibrium modelling, present additional problems. For example, serious efforts have been made to develop general equilibrium models of the Chinese economy by incorporating a two-tier price system, but this is done with considerable difficulty and by simplifying assumptions.[8] Financial closure of computational equilibrium models is complicated for any country, but more so in the case of developing countries.[9] Estimation of import and cross-elasticities of demand, particularly at appropriate levels of disaggregation, tends to border on the impossible, given the paucity of reliable data, the limited number of observations (usually on an annual basis except at the very highest order of aggregation), and the rapid structural change leading to paradigmatic shifts.[10] Usually, modellers attempting to estimate the effects of economic integration in developing countries either borrow estimates from (often weak) developed-country estimates or assume a "reasonable" domain for them and apply sensitivity analysis. Finally, as the "shocks" that drive these models pertain to changes in prices through the liberalization of tariff and non-tariff barriers, the fact that developing countries tend to have far less transparency in these areas precludes reliable estimation. These inherent difficulties have rendered the "natural economic bloc" approach that much more appealing.

Third, developing countries encounter greater constraints in tapping global liquidity. Although international capital markets have become far more fluid, and access

---

[7]   One such constraint is the ability to remove popular but inefficient subsidies such as those on gasoline, electricity or public transportation, or in even deregulating the price of such staples as rice, as these moves are seen as mostly affecting the poor. The worse the distribution of income, the more convinced people are of this (Rodrik, 1996). Attempting to change such policies, even when clearly essential to sound macroeconomic management, is difficult.

[8]   For example, the two-tier price system in China has been gradually changed into a more market-oriented system, making modelling of the Chinese economy a bit of a moving target, not unlike many other developing countries in the process of reform.

[9]   See Devarajan, Lewis, and Robinson (1994) for a thorough discussion of the difficulties in choosing the correct form of macroeconomic closure in CGE models.

[10]   For a review of these problems, see Plummer (1991), and Lee and Roland-Holst (1994).

for developing countries (especially since the debt crisis of the 1980s) has increased tremendously, financial risk and information costs tend to be higher in the case of developing countries, and, hence, they face a fairly high risk premium. They are also more prone to short-run capital flight.

Fourth, because of the financial risks associated with developing countries, poorly developed financial markets, and the tendency to be more open (in the sense that trade as a percentage of GDP is higher), they have less flexibility in the choice of exchange rate regimes.

Fifth, developing countries rely more on technology transfer than developed countries. It is obvious that one reason developing countries are classified as such is their low level of technological sophistication. At the margin, they therefore tend to rely more on the transfer of (appropriate) technology from developed countries (or advanced developing countries[11]). In this sense, they are more dependent on FDI, not only as a source of longer-term capital flows, but especially because of the technology transfer dimension.

Real sector constraints

Sixth, developing countries face different domestic resource mobilization constraints. Unemployment and/or underemployment tend to be higher in developing countries, and internal financial markets are less efficient. At the margin, this makes the reallocation of resources more costly. Still, unemployment rates differ greatly between developing countries, with some of the richer ones (such as Singapore and Malaysia) having lower rates than even some developed countries, and the poorer ones having sometimes severe problems. In the case of rapidly growing developing countries, such as those in East Asia, while resource mobilization may be constrained (as it is in all traditional and many modern societies), structural change becomes easier because of the internal economic dynamics of the economy.[12]

This is an important point. The entire neoclassical literature developed since Jacob Viner's seminal contribution to the customs union theory is based on the assumption of full employment of resources. Relax this assumption, and trade creation and trade diversion may generate opposite effects on allocative efficiency and, hence, welfare.[13] In this sense, the attractiveness of using regional economic integration as a means to close off the rest of the world would be larger at the margin. Moreover, regional economic integration agreements used to support such regimes are often stillborn or short-lived, as one must find a partner country that is willing to let it benefit from trade

---

[11] In fact, advanced developing countries and areas, such as the Republic of Korea and Taiwan Province of China, have recently been major investors in developing Asian countries and, arguably, the source of technology transfer in areas in which these countries have comparative advantage.

[12] This is one reason why the process of economic policy reform is easier in a rapidly growing economy than in a stagnant one.

[13] For a more in-depth discussion, see Plummer (1996).

Asia-Pacific Development Journal   Vol. 4, No. 1, June 1997

diversion without asking for benefits it might reap from trade creation, in essence assuring that the agreement will not go through.[14]

Seventh, developing countries tend to have small markets. Thus, these countries have less potential for internal scale economies. Of course, to the extent that they are members of the World Trade Organization (WTO) and benefit from Generalized System of Preferences (GSP) programmes, they have access to the international market place on (at least) a most-favoured-nation basis. However, protection in developed-country markets continues to be quite high in many of the sectors in which these countries have comparative advantage, even accounting for Uruguay Round cuts. For example, with respect to textiles and clothing, developed countries will be phasing out the Multi-fibre Arrangement very slowly, with up to 49 per cent of the quotas remaining intact until the end of the 10-year phase-out; tariffs will stay high in textiles and clothing (in double-digits); and arrangements within certain regional groupings (for example, the rules of origin in textiles in NAFTA) can be highly discriminatory.[15] Moreover, items of interest to developing countries (such as, labour-intensive manufactured products) are often excluded from GSP schemes.

Political-economy considerations

Eighth, developing countries tend to face a different set of political variables. Rodrik (1995) points out an interesting paradox in the economic reform debate: if economic reform is clearly in the best interests of the nation, why should it be politically unpopular? He notes, as does a great deal of economics and political literature, that there could be a number of reasons for this, but in most cases it is related to the fact that voters do not pay gladly for long-run improvements if the short-run costs are high. Part of this is due to the uncertainties of future success, especially when measured according to the "good old days". Moreover, the short-run perspective of politicians and the well-defined economic incentives of special interest groups often result in resistance to reform.

These influences tend to be much stronger in the developing world. In many countries, a small group of industrialists can exert enormous political influence. Often, protection can be promoted under the guise of national prestige in order to gain domestic popularity, an argument that is all too common in South-East Asia. In most developing countries, the demand for greater democracy (or a weaker central government in politics) could even exacerbate these problems, as weaker governments are more prone to such demands than strong governments.

Ninth, developing countries suffer from shortcomings associated with being smaller and weaker participants in the international system. This puts them at a disadvantage

---

[14] Arguably this was the case for formal regional economic integration agreements in Africa and Latin America in the 1960s and 1970s (Petri and Plummer, 1996).

[15] See, for example, Rugman (1994), PECC (1995), and Fukasaku, Plummer and Tan (1995).

in multilateral, regional and bilateral negotiations, a fact emphasized by Johnson (1965) and others.

In sum, there are a number of structural differences between developed and developing countries that require consideration in economic modelling and in theoretical model construction. Often, it is a matter of differences in the *extent* of real/financial distortions. This is not to say that existing theories created primarily for developed-country applications are necessarily inappropriate; rather, *they suggest a different emphasis in certain areas.* As it turns out, these areas tend to be those that are most difficult to capture in formal models. The case of formal regional economic integration in the context of policy reform is a salient example of this.

III. POLICY REFORM AND REGIONAL INTEGRATION IN DEVELOPING ASIA

As noted above, regional economic integration groupings became increasingly popular in the mid-1980s, prompting considerable interest from the academic community. Although there were new innovations in regional economic integration theory over this period, the overriding framework for understanding economic integration continued to be based on the customs union literature developed since Viner (1950).[16] From the 1960s to the 1980s, the most common empirical work (again, based on traditional theory) related to partial equilibrium analysis of various regional groupings. However, new empirical studies, especially those applying the general equilibrium theory,[17] did allow for a more comprehensive treatment of the economic implications of these sorts of trade accords, though most of the analysis remains static in that it focuses on relative price changes rather than the dynamic elements of regional economic integration accords.

It is really these dynamic elements of regional economic integration arrangements as well as other forms of economic integration, be they unilateral or multilateral in nature, that are the most important in the developing-country context. The reasons why formal regional economic integration can be useful to developing countries are delineated below, making use of the stylized characteristics of developing countries delineated above.

Macroeconomic stability. There is consensus in economics that macroeconomic stability is critical to the continued success of any development strategy. Even short-term bouts of instability can haunt an economy for many years. Latin America's long struggle with inflation is only now beginning to be won, and this has been accomplished at considerable economic cost (through unemployment and foregone output) and with

[16]   Even new approaches, such as the "natural economic bloc" literature, couch their analysis in terms of the standard neoclassical analysis, in particular with respect to the General Theory of Second Best (i.e., static allocative efficiency effects such as trade creation and trade diversion).

[17]   Shoven and Whalley did pioneering work in the area of computational general equilibrium modelling in the early 1980s (see, for example, Shoven and Whalley 1994), but it has really been in the 1990s that these models have become common.

much social tension.[18] In view of the financial problems noted above, promoting macroeconomic stability tends to be difficult in developing countries, and an external means to support this process is often a necessary part of the stabilization process.

Fortunately, developing Asia has had less difficulty in keeping a stable macroeconomic environment, if by this we mean low inflation. However, in many areas, developing Asian countries have had difficulty maintaining low fiscal budget deficits; inflation has been a problem in some countries; and current account imbalances[19] supported by strong FDI and, more recently, portfolio investment flows have become worrisome (see table 1). Movements in the long-run interest rates of some countries show what is apparently a high-risk premium, reflecting market concern over the macroeconomic stability of the country.

Exchange rate stability is also a vital area for the smooth functioning of the economy, particularly in the tradeables sector. Developing countries tend to rely on variations of fixed exchange rate regimes for a number of reasons, including vulnerability to inflation. As noted in the "optimum currency area"– and subsequent related literature – the more open the economy, the less useful are expenditure-switching policies in addressing macro imbalances. In addition, weak forward exchange markets and other means of privatizing currency risks make fixed rates more attractive in order to facilitate international trade. Even in the case of fixed exchange rates, the financial uncertainties associated with short-term capital inflows in developing nations leave them open to currency attacks, underscoring the importance of prudent fiscal and monetary policies and sufficient reserves to protect the currency against speculation.

In this sense, the most important contribution that regional economic integration accords can make to developing countries is to help support stable macroeconomic policies. Obviously, it is possible to do this in the absence of a regional grouping, as Asia has done thus far.[20] But regional economic integration accords can help to encourage macroeconomic stability in a number of ways. In particular, real-financial links endemic to regional economic integration agreements require stable macroeconomic policies if the agreements are to function smoothly. For example, a major push for monetary union

---

[18] Argentina is probably the most obvious in this regard. Hyperinflation in the 1980s has now been brought down to the single-digit level by anchoring the new currency (the peso) to the dollar, a parity that is protected by a currency board. While Argentina has been able to keep inflation down and has successfully protected the (Argentine) peso in the wake of the Mexican peso crisis "tequila" effect, this has been done with an increasingly overvalued exchange rate and high unemployment. Many experts believe that Argentina will need to continue such austere policies – and forcing internal price adjustments – until the market is confident in its willingness to promote stability, which may take a long time. In short, Argentina has paid an extremely high price for its legacy of macroeconomic profligacy.

[19] Current account deficits such as those being experienced by ASEAN countries are not necessarily detrimental to economic development if they are a result of investment in beneficial projects. However, if such borrowing is required to finance the government deficit or, arguably, a consumption boom, the country may face problems.

[20] There are, however, some regional organizations which are used to promote macroeconomic cooperation, such as under SEACEN, a group of South-East Asian central banks.

Table 1. Basic Financial Indicators ASIA-PACIFIC Developing Countries (Selected Years)

	GDP Growth (per cent)			Inflation (per cent)			Cur Act Bal (per cent of GDP)			Debt service (per cent of expts)			Fiscal sur/def (per cent of GDP)		
	1981–1990	1994	1996[a]	1981–1990	1994	1996[a]	1989	1994	1996[a]	1989	1994	1996[a]	1989	1992	1994
Newly Industrializing Economies	9.4	7.4	6.7	6.4	5.7	5.1									
Hong Kong	6.9	5.5	5.6	8.3	8.1	8	4.1	1.1	1.6	–	–	–	2.1	2.8	0.8
Republic of Korea	10.7	8.3	6.8	6.4	6.4	5.5	2.3	–1	–1.1	11.8	5.1	4.8	0.2	–0.5	0.6
Singapore	6.3	10.1	8.5	2.5	3.8	3	9.5	9.6	8.8	–	–	–	4.4	6.2	6.8
Taiwan Province of China	7.8	6.5	6.8	3.1	3.9	3.7	7.8	2.7	4.6	–	–	–	1.4	–5.4	–1.8
China	10.4	11.8	8.9	7.5	21.7	8	–1	0.9	0.2	11.4	11.3	9.6	–2.3	–2.5	–2.4
South-East Asia[b]	6.1	7.5	7.4	6.4	7	6.3	–2.2	–3.9	–3.2						
Indonesia	5.5	7.4	7.1	8.5	9.2	7.6	–1.2	–1.9	–1.6	35.4	32.9	32.3	–1.4	–0.1	0
Malaysia	5.2	8.5	8	3.6	3.8	4.4	0.7	–9	–4	15.1	4.7	6	–3.3	–0.8	0.4
Philippines	1	4.3	5.5	13.4	9	8	–3.4	–5	–4	25.9	18.7	17.2	–2.1	–1.2	1.1
Thailand	7.9	8.5	8	4.4	5	4.5	–3.5	–5.2	–4.2	16.3	11.2	12.5	3.5	2.5	2.5
Viet Nam	7.1	8.8	9	195	9.9	11	–9.8	–5.4	–6.1	18.9	11.9	11	–7.1	–1.7	–4.1
Other															
Papua New Guinea	–	0.8	–	5.8	6.1	–	–10	4.9	–	29.3	32[c]	–	–7.4	–10	–5.5

Source: Asian Development Bank, *Asian Development Outlook 1996* (Manila: ADB, 1996).

Notes: a   1996 figures are forecasts.
   b   Figures for South-East Asia are weighted and include (the much smaller) economies of Cambodia and the Lao People's Democratic Republic.
   c   1993 figures were the latest available for Papua New Guinea.

in Europe came from the need to promote the single market, for example, by abolishing the possibility of competitive depreciation and allowing for the removal of border controls.[21] The NAFTA agreement was signed without any provision for exchange-rate cooperation (a very small currency stabilization fund was set up later), a decision that leaders came to regret by December 1994. From the perspective of the Government of the the United States, the peso crisis created problems not only because of the ensuing economic crisis in Mexico but also the effect of the steep fall in the Mexican peso turned an American surplus into a deficit in a short period of time. As noted by Bhagwati (1991) in the context of fostering overall stability in international trade in the area of flexible exchange rates:

> Dramatic shifts, such as the yen-dollar rate before and after the 1985 Plaza accord, underline the intensity of the problem that can arise. I think it is pretty obvious that unless some degree of stability in the structure of exchange rates is achieved by coordination of underlying macroeconomic policies, the rise of unfair trade allegations will be hard to contain and will lead to demands for a fix-quantity rather than a fix-rule trading regime. The choice in practice may well be between managed exchange rates and managed trade (Bhagwati, 1991, p. 17).

Hence, in order to ensure a stable partnership, countries must share information, cooperate in advocating stable fiscal and monetary policies, and engage in strong "peer pressure" against unstable policies. For instance, an important *quid pro quo* for Viet Nam's access to ASEAN was the taming of its triple-digit inflation rate; now that it is in ASEAN, it is facing strong pressure to keep fiscal policy under control (especially with respect to the subsidization of State-owned firms).

Perhaps more importantly, in advanced regional agreements (and, as is noted later, there is evidence that regional groupings such as ASEAN are moving in this direction), countries find that they must focus on non-traditional areas affecting trade and investment if they are to advance economic integration, including competition policy and government procurement. These "non-border" measures force a stronger market-orientation, inject greater microeconomic competition by reducing the power of domestic monopolies and "rent-seeking," and place constraints on government spending through, for example, the abolition of export subsidies and restrictions on industrial policies. Furthermore, as noted in De Melo and Panagariya (1992), the influence of special interests groups seeking protection will diminish, a dynamic policy element that should facilitate openness. As these policies exacerbate transparency problems and make micro and macro reform difficult, they are often the greatest culprits when instability and/or economic stagnation is in evidence in developing countries. Thus, such "forced macroeconomic stability" could be highly beneficial to the economic development strategies of participating countries. Moreover, these "deep" integration schemes tend to be far more difficult to achieve in multilateral negotiations.

---

[21] For example, as noted by Pomfret (forthcoming 1997), implementation of the Common Agricultural Policy (CAP) requires the (expensive) administration of monetary compensatory amounts (MACAs), which, in turn, requires border controls.

Technology transfer and foreign direct investment. Increasingly, developing countries have been placing stronger emphasis on technology transfer in their multilateral and bilateral relationships. The evidence of this is ubiquitous, from the preponderance of requests for technical assistance in development aid and cooperation programmes to the "virtuous cycle" of policy liberalization stemming from the desire to promote FDI capital inflows as a means of private-sector-led technology transfer. Regional economic integration accords can promote FDI inflows through reductions in transaction costs (be they border or non-border in origin) and in doing so, they are able to establish an attractive business environment within which multinationals can easily profit from a vertical division of labour, as well as facilitating the emergence of multinationals within the developing region itself.[22] Of course, the same is true for developed countries (see Dunning and Robson, 1988). Nevertheless, developing countries will, at the margin, gain more from technology transfer, in view of the greater technological gap taking the form not only of production technologies but also management techniques, other business practices, corporate culture and various training programmes. AFTA, for instance, was created mainly as an instrument to attract greater FDI to the region at a time when competition for such flows was deemed to be increasing (especially from China, but also South Asia and Latin America). Some have even described AFTA as more of an investment pact than a trade pact.[23]

Although the link between FDI and technology transfer has been firmly established, the relationship between trade and technology transfer is less well known. Through trade liberalization, countries are also able to stimulate technological development. For example, trade leads to the adaptation of new technologies from abroad by increasing the potential for success in using those technologies to crack foreign markets; in addition, increased competition forces domestic firms to place a higher priority on creating their own or importing new technologies (Pissarides, 1995). This implies a strong incentive for developing countries emphasizing technology transfer (such as, all East Asian countries) to liberalize even unilaterally.

Moreover, to best take advantage of these new technologies, countries find that they must establish strong intellectual property protection laws and means of enforcement. Without an attractive, protective environment in which multinationals can operate and in which domestic firms can invest in new innovations, the process of technology transfer is significantly inhibited. Formal regional economic integration agreements can help in creating a strong underlying framework for the protection of intellectual property and "peer pressure" in the implementation of associated laws.[24]

---

[22] ASEAN multinationals, for example, have been increasing in number and importance since the creation of AFTA. In fact, some of the largest investors in Viet Nam are ASEAN-based, with ASEAN FDI accounting for fully 20 per cent of the country's total.

[23] Ariff (1996) and Petri and Plummer (1996).

[24] Having recognized this, the ASEAN countries have developed a regional framework for intellectual property protection.

In the area of technology transfer, using the above analysis might suggest that developing countries should seek partnerships with developed countries, a conclusion that runs as counter to Vinerian analysis as it does to the structuralists/dependencia school. It does, however, present a powerful (though perhaps not overriding) argument; McCleery (1992), for example, incorporates some aspects of investment and other dynamics into a regional model of NAFTA and finds much larger effects for Mexico than in a static model.

Nevertheless, developing-country groupings can encourage technology transfer together, either through internal promotional means (for example, in terms of training facilities, regional research and academic institutes, and research consortia) or in jointly devising means to bring in appropriate technologies from abroad.

In any event, regional economic integration can have an important impact on inflows of FDI and, implicitly, technology transfer. Moreover, the use of regional economic integration in this way serves to reinforce economic liberalization.[25]

Economies of scale. As developing nations are small (from an economic perspective), access to larger markets is important in industries in which economies of scale are apparent. Modern technologies ensure that this is the case for many industries. Regional trading agreements can be used as a means to expand production at the margin and, hence, reap cost-reduction benefits. The need to obtain economies of scale is often cited by the private sector as a useful element of regional economic integration and by policy makers as an important goal.

The importance of economies of scale for developing countries is formally developed in Cooper and Massell (1965) and elaborated by Bhagwati (1968). They note that the costs of import-substitution policies used to attain a given level of "industrial production" as a public good could be reduced through regionalism. This is possible because it allows for internal specialization in more efficient (from a regional viewpoint) industrial areas and the possibility of realizing scale economies.

However, gains from economies of scale may be less than one might first guess for three reasons: (a) global markets tend to be fairly open already (though, as noted above, there are important exceptions); (b) as developing nations have small markets themselves, there are fairly strict limits as to how much can be gained; and (c) the benefits of economies of scale themselves have been questioned (for example, Pomfret 1997). But in the rapidly growing Asian economies characterized by an emerging middle class and greater consumer orientation, scale considerations are becoming important.[26]

Harmonization issues. The largest effects of the single market programme in the European Union (EU) were gauged to be in many of the "non-border areas" listed above, but, perhaps, one of the most important areas of cooperation can be classified

---

[25] For further discussion, see Yamazawa and Asano (1996), Petri and Plummer (1996), and Plummer (1996).

[26] One bit of evidence of this is in the big push by American automobile companies into Asia to serve regional markets.

under the rubric of "harmonization issues," such as in product testing, professional certification and standards conformance. Asian developing countries have greater divergence in these areas than the EU, not only because of the colonial history of the region (that ended up reflecting varied European and other differences) but also because nation-State building has often meant taking pride in creating such differences. They therefore stand more to gain from regional economic integration. For Asia, such categories as investment codes, customs harmonization, and various legal impediments must be added.

Again, gains in all of these areas would be maximized by adopting global harmonization standards. Nevertheless, doing so at the global level is much more difficult, particularly for developing countries which often feel threatened by such programmes. By conforming as a group to some global standards, the agreement clearly reinforces the global system, but even when they do not, such agreements will reduce the "stock of divergencies," making global agreements that much more feasible.

Political-economy issues. All existing formal regional economic integration accords either were created as economic arrangements in support of political goals or were at least consistent with the diplomatic strategy of the founding countries. For example, the European Economic Community was formed as a means to strengthen European economies in the face of a Cold War aggressor, as were subsequent arrangements to develop association agreements with Greece and Turkey. ASEAN was created at a time of instability in South-East Asia (the Cultural Revolution in China; war and a communist threat in Viet Nam), and the First ASEAN Summit was convened in 1975, when the communists unified Viet Nam. NAFTA had as a special purpose the promotion of economic liberalization and (indirectly) stable political reform in Mexico, as was the case with the proposal to create a Free Trade Area of the Americas (FTAA). Economic cooperation in these arrangements was seen as an important vehicle through which political goals could be pursued (which, in themselves, have important economic ramifications[27]).

To the extent that these regional economic integration arrangements add to the political stability of the region, they do service to economic development in general and the goal of policy reform in particular, even if the arrangements have very weak substance to them. This, of course, is an important part of the early success story of ASEAN. Although most ASEAN countries had only recently achieved independence, were often characterized by unstable domestic political situations and were struggling to create nation-States (with many territorial disputes, a number of which continue to date), the arrangement established an important dialogue process that prevented overt hostilities between these countries.[28] Moreover, ASEAN created a united front in the face of any

---

[27] It should be noted also that the ASEAN countries did not collude extensively at the Uruguay Round, though they did keep each other well-informed of their individual positions. Moreover, the resource-rich ASEAN countries were part of the Cairns Group, which strongly supported agricultural liberalization, but this group included a number of other countries as well (including the United States).

[28] See Sandhu and Siddique (1992), for a series of reflections on the political and economic evolution of ASEAN economic integration.

potential communist "domino" effect, which, interestingly, turned into a "reverse" domino effect with respect to market reform in the rest of Indochina. Today, the "constructive engagement" of the ASEAN countries vis-à-vis the transitional economies of South-East Asia, though controversial in the West, has strong political intentions. ASEAN understands the critical need to use economic cooperation as an essential "carrot" when direct political dialogue is extremely sensitive.

As developing countries throughout the world tend to have weaker political (and economic policy) traditions, instability is always a potential problem. This is not as true for developed countries. Hence, the beoeficial economic effects of formal regional economic integration in, for example, the enlargement of the EU to include the EFTA countries might be estimated, and the indirect political stability factors could be ignored without serious fear of underestimation. This is not true of developing-country or developed-developing country groupings. To say that the (intentionally) weak economic cooperation initiatives in ASEAN had nothing to do with the subsequent dynamic growth in the region is to understate its role seriously.[29]

Static efficiency effects. While the five preceding items were not listed in any special order of importance, "static efficiency effects" are deliberately mentioned last, for they are probably the least important, especially in the context of developing countries. As part of an import-substitution development strategy, regional economic integration agreements are used as a means to promote regional industrial development and displace extraregional imports. In this sense, Vinerian trade creation in which inefficient domestic industries are replaced by more efficient partner-country exports can still play a positive role, particularly in the light of the Cooper-Massell-Bhagwati analysis. Still, from the individual interests of an acceding country, an inward-oriented development perspective looks unkindly on any imports, even if they come from partners. Strong political interests are also opposed, making trade creation a hard sell in regional economic integration bargaining. On the other hand, trade diversion displacement of efficient non-partner imports with less efficient partner country imports would technically be pleasing to policy makers if they were one integrated political unit, as it implies a reduction in imports. However, this is not the case with a standard regional economic integration arrangement. The partner country reaps the benefits of trade diversion, and the government of the home country loses tariff revenue (and buys from a higher-cost source), meaning that trade diversion does not help adoption of the agreement. It is not hard to predict, therefore, that inward-looking regional economic integration arrangements in the developing world will not last.

On the other hand, if regional economic integration is used as part of an outward-oriented development strategy, formal regional economic integration is actually a useful approach even from a static efficiency perspective. The reason for this is that the countries not only reap efficiency gains due to trade creation (a goal of the outward-looking regime) but they have a strong disincentive to bear the costs of trade diversion.

[29]   Naya and Plummer (1991).

Hence, instead of importing inefficient goods from the higher-cost partner country, an acceding nation has a strong incentive to lower its external barriers to trade.[30] This unambiguously reinforces its outward-oriented development drive.

Thus, it becomes difficult to separate the logic of pursuing formal regional economic integration in lieu of a unilateral/multilateral stance, which is undoubtedly why the economics profession in normative and positive analysis has felt uncomfortable with such regional accords. It is argued here, however, that regional economic integration is useful as a means of reaping the numerous "dynamic" benefits discussed above; moreover, the static economic effects will, through an endogenous policy process, create a strong incentive to push the country toward unilateral liberalization. As noted by Sachs and Warner (1995) in a more general context:

> Trade liberalization not only establishes powerful direct linkages between the economy and the world system, but also effectively forces the government to take actions on the other parts of the reform programme under the pressures of international competition. (Sachs and Warner, 1995: 2).

Outward-looking developing countries are therefore "forced" by the market to minimize any negative consequence of trade diversion and to use regional economic integration as a means of rendering the grouping more competitive (some evidence of which is discussed in the next section).

It is therefore unfortunate that studies which estimate the effects of an ASEAN (for example, Adams 1995 and DeRosa 1995) or Asian (for example, World Bank 1994 and Brown, Deardorf, and Stern 1995) free-trade area are mainly confined to measuring static economic effects rather than focusing on the dynamic economic effects and the endogenous effects on policy formation. After all the preceding five topics are potentially much more important to developing countries, and such static models do not even capture the most important element of the sixth topic: the salutary effect of regional economic integration on policy formation.

IV. THE DIRECTION OF REGIONAL ECONOMIC INTEGRATION AS PART OF THE ECONOMIC REFORM PROCESS

To summarize the above analysis: (a) the role of regional economic integration in policy reform in Asia, as a developing region, takes on special significance; (b) while the economics of regional economic integration applied to developing countries may be evaluated using the same general framework as that of developed countries, one is required to place a different emphasis on major aspects of inquiry (especially with respect to economic and political-economy dynamics), and, further, one must respect the limitations of modelling in capturing the most important economic development elements; and (c) there is a strong case to be made for regional economic integration as a parallel strategy to multilateral liberalization.

[30] See Petri and Plummer (1996) for further discussion.

Asia-Pacific Development Journal   Vol. 4, No. 1, June 1997

Regional economic integration was evaluated above in the context of the overall global economic system. In other words, regional economic integration was a means, to be used together with multilateral levers, to advance economic policy reform in the direction of openness and macroeconomic stability. This section addresses more fully the essential issue of the relationship between regional economic integration and the process of economic policy reform in developing Asian countries. More specifically, has regional economic integration thus far reinforced outward-oriented economic policy reform? This is a critical question that has escaped close inspection, mainly because the answer is so difficult to confirm. Much of the literature related to the topic seems to doubt the usefulness of regional economic integration as a vehicle of economic reform. The reasons are many, but mainly they relate to the possibility of a region becoming inward-looking, or the inefficiency of REI as compared with multilateral liberalization.

Developing countries rely on the global market place for openness; why should they settle merely for discriminatory regional groupings? Trade diversion is a consideration, but there is probably a more important detrimental side effect of regionalism: with a given stock of human capital devoted to international trade and investment issues, efforts applied to promote regionalism might affect resources devoted to multilateralism. Even though the Johnson argument for closer cooperation within a region to push global trade negotiations may be applicable, empirical evidence is lacking in this regard. For example, although the ASEAN countries did cooperate in creating the "Kuching Consensus" to limit the role of regional economic liberalization in APEC, there has been little effective cooperation between these countries at the annual APEC summits, much to the chagrin of its chief policy makers.[31] Besides, if Asian countries are reforming so rapidly on a unilateral basis, will not regionalism slow this process down?

It is no mean feat to show a causal effect between REI and policy reform in developing Asia. Petri and Plummer (1996) show empirically an association between regional group formation in Asia and greater openness, but with no necessary pretension as to causality. The problem, of course, is that Asian regionalism gained momentum in the late 1980s and early 1990s, at the same time that Asian countries were implementing their impressive liberalization programmes. For example, ASEAN economic integration began to deepen in the late 1980s, expanding to take the form of AFTA and subsequent ancillary agreements in the early to mid-1990s. The commitment to create a region of "open trade and investment" under APEC (the Bogor Agreement) was made in 1993. This creates an intractable "chicken and egg" problem.[32] Moreover, standard *ex post* analysis in which a counter-factual scenario can be erected would be highly questionable in the context of modern policy reform.

However, it is just this simultaneity problem that gives strong credence to the idea that regional economic integration is part of the policy reform process in Asia, rather than a separate development with, perhaps, ulterior motives. In referring to the

---

[31]   See note 27.

[32]   For more information on empirical difficulties, see Plummer (1996) and Petri and Plummer (1996).

possible diversionary effects of regional integration schemes such as NAFTA, Ariff (1996) notes that:

> ASEAN has carefully avoided integration schemes that would reorient member economies. Even its newest trade initiative, the ASEAN Free-Trade Area (AFTA), is designed in such a way as to not weaken ASEAN extraregional linkages....A laudable feature of AFTA is that it is aimed not at increasing intra-ASEAN trade but at making ASEAN products competitive in the world market and making the ASEAN region attractive as a centre for FDI. (Ariff 1996, p. 218)

In view of these quantification problems and those mentioned earlier, we consider the relationship between regional economic integration and policy reform in the cases of ASEAN and APEC can be considered examples of policy dynamics in regions that are embracing outward-looking development strategies. In the context of the developing country policy framework presented above, these two regions also present some interesting comparisons as they represent developing-country and developed-cum-developing country groupings, respectively.

Regional economic cooperation in ASEAN

One way to sort out the intentions and motives of policy makers in creating regional economic integration schemes is to ask them. Alternatively, it is possible to survey the statements that they have made to the (domestic and international) press to get a better idea of their thinking beyond joint statements made at regional meetings (which can be obviously biased). For example, during the NAFTA debates, the anti-NAFTA camp tended to campaign against trade in general (for example, certain environmental and labour groups), and a number of NAFTA proponents encouraged it on its trade-diversion merits (including business leader Lee Iacocca). Statements from policy makers tended to be mixed, with most of them advocating the importance of free trade and sustaining liberalization within Mexico.

In order to gauge such sentiments among ASEAN leaders in AFTA, a media search was undertaken as one (indicative) means of classifying their intentions in AFTA.[33] The period 1 January 1996 to 7 October 1996 was chosen as a suitable period for such a survey, under the assumption that, first, it would include comments from government officials at a time when ASEAN was undergoing significant change; second, its leaders would have four years of "thinking about AFTA" behind it; and third, it would allow for some analysis of Viet Nam, which is the newest member of ASEAN and its only transitional economy. The results were illuminating:

(a)   Out of hundreds of quotes, in no case did an ASEAN official ever say that AFTA should be used as a means of closing off the ASEAN market as a discriminatory trade bloc. The majority of statements were strongly supportive

[33] This was done for *The Strait Times* (a daily based in Singapore with a reputation for having some of the most extensive coverage of ASEAN affairs); and the *Far Eastern Economic Review* (a weekly magazine). The search was conducted simply using the keyword "ASEAN Free-Trade Area" and was undertaken for all issues between 1 January and 7 October 1996.

Asia-Pacific Development Journal   Vol. 4, No. 1, June 1997

of using ASEAN as a means to enhance competitiveness and economic development in the region;

(b) Only two sets of quotes might suggest a lack a complete "opening" intentions: (i) Malaysian Trade Minister Rafidah said (*Strait Times*, June 6) that while she supported AFTA, she did not necessarily advocate the MFN-ization of AFTA cuts because then it would no longer technically be a free-trade area (possibly alluding to a willingness to gain preferential treatment within the region): and (ii) the Trade and Industry Minister of Indonesia, Tunky Ariwibowo, mentioned (*Strait Times*, March 16) that, while Indonesia would respect its commitments to liberalize under AFTA and APEC, it would use various forms of industrial policy in the transitional period in order to support certain industries. It should also be noted that some officials (for example, B.G. Lee of Singapore) were sceptical that ASEAN could hope to include all goods under AFTA with no exceptions; certain others believed that Viet Nam had a very long fight ahead of it in order to keep its terms under AFTA (though all, including Vietnamese officials themselves, noted that Viet Nam had undertaken a tremendous amount of policy reform toward this end);

(c) ASEAN leaders continued to advocate more comprehensive lists for trade liberalization (with an agreement in 1996 to include even sensitive unprocessed agricultural goods such as rice and sugar by 2010, though with extra time and some differences between parties about interpretation);

(d) ASEAN committed itself to cooperation on a host of "non-border" and trade facilitation issues, in the form of either formal agreements or initiatives to work toward this end, such as: the ASEAN investment cooperation scheme; the ASEAN investment area; intellectual property protection; a dispute-settlement mechanism; a harmonized and integrated mass transit system to facilitate the implementation of AFTA; advanced means of regional investment promotion; harmonization of customs laws and other legal areas; cooperation in standards and conformance; development of closer ASEAN capital markets, including the possible adoption of "ASEAN Capital Time" (common time to facilitate business links); and support for the development of greater transparency in doing business;

(e) ASEAN enlargement to include all of South-East Asia was an important area of discussion. A major motive in doing this was to reinforce and augment liberalization in the transitional economies of Cambodia, the Lao People's Democratic Republic and Myanmar;

(f) ASEAN expanded negotiations with other countries and groupings, such as strengthening links with India (making it a full dialogue partner); signing an agreement on "Cooperation on Standards and Conformance" between AFTA and the CER (Australia and New Zealand); strong interaction at the Asia-Europe Meeting while at the same time stressing links between ASEAN and the EU; and stepped up plans for cooperation within WTO;

Hence, from this indicative survey, it would appear that ASEAN economic integration has moved well beyond the textbook variety and includes many of the items associated with even the most advanced economic integration areas, though, obviously, these ambitious plans will continually confront difficulties. For our purposes of this paper, evidence would seem to support the view that regional economic integration within the region has helped to promote domestic economic reform; indeed, regional economic integration does seem to be part of the economic reform process. This is most evident in the case of Viet Nam but applies to all ASEAN countries. In addition, while studies focusing on the statics of economic integration and traditional neoclassical analysis in general might suggest that AFTA makes no sense as formal regional economic integration, the dynamic effects on domestic policy formation and in lowering transaction costs within ASEAN and between ASEAN and the rest of the world are arguably more relevant to these developing countries.

Regional economic integration in APEC

Since its creation in 1989, APEC has received a great deal of attention as the first "post-Cold War" international organization. While it was originally created as mainly a means of economic dialogue, it rapidly grew into much more. Once the "membership issue" regarding the three Chinas was solved, APEC became free to explore a wider variety of cooperative ventures. In 1993, President Clinton of the United States invited the heads of state of APEC to Blake Island, which was the beginning of a yearly APEC summit. In 1994, APEC countries committed themselves in Bogor, Indonesia to creating a region of "open trade and investment" by the year 2010 (2020 for developing countries). Based on the (yet to be clearly defined) "open regionalism" concept, APEC has three pillars of cooperation: trade and investment liberalization; trade and investment facilitation; and development cooperation.

APEC is special for a number of reasons, including its sheer size and composition, involving both developed and developing countries, and its basic dedication to the goal of creating a free and open international market place. In practically all APEC declarations, the association commits itself to shunning an inward orientation and instead embracing open regionalism. It is not clear if by "open regionalism" APEC means that all reductions in trade barriers will be non-discriminatory vis-à-vis the outside world, or just non-discriminatory vis-à-vis APEC members (with possible reciprocity for non-members accepting APEC conditions). There has been a lively academic debate on the subject; almost all economists who believe in the goal of free trade would like to see the first option pursued. However, within this group there are a number of economists who believe that the non-reciprocity option is politically a non-starter, and since APEC can be a stepping stone to multilateral free-trade, it is important to work on a reciprocal basis.[34]

---

[34] Peter Drysdale, Andrew Elek, and Ross Garnaud at the Australian National University have been major supporters of the non-reciprocal camp, and Fred Bergsten at the Institute for International Economics a protagonist of reciprocity.

Although there are differences between countries regarding the means to promote cooperation in APEC, the overriding goal is ostensibly shared by all: to create an Asia and Pacific region in which the transaction costs of international interchange are as low as possible. The idea of exchanging "down payments" and "action plans" at APEC summits has received a great deal of attention. The lack of agreement on how to compare liberalization offers in such a loose, voluntary organization (working in a framework of "concerted, unilateral action") has left some disillusioned, but the analysis in this paper suggests that regional economic integration through tariff liberalization is only a small part of the overall liberalization package to be expected from a modern regional economic integration accord, especially for developing countries. Extensive work is being undertaken by APEC working groups to improve customs clearance procedures, the creation of a business person's "smart card", APEC investment agreements, development cooperation, exploration of the means to facilitate technology transfer, cooperation in infrastructure, standards and conformance, harmonization of product standards, enhanced dialogue between APEC countries, and the means for improving other areas generally classified under "deep integration." While often tedious and seemingly mundane, work in these areas will go much further in attaining the two most important aspects of regional economic integration for developing nations: "economic dynamics" and reinforcement of the economic reform process.

Note that the debate surrounding the discriminatory effects of regional economic integration in APEC misses the important point that all these activities, even those that are clearly non-discriminatory, will have the effect of creating a more integrated region, which will no doubt lead to a greater concentration of regional economic activity as a percentage of total economic activity (even though the latter will grow as well). For example, the European Community's single market programme was estimated by Cecchini (1988) to have a fairly large effect on growth in Europe (a 2.5 per cent to 6.3 per cent increase in GDP). This would lead to some "trade creation" and "trade diversion" affecting Asia (Asian Development Bank 1994, Plummer 1994) but not in the Vinerian sense, as the single market was not about changes in external and internal tariffs (the EC was already a customs union). In general, trade creation would take place because of the growth effect of the programme, and trade diversion would derive from increased competitiveness in Europe due to the displacement of external imports. Hence, while regional economic activity would increase its share in Europe, this would be due to a more efficient rather than less efficient allocation of resources, as implied by the Vinerian trade diversion policy scheme, from which the outside world would also benefit to some degree.[35]

An even stronger case can be made for APEC in this regard. As was noted above, developing countries are likely to gain more in terms of dynamic effects from

---

[35] The Asian Development Bank (1994) uses a general equilibrium model to show that, on the whole, developing Asia would be better off with the Single Market Programme. Plummer (1994) uses an *ex post* technique to show that some countries would gain and others would lose in Asia but that, on the whole, the private sector and policy makers in Asia and the Pacific (including the United States) were convinced that the Programme was, indeed, outward-oriented and generally good for the world economy.

regional economic integration agreements, but the inclusion of developed countries in such groupings implies added advantages in terms of advancing, for example, technology transfer and economies of scale. While a Cecchini-like report does not exist for APEC, one can venture to guess that APEC will lead to a greater concentration of regional activity but this will not be to the disadvantage of the outside world.

This conclusion should hold unless APEC does any of the following: (a) it causes economic reform in developing (or developed) countries to slow down or reverse; (b) APEC leads to explicitly discriminatory policies vis-à-vis the outside world (meaning that APEC becomes an inward-looking bloc); (c) it detracts from the GATT/WTO process; or (d) it causes increased political tensions. The first two are highly unlikely: as noted above, APEC has explicitly dedicated itself to openness; the analysis of this paper strongly supports the view that liberalization within APEC will actually strengthen the reform process (and should even induce non-members wanting to join to speed up liberalization); such discriminatory policies could be taken to task in a much improved dispute-settlement mechanism within WTO; and recent arrangements between Europe and NAFTA (for example, discussions to create a "transatlantic free-trade area"), and between Asia and Europe (for example, the Asia-Europe Meeting ASEM and the ASEAN-EU framework agreement), give Europe an indirect channel through which it can raise objections to policies that might be aimed at it. Regarding detrimental effects on the GATT/WTO negotiations, APEC could cause problems, particularly since developing countries have a human capital scarcity problem in external negotiations. However, this problem was much more pertinent before the conclusion of the Uruguay Round (and, in fact, some have credited the emergence of the APEC Summit as a potent inducement to the Europeans to agree to the final document). Moreover, the next Round of WTO is probably a long way off; (for example, Bergsten, 1996) some believe that there will never be another comprehensive GATT round. Besides, APEC has firmly committed any policy developments to be supportive of the GATT/WTO process; in fact, recent "down payments" for APEC trade liberalization for the most part merely expedite Uruguay Round commitments.

Nevertheless, political developments within APEC may lead to problems which create negative externalities for the global system. Disagreements regarding sensitive economic policy areas (such as environment-trade and labour-organization issues) as well as political ones (such as human rights and "constructive engagement") could jeopardize bilateral, regional and multilateral economic relations. As APEC is by the far the most diverse grouping in the world in terms of both economics and politics, it will be walking a fine line on these issues.

V. CONCLUDING REMARKS

Developing countries are different. While economic policies promoting macroeconomic stability and microeconomic efficiency are essential to all countries, developing nations often have special needs, a result of being on a lower rung of the economic development ladder. In this sense, developing countries place an even stronger weight on areas such as technology transfer, access to larger markets and FDI flows. Moreover, they face different challenges with respect to macroeconomic stability, exchange-rate management and capital flows. Since these areas are often the most difficult to grasp empirically, it is likely that the importance of pro-market economic reform is significantly underestimated in this paper.

This paper has argued that outward-looking developing countries can gain significantly from regional economic integration as part of their economic reform packages. Scholars using Vinerian and neoclassical models derive results that would suggest that regional economic integration arrangements do not make sense because they tend to be trade-diverting on the whole and could negatively affect economic reform. Furthermore, multilateral liberalization may dominate the regional alternative. It is argued here that the dynamic benefits of regional economic integration outweigh the potential static costs and, in fact, will set in motion pro-liberalization measures to reduce these static costs. This process will support the economic reform efforts of member countries.

Two case studies were used to show how, in practice, this dynamic policy process works in developing Asia, first applied to ASEAN and then to APEC. But the same analysis could be applied to other developing regions as well. For example, unlike the moribund Latin American Free Trade Area, which tried to use regional economic integration to further import substitution, MERCOSUR is outward-looking in its orientation and is being used to help the economic reform drives of its member States (Nishijima and Smith, 1996). Economic integration in Western Europe was a major factor behind liberalization moves in Eastern Europe; the prospect of joining the world's most successful formal regional economic integration arrangement has been an important incentive for reform in these countries, some of which may join by the year 2000.[36]

Economic reform still has a long way to go in the developing world. Regional economic integration cannot be a substitute for the primacy of domestic or multilateral liberalization; in fact, groupings that have tried to use regional economic integration as a substitute for global economic integration have not been successful. Instead, regional economic integration must be seen as an option through which a country can enhance the economic reform process.

---

[36] African nations have not yet risen to this level (though there are positive signs in the Preferential Trading Area), but neither have they necessarily been convinced of the importance of outward-looking economic development (and have been severely plagued by political instability).

REFERENCES

Adams, F. Gerald, 1995. Measuring the impact of AFTA: an application of a linked CGE system, *Journal of Policy Modeling*, vol. 17, No. 4, pp. 325-365.

Anderson, Kym and Richard H. Snape, 1994. European and American regionalism: effects and options for Asia, *Journal of Japanese and International Economies,* vol. 8, No. 4, pp. 454-477.

Ariff, Mohamed, 1996. Outlooks for ASEAN and NAFTA externalities, Ch. 12 in Nishijima, Shoji and Peter H. Smith, eds., *Cooperation or Rivalry? Regional Integration in the Americas and the Pacific Rim*, (Boulder, Westview), pp. 209-224.

Asian Development Bank, 1994. *The Effects of the Single Market Programme on Developing Asia* (Manila, Asian Development Bank).

Bergsten, C. Fred, 1996. Globalizing free trade, *Foreign Affairs*, vol. 75, No. 3, May/June, pp. 105-120.

Bhagwati, Jagdish, 1968. Trade liberalization among LDCs, trade theory and GATT rules, in J.N. Wolfe, ed., *Value, Capital and Growth: Papers in Honour of Sir John Hicks* (Edinburgh, University of Edinburgh Press).

Bhagwati, Jagdish, 1991. *The World Trading System at Risk* (Princeton, Princeton University Press).

Bhagwati, Jagdish, 1994. The world trading system, *Journal of International Affairs*, Summer, vol. 48, No. 1, pp. 279-85.

Bhagwati, Jagdish and Arvind Panagariya, 1996. The theory of preferential trade agreements: historical evolution and current trends, *AEA Papers and Proceedings*, May, pp. 82-87.

Brown, Drusilla K., Alan V. Deardorf, and Robert M. Stern, 1995. Computational analysis of the economic effects of an East Asian preferential trading bloc, paper submitted to the United States Department of Labor, January.

Cecchini, Paolo, 1988. *The Costs of Non-Europe* (Bruxelles, Commission of the European Communities).

Cooper, Charles A., and B.F. Massell, 1965. Towards a general theory of customs unions for developing countries, *Journal of Political Economy*, vol. 73, No. 5, pp. 461-76.

Cuyvers, Ludo, 1995. The trade diversion effects on ASEAN of the European Union enlargement with EFTA countries and the association agreements with Eastern Europe, *CAS Discussion Paper*, No. 4, December.

De Melo, Jaime and Arvind Panagariya, 1992. The new regionalism, *Finance and Development*, vol. 29, December.

DeRosa, Dean A., 1995. *Regional Trading Arrangements Among Developing Countries: The ASEAN Example* (Washington DC, IFPRI).

Devarajan, Shantayanan, Jeffrey D. Lewis, and Sherman Robinson, 1994. *Getting the Model Right: The General Equilibrium Approach to Adjustment Policy,* mimeo, May.

Dollar, David, 1992. Outward-oriented developing countries really do grow more rapidly: evidence from 95 LDCs, 1976-1985, *Economic Development and Cultural Change*, April, pp. 523-44.

Dunning, John and Peter Robson, eds., 1988. *Multinationals and the European Community* (Oxford, Blackwell).

Edwards, Sebastian, 1993. Openness, trade liberalization, and growth in developing countries, *Journal of Economic Literature*, 31, September, pp. 1358-1393.

Frankel, Jeffrey A., 1992. Is Japan creating a Yen block in East Asia and the Pacific?, NBER Working Paper No. 4050, April.

Fukasaku, Kiichiro, Michael G. Plummer, and Joseph Tan, eds., 1995. *OECD and ASEAN Economies: The Challenge of Policy Coherence* (Paris, OECD Development Centre, 1995).

Grossman, Gene M. and Elhanan Helpman, 1995. The politics of free-trade areas, *American Economic Review*, vol. 85, No. 4, September, pp. 667-690.

Grossman, Gene M. and Elhanan Helpman, 1991. *Innovation and Growth in the Global Economy* (Cambridge, Masachusetts Institute of Technology Press).

James, William E., Seiji Naya, and Gerald Meier, 1991. *Asian Development* (Madison, University of Wisconsin Press). .

Johnson, Harry, 1965. An economic theory of protectionism, tariff bargaining, and the formation of customs unions, *Journal of Political Economy*, June, vol. 73, No. 3, pp. 256-283.

Kreinin, Mordechai E. and Michael G. Plummer, 1992. The effects of economic integration in industrial countries on ASEAN and the Asian NIEs, *World Development*, vol. 20, No. 9, September, pp. 1345-1366.

Kreinin, Mordechai E. and Michael G. Plummer, 1994. 'Natural' economic Blocs: an alternative formulation, *International Trade Journal*, vol. 8, No. 2, summer, pp. 193-205.

Krugman, Paul, 1991. Is bilateralism bad?, in E. Helpman, and A. Razim, eds., *International Trade and Policy* (Cambridge, Massachusetts Institute of Technology Press).

Lawrence, Robert Z., 1991. Emerging regional arrangements: building blocks or stumbling blocks?, in Richard O'Brien, ed., *Finance and the International Economy*, 5 (Oxford, Oxford University Press).

Lee, Hiro and David Roland-Holst, eds., forthcoming 1997. *Economic Development and Cooperation in the Pacific Basin: Trade, Investment, and Environmental Issues* (New York, Cambridge University Press).

Lewis, Jeffrey D., Sherman Robinson, and Zhi Wang, 1995. Beyond the Uruguay round: the implications of an Asian free-trade area, mimeo, February.

Pacific Economic Cooperation Conference, 1995. *Milestones in APEC Liberalization: A Map of Market Opening Measures by APEC Economies* (draft), November.

McCleery, Robert, 1992. An intertemporal, linked macroeconomic CGE model of the United States and Mexico focusing on demographic change and factor flows, in USITC, ed., *Economy-Wide Modelling of the Economic Implications of a FTA with Mexico and a NAFTA with Canada and Mexico* (Washington DC, USITC).

Naya, Seiji, and Michael G. Plummer, 1991. ASEAN economic cooperation in the new international economic environment, *ASEAN Economic Bulletin*, vol. 7, No. 3, March, pp. 261-276.

Nishijima, Shoji and Peter H. Smith, eds., 1996. *Cooperation or Rivalry? Regional Integration in the Americas and the Pacific Rim* (Boulder, Westview).

Petri, Peter A., 1992. Platforms in the Pacific: trade effects of direct investment in Thailand, *Journal of Asian Economics*, vol. 3, No. 2, pp. 173-196.

Petri, Peter A. and Michael G. Plummer, forthcoming 1997. The determinants of direct foreign investment: a survey with applications to the United States, in Lee, Hiro and David Roland-Holst, eds., *Economic Development and Cooperation in the Pacific Basin: Trade, Investment, and Environmental Issues* (New York, Cambridge University Press).

Petri, Peter A. and Michael G. Plummer, 1996. *The Multilateralization of Regional Preferences: The Case of the Asia-Pacific*, Brandeis University Working Paper, March.

Pissarides, Christopher A., 1995. Trade and the returns to human capital in developing countries, mimeo, October.

Plummer, Michael G., 1991. Static efficiency effects of the accessions of Spain and Portugal to the EC, *Journal of Common Market Studies*, vol. 29, No. 3, March, pp. 317-325.

Plummer, Michael G., 1996. Policy reform in Asia and trade-investment links, presented at the East Asian Economic Association meetings, Bangkok, Thailand, October 1996.

Plummer, Michael G., 1994. Implications of economic integration in Europe for the Asian industrializing region, in Toida, Mitsuru and Daisuke Hiratsuka; eds.; *EC1992 and the Pacific Asian Industrializing Region* (Tokyo, Institute of Developing Economies).

Pomfret, Richard, forthcoming 1997. *The Economics of Regional Trading Arrangements* (Oxford, Oxford University Press).

Rodrik, Dani, 1996. Understanding economic policy reform, *Journal of Economic Literature*, vol. 34, March, pp. 9-41.

Rugman, Alan M., 1994. *Foreign Investment and NAFTA* (Columbia, University of South Carolina Press).

Sandhu, Kernial S., and Sharon Siddique, eds., 1992. *The ASEAN Reader* (Singapore, ISEAS).

Sachs, Jeffrey D. and Andrew Warner, 1995. Economic reform and the process of global integration, *Brookings Papers on Economic Activity*, vol. 1, 1995, pp. 1-95.

Sazanami, Y., Shujiro Urata, and Hiroki Kawai, 1995. *Measuring the Costs of Protection in Japan* (Washington DC, Institute for International Economics).

Shoven, John and John Whalley, 1994. Applied general equilibrium models of taxation and international trade: An Introduction and Survey, *Journal of Economic Literature*, September, pp. 1007-1051.

Taylor, Lance, 1991. Economic Openness: Problems to the century's end, in Tariq Banuri, ed., *Economic Liberalization: No Panacea* (Oxford, Oxford University Press), pp. 99-147.

Viner, Jacob, 1950. *The Customs Union Issue* (New York, Carnegie Endowment for International Peace).

World Bank, 1993. *The East Asian Miracle: Economic Growth and Public Policy* (Washington DC, IBRD).

World Bank, 1995. *Managing Capital Flows in East Asia* (Washington DC, IBRD).

World Trade Organization, 1995. *Regionalism and the World Trading System* (Geneva, World Trade Organization, April).

Yamazawa, Ippei and Akihito Asano, 1996. Trade-investment and productivity nexus in Asia-Pacific: Review of Existing Studies, *Working Paper APEC/SC/HIT/DP, No. 7*, March.

[13]

Corporate interaction, direct investment and regional cooperation in industrializing Asia

Economic growth in Asia over the past decade has been the envy of the world. During the 1980s and early 1990s, economic ties between East Asian countries intensified, and closer regional trade links have made an important contribution to the region's economic growth. Significantly, deeper regional integration in East Asia has coincided with greater overall openness of their economies and an ongoing liberalization of their trade and investment regimes. Through policy reform, the structure of East Asian countries' production is becoming increasingly based on comparative advantage, and their ability to absorb more sophisticated foreign technology was enhanced by rapidly growing direct foreign investment (DFI) flows. *Prima facie* evidence suggests that a virtuous cycle is at work in East Asia, with DFI contributing to export growth, which in turn creates pressures for further trade and investment liberalization and even greater volumes of DFI flows.

The increase in regional interdependence is unique in that it has not been due to one hegemon at the 'core' that leads integration, though surely Japan has played an important role. In fact, over the 1986–92 period, the sources of East Asian DFI were primarily intraregional: half of all DFI flows in the region originated in other East Asian countries (predominantly Hong Kong, Singapore, Korea and Taiwan); less than one-fifth originated in Japan and only one-tenth came from the United States and Western Europe (United Nations 1995). The sectoral composition of DFI has also been changing. In earlier periods, investment from advanced industrial countries were channelled primarily into natural resource-based industries and related sectors, while in more recent years the newly industrialized economies (NIEs) have been investing primarily in manufacturing, especially in electrical machinery, electronics, non-ferrous metals and chemicals.

This chapter considers the emergence of Asian developing countries as a source of DFI in the region and their role in spurring regional interdependence. While triad countries continue to be critical investors in the region, developed-country DFI in Asia has been extensively analysed elsewhere in the literature, as well as in other contributions to this volume. The role of developing Asian countries is often under-estimated and, hence, the bulk of our analysis is focused on non-triad investment. We begin in the next section with a theoretical approach to corporate strategies and policy formation, with a special application to developing Asia. While this model can be generalized, it is particularly relevant in explaining the role that foreign investors have played in the Asian liberalization process. Next, as a large part of Asian economic integration is due to the interaction of (overseas and Mainland) Chinese firms, we consider the web of Chinese corporate connections in regional trade and investment. While the literature on the interactions of overseas Chinese in Asia is fairly extensive, it mainly pertains to social and cultural considerations rather than explicit empirical evidence. Hence, much of this analysis is anecdotal, except at the national level where data are more easily retrievable (but in which case analysis of overseas Chinese interactions are indirect). In the subsequent section we discuss the case of DFI in mainland China, where overseas Chinese are clearly the most important foreign investors.

However, it is not only the Chinese who have emerged as major investors in the region; DFI from Korea has increased rapidly since the mid-1980s when regulations on outward DFI began to be lifted and the structural change in the Korean economy provided a push to such investment. We therefore analyse some econometric evidence of the determinants of Korean investment abroad as an example of 'non-triad' DFI.

Policy-led regional economic integration has not been a force in Asian economic integration to date, but the creation of the ASEAN free trade area in 1992 is a sign of things to come. Arguably, formal economic integration accords will play an important part in facilitating corporate integration in the region. In the final section we consider new developments in regional integration, as well as the mechanisms through which these accords will affect corporate strategies, and we offer some concluding remarks.

A model of DFI and policy formation

Although there is no general consensus as to what the 'Asian model' of economic development is (or, in fact, if one exists), an important feature which is generally accepted as an integral component is the focus on outward orientation, as opposed to an import-substitution approach to industrialization. In fact, most Asian 'tigers' are essentially transitional economies, in which they are changing from import substitution to outward orientation and export promotion. They have succeeded to varying degrees; the Asian currency crisis of 1997 will no doubt affect the speed of economic reform, but it is not clear in which direction.

While the international trade aspects of an import-substitution paradigm have been analysed extensively in the literature, the role of DFI as an important force for liberalization has been almost totally ignored. Yet liberalization of trade policies in Asia has taken place simultaneously with rapid increases in DFI inflows.

In an import-substitution orientated regime, there exists an investment policy dimension that is predicated on the same notion that countries should be self-sufficient and, to the greatest extent possible, independent of 'core-country' dominance, which has not only detrimental economic but also political implications.[1] In principle, the rule-of-thumb is to restrict or even ban DFI from sectors in which indigenous investors are able to function, and to put very stringent investment restrictions (for example, in the form of severe performance requirements) on others, especially in more advanced areas such as automobiles, electronics and capital equipment production in which there is little or no hope of successful domestic undertakings without foreign participation. In order to bring DFI into these latter areas, countries have to compensate for the high transactions costs of functioning in the inward-looking economy. This is redressed through the provision of tax and other fiscal incentives, but especially through high external protection, which is consistent with the overall development strategy anyway. Hence, DFI is directed to areas in which the country has comparative *disadvantage*.

The effects of DFI 'tariff hopping' has been explored fairly extensively in the literature.[2] Neoclassical theory argues that DFI in such sectors tends to stifle economic growth and development because it distorts relative prices, draws resources into inefficient sectors, creates incentives for rent-seeking, imposes demand constraints, and limits productivity-enhancing interaction with the international market place.

What do inward-looking policies imply for domestic policy formation? Import substitution is designed to reduce exposure to international markets; restrictive DFI policies also try to do this. In fact, DFI is permitted into the country *only as a means to support import substitution*; that is, DFI is allowed to flow to sectors in which the country has comparative disadvantage and, hence, can substitute for imports. Investment and trade are 'path dependent', that is, increases in investment into the country will be followed by increases in trade, similarly, increases in trade will be associated with increases in investment (Lee and Roland-Holst forthcoming; Petri and Plummer 1996). Hence, if investment and trade policies become more restrictive, it follows that the path will lead toward zero trade (extreme import substitution). This appears to be the logical conclusion to an 'effective' import-substitution regime.

However, this analysis is static in nature and arguably misses a critical policy dynamic that might distort the ostensible linearity of such 'path dependency', at least in the downward direction. In fact, it is possible that the DFI–trade interdependency sows the seeds of policy reform even in a standard import-substitution model.[3]

The argument could be advanced as follows. Suppose, as is typical, that foreign investors are attracted to a country in order to gain a special tax holiday and to enjoy protection in the manufacturing sector. With captive internal markets, affiliates of foreign multinationals will be able to reap extra-normal profits and, at least in the short run, may have little incentive to alter the current policy regime. Nevertheless, the presence of a foreign investor (who, since DFI in capital-intensive sectors is not footloose, will be present in the country for at least the medium term) adds an international dimension to the domestic economy that would not exist if DFI were prohibited. Foreign affiliates by their very nature are more dependent on imported inputs (often from their parents); relative to domestic firms, they will suffer more from a highly restrictive commercial policy regime and would tend to exert more pressure for liberalization. And as changes in tariff structures have the characteristics of being 'public goods', in that lobbying by one firm in a given sector will affect all firms in the sector, the influence of foreign affiliates may be disproportional. Additionally, since we have assumed that DFI is permitted in capital-intensive and high-tech sectors that often serve as inputs to the production of final goods, the effective rate of protection for these goods will increase, *ceteris paribus*. This allows the government to reduce nominal protection in the final-goods sector without changing the amount of protection accorded domestic value added.

Moreover, the evolving modern economy is characterized by an increasing global division of labour in which international affiliates become part of a larger production chain. Foreign affiliates in inward-looking economies will be cut off from these networks, and the pace of globalization of production makes such a situation increasingly costly.[4] One might also consider the international ramifications of such incentives for liberalization, as a country may need to be more responsive to the demands of foreign affiliates if they must compete for DFI with other countries.[5]

Linking the effects of trade policy innovations to changes in investment is certainly not new to the literature. However, existing work tends to focus on how altering tariffs induces changes in relative factor demands and, hence, factor returns (in the case of a fixed capital stock). If endogenous capital accumulation is permitted, protection could have a permanent effect on the growth rate, no doubt one incentive for an import-substitution regime. As noted by Baldwin and Seghezza (1996), there is a problem with this approach, not the least of which is that it ignores the stylized facts. They develop a dynamic model to test for 'trade-induced, investment-led growth' taking into account the cost of protection on imported intermediate goods, which has an 'anti-investment' aspect to weigh against the 'pro-investment effect'. While they do not consider DFI in the same way as we do here, the intuition is the same, in that they focus on the secondary distortions caused by the protective environment. On the other hand, Froot and Yoffie (1993) construct a model in which 'traditional' sectors not characterized by economies of scale will have a weakened incentive to protect (and, in fact, will push for liberalization) as production becomes increasingly mobile internationally. Ultimately over time, this will be true even for sectors exhibiting increasing returns:

> And to the extent that foreign direct investment occurs, and as long as it is an imperfect substitute for trade, it should diminish the force of increasing returns-based arguments for domestic protection. Foreign firms with local production (and local employment) will advocate liberalization. (Froot and Yoffie 1993: 146)[6]

Figures 7.1 and 7.2 present our argument more formally from the perspective of foreign affiliates of multinationals ('foreign firms') operating in a developing country. Figure 7.1 shows the costs and benefits associated with a protected environment using the framework outlined above. Benefits from 'special preferences' take the form of special protection through tariffs and non-tariff barriers, fiscal incentives, and so on. We assume that these benefits can be quantified in money terms for the firm and reflected in a 45-degree line through the origin. The 'demand costs' (DC) associated with the protected environment are increasing in special preferences, as the efficiency costs associated with greater protection grow at an increasing rate.[7] Hence, the DC curve exhibits positive first- and second-order conditions; its slope will be a function of a number of national characteristics of the host country, for example, its dependence on international trade. A country like Singapore, for example, will have an extremely steep DC curve (see DC), as its international trade comes to over three times national value added. However, the slope of the curve will also depend on the production function of the industry, with more imported-input-dependent sectors having steeper DC curves.

In addition, we could include the cost of lobbying in this model. After all, this is the essence of the endogenous tariff literature: the higher the level of protection that politicians[8] grant, the greater the cost to the economy and, hence, the larger the cost to them in terms of votes. Politicians force lobbyists to pay more in order to obtain marginal increases in protection. The tariff level that optimizes the private-welfare functions of economic agents and politicians will be the one where the marginal cost of lobbying is exactly equal to the marginal (private) benefits of increased protection. This is the 'endogenous tariff'. However, while it is debatable how well this form

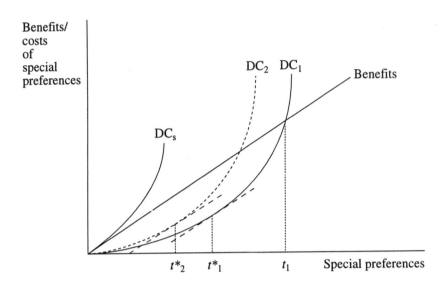

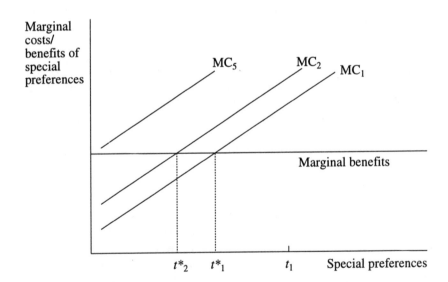

Note: DC = Demand Costs

Figure 7.1 Costs and benefits of a protective environment to foreign firms

of bargaining reflects the commercial policy determination process in developed countries (for which the model was created), the process in developing countries – particularly in Asia – is fundamentally different. While it still may be reasonable to assume that the costs associated with lobbying are positive, it is not necessarily true that these costs will be increasing in special preferences. Nevertheless, assuming zero, linear or increasing costs associated with lobbying will not affect our analysis here; rather, it will merely affect the slope of the DC line.

In Figure 7.1, foreign firms will break even at the point where the DC_1 curve cuts the benefits curve (t_1). However, from its perspective, the optimal level of protection will be at t_1^*, that is, where the marginal costs of the protective regime to foreign firms are exactly equal to marginal benefits. Now, suppose that, over time, the costs associated with protection change in the light of a more sophisticated division of labour (and, hence, greater reliance on international sources) and of dynamic inefficiencies spawned by the import-substitution regime. In this case, any given level of special preferences will be associated with higher demand costs; the DC shifts to the left (to DC_2) and the endogenous tariff decreases to t_2^*. In other words, foreign firms either reduce their lobbying activities or, perhaps, lobby proactively in favour of liberalization. Once again, the magnitude of the DC curve shift and, hence, the change in the endogenous tariff will be a function of both host-country-specific and industry-specific characteristics.

Another way to look at this problem from the foreign firms' perspective is to consider the effective rate of protection (ERP) facing the industry, which captures the degree to which actual value added in an industry is being protected.[9] Figure 7.2 focuses on the effects of a changing international division of labour on the structure of net benefits accruing to the foreign firm (that is, as proxied through ERP). We adopt the same notation from the ERP literature for simplicity. Advantages of a protective environment

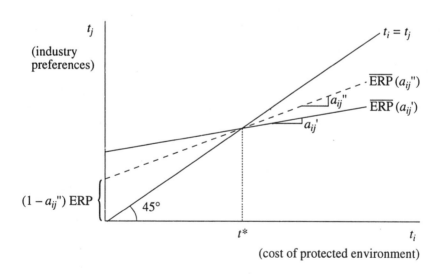

Notes:
1. $ERP = (t_j - a_{ij}t_i)/(1 \times a_{ij})$, $t_j = (1 \times a_{ij}) ERP + a_{ij}t_i$.
2. At t^*, $t_i = t_j = ERP$.

Figure 7.2   Costs of protection under alternative input–output coefficient assumptions

are grouped into t_{ji}, whereas the costs of the protected environment are denoted by t_i. Along the ERP (...) lines, the ERP is constant; as protection increases, the ERP lines show by how much industry preferences have to increase in order to prevent the ERP from changing, given a_{ij}. Hence, at $t_i = 0$, $t_j = (1 - a_{ij})$ ERP and, of course, $t_i = t_j =$ ERP where ERP (...) crosses the 45-degree line (for example, at t^* in Figure 7.2).

The curves ERP (a_{ji}') and ERP (a_{ij}'') correspond to the same ERP under different assumptions of the input–output coefficient a_{ij}. The larger a_{ij} the greater the change required in t_j for a given change in t_i if the ERP is to remain constant. Therefore, with a changing international division of labour such that foreign affiliates engage in a greater degree of specialization and rely more on imported inputs, a_{ij} increases and, at the margin, the cost of the protected environment to foreign firms increases. This implies a stronger incentive to push for liberalization.[10]

It should be noted that many of the arguments developed above can be applied to domestic firms as well, especially in terms of the direction of the marginal incentives for liberalization. In fact, it would be a great stretch indeed to attribute the rapid liberalization programmes of East Asian economies to foreign firms alone; clearly, many domestic firms, as well as growth-minded policy-makers with their minds on the economy rather than votes, played essential roles. In fact, while DFI can sometimes constitute a significant amount of capital formation in certain sectors, only in a few East Asian countries (for example, in city-states of Singapore and Hong Kong and in Malaysia) has DFI constituted much more than 10 per cent of domestic capital formation. However, as argued here, it is likely that affiliates of foreign firms will be affected more at the margin by these trends and, hence, will be more inclined to push for reform (though, clearly, they will not be the only ones).

In sum, in the modern international economy, there exist strong incentives for countries to keep open trade and investment regimes, and DFI can serve as an important catalyst, regardless of whether it comes from developed or developing countries.

Overseas Chinese and corporate relationships
The private-sector economy in South East Asia is controlled largely by ethnic Chinese, a fact that has led to delicate social considerations and balancing over the years. For example, prior to the New Economic Policy in Malaysia in 1969, which led to a highly aggressive affirmative action programme in favour of indigenous Malays (*bumiputra*), up to 90 per cent of the private sector was controlled by ethnic Chinese; 25 years later, that ratio would fall to around two-thirds, but still a high proportion considering that ethnic Chinese in Malaysia comprise approximately one-third of the population. It is, perhaps, easiest to ascertain the magnitude of Chinese capital in South-East Asia in the cases of Malaysia and Indonesia, where they stand out culturally, but it is much more difficult to do so in the case of Thailand, where Chinese over the years have been closely integrated into the indigenous population. Clearly, the vast majority of the populations of Singapore, Hong Kong and Taiwan is Chinese, and these economies form the core of Chinese corporate interaction.

This is not to suggest that the *economies* of South-East Asia are necessarily dominated by ethnic Chinese. After independence, South-East Asian economies became largely state-directed, with abundant natural resources allowing for the perpetuation of myriad state-owned and/or state-directed enterprises. Hence, the private sector was restricted to various degrees in each economy, thereby limiting the potential for a strong 'dominance' on the part of the ethnic Chinese. Yoshihara (1988) in his oft-cited study refers to the 'rise of ersatz capitalism in Southeast Asia', with ersatz capitalism denoting state-control, rather than ethnic-Chinese or foreign dominance.

According to Yoshihara (1988: 51), in the resource-rich ASEAN countries Chinese capital is dominant in the banking and light industries sectors and has a substantial presence in property development, mining, plantation agriculture, trade and machinery. Private indigenous capital, on the other hand, is dominant in no sector and has a substantial presence only in banking, property development and plantation agriculture. In all manufacturing sectors, indigenous capital plays a minor role.

The large presence of ethnic Chinese in the private sector of South-East Asia has been ascribed to many factors, including the influence of colonialists in bringing Chinese into their colonies as merchants, as well as cultural dispositions on the part of both the Chinese and the indigenous population (Yoshihara 1988).[11] Thus, the success of Chinese corporate strategies relied not only on a unique system of relationships but also on state patronage at a crucial period.

Overseas Chinese corporate interactions tend to be based on informal relationships that place a strong emphasis on trust. As these relationships often evolve in an under-developed legal environment – compounded by problems associated with more than one country in the case of an overseas joint venture – informal contracts and commitments must be enforced somehow, and this is done by reputation. If a party reneges on a contact or does not pull through, this 'loss of face' could be devastating and might severely impede the ability to undertake future business.

Thus, it is understandable that business partnerships are arranged between parties who are not only familiar to each other on a personal level but also have established a strong bond of trust. These ventures usually begin within families or extended families and often stay family-centred (Yoshihara 1988). Moreover, in overseas Chinese communities, common regional roots and language tend to be important (according to the many Chinese dialects) and a strong emphasis is placed on interactions at the communal level.

These types of arrangements tend to be flexible, long-lasting, and lucrative, as evidenced by the great success of overseas Chinese. However, there have been social problems in host countries, as the Chinese are often seen to be exclusionary *vis-à-vis* non-Chinese. This in turn has led to a less-favourable social and business environment for the Chinese, at times leading to bloodshed.

Direct investment in mainland China
Given the strong linguistic and cultural affinities between overseas Chinese and mainland China, it is not difficult to predict that ethnic Chinese capital would be among the first to take advantage of the opening up of the Chinese market which began with Deng's Four Modernizations in 1979. With rising wages in key markets such as Singapore, Hong Kong, Thailand and Malaysia, coupled with increasingly fluid international capital markets as the 1980s progressed, the locational advantages of cheap and abundant labour in mainland China and an increasingly hospitable local investment environment proved extremely attractive. Moreover, the traditional nature of doing business between ethnic Chinese made the lack of a strong legal framework

less problematic in arranging business ventures, though they clearly influenced the type of arrangement.

A number of studies (for example, Thoburn *et al.* 1990) survey issues pertinent not only to the importance of overseas Chinese investment in China but also to the rationale for mainland China's courting of this capital. Four major motivations on the part of the Chinese government are frequently cited:

1. to diversify and modernize the economic structure of China;
2. to bring in foreign know-how, business practices, expertise and especially new technologies;
3. to tap into ready-made foreign markets and international production chains; and
4. to create additional sources of capital and foreign exchange.

These motivations are not unlike those of other developing countries; however, the size and transitional nature of the Chinese economy, coupled with the strong desire to catch up after years of autarky under Mao, in many ways made these needs more acute.

Pan and Tse (1996) test a series of hypotheses regarding investor motivations in China and corporate strategies. In particular, they focus on the strategies of foreign firms in forming cooperative relationships with *other* foreign firms. *Inter alia*, they find that a foreign firm would be more likely to bring another foreign firm into a cooperation venture as: (a) the risk level in China increases; (b) foreign firms choose a high-control mode of operation, such as equity joint ventures instead of contractual joint ventures; and (c) bilateral trade with China increases. Moreover, they note that Japanese firms in China are more likely to form a joint venture with another foreign firm than is the case for other triad countries.

Aggregate data on DFI give a strong indication of the importance of ethnic Chinese investment in mainland China at the macro level. Table 7.1 shows actual DFI flows in China by investing country/region. Total DFI flows into China have grown rapidly, from under $2 billion in 1985 to $3.5 billion in 1990 (Plummer and Montes 1995).

Table 7.1   Direct investment in China: actual investment flows ($ million)

	1985	1988	1990
Total	1956	3199	3487
of which			
Japan	315	515	503
United States	357	236	456
Hong Kong/Macau	956	2095	1913
Germany	24	15	64
France	33	23	21
United Kingdom	71	34	13
Australia	14	4	25
Singapore	10	28	50

Source: China Free Trade and Price Statistics/China Statistical Yearbook, various years.

More recent data show that DFI inflows in the 1990s were many times as large, growing to $34 billion in 1994 and $38 billion in 1995.[12] The data are more impressive when it is considered that before the 1980s DFI in China was essentially zero.

Hong Kong/Macau continue to be the largest investors in China, particularly in Guangdong Province, with a total of $1.9 billion in 1990, which has increased from less than $1 billion in 1985. The second largest investors are Japan and the United States, with investments of $503 million and $456 million, respectively. However, Singapore exhibits the fastest increase in China over the 1985–90 period, rising from $10 million to $50 million. Official and unofficial investment from Taiwan, which is not reported in the statistics, and from Korea, whose presence is undoubtedly large in north-east China, are also large and are growing in importance (Kim 1995).

Clearly, the rapid increase in ethnic Chinese DFI is noteworthy. In fact, a great deal of DFI in China flows through Hong Kong in partnership with developed-country multinationals, which form joint ventures with Hong Kong firms due to its 'competitive advantage' in investing in China. While the return of Hong Kong to China in 1997 holds some political risks, it could reduce significantly the transactions costs of doing business in China through Hong Kong and, hence, the latter might serve as an even more attractive conduit of international investment into the mainland. This was probably a motivation behind the business community's pro-Chinese stance in the years leading up to the changeover.

Economic growth in China is concentrated in the coastal regions (see, for example, Lardy 1994). By far, Guangdong Province is the largest recipient of direct investment, with $1.2 billion in 1989 alone, followed by Shanghai ($422 million), Fujian ($329 million) and Beijing ($318 million) (Plummer and Montes 1995). This investment flows from Hong Kong or from Hong Kong–foreign joint ventures (often with Taiwan). Liaoning and Shandong Provinces, which have benefited from Korean DFI, also have DFI projects amounting to over $100 million. In part, these figures are a reflection of the increase in outward DFI from South Korea. This DFI flow has been induced by a combination of Korean restructuring, fundamental economic and political policy changes and rapidly rising wage rates. Thus, reforms in the NIEs as well as in China have generated the DFI flows to China (see Lee and Plummer 1992).

Direct Taiwanese investment flows appear to have concentrated mainly in Fujian Province. Total approved Taiwan investment flows in China came to $5.1 billion over the 1991–95/6 period, electronics and electrical machinery ($775 million), food and beverages ($591 million) and plastic products ($563 million) being the three largest sectors (Tu 1997). As noted above, these figures generally exclude DFI flows through Hong Kong and other vehicles. Interestingly, the size of Taiwanese investment in China has been kept relatively low by Taiwanese – rather than mainland Chinese – government restrictions, as officials are nervous about the political ramifications of an unduly large presence of Taiwanese investment in the mainland.

Thoburn *et al.* (1990) survey the distribution of foreign investment under various kinds of contracts in China. This is done for the 1985–88 period for both China and Guangdong Province, where the role of overseas Chinese capital is arguably strongest. They find that equity joint ventures in 1988 constituted 51 per cent of contracts in China compared to 39 per cent in Guangdong, whereas contractual joint ventures are more popular in Guangdong (39 per cent compared to 26 per cent). However, in both cases, the share of equity joint ventures had increased substantially since 1985. Moreover, the share of contracts associated with 'processing and assembly, compensation trade and international leasing' experienced a rapid growth rate for China and Guangdong, comprising 14 per cent and 18 per cent respectively, of all contracts in 1988.

Determinants of outward DFI from industrializing Asia: the case of Korea

There is no reason to believe that outward DFI from developing countries should be determined by different motivations than developed countries on the whole, though the divergent stages of economic development suggest that DFI would flow to different industries and countries than might be the case of developed-country DFI. It could be expected that the major contribution to the theory of the determinants of DFI (see, for example, Rugman 1980, and Dunning 1988) should, therefore, be generally independent of the stage of economic development of the capital-exporting country. In this section, we try to gauge the determinants of Korean DFI using a simple cross-sectional model. We limit the analysis to Korea, given the difficulties of obtaining reliable, disaggregated DFI data for the other NIEs.

As noted above, the Korean government severely restricted outward DFI outflows before 1985. Since then, they have been gradually liberalized, and Korea has emerged as an important investor not only in north-eastern China but also in the ASEAN countries. Moreover, it has been involved in 'reverse DFI' in developed countries; that is, outward investment to the United States and Europe in order to set up distribution networks and acquire new technologies.

DFI theory suggests a wide variety of potential determinants to be examined in empirical analysis. While estimation of ownership and internalization motivations are beyond the scope of our study, we focus on locational considerations, which have been at the heart of empirical analysis of DFI determinants in the economics literature.

We use DFI data from the Bank of Korea, *Overseas Direct Investment Statistics*, 1992 and 1995, in order to gain intuition into the determinants of Korean investment abroad, including the trade–investment nexus.[13] The model estimated includes standard variables suggested by theory, such as distance, general measures of market supply potential (GDP), and potential market demand (population), as well as exports. Because of this selection of variables, the model resembles the familiar gravity models of the empirical trade literature. Although sometimes criticized for their weak theoretical foundations in the trade context, gravity models also provide a natural framework for the analysis of DFI flows.

Our model specification is of the following form:

$$\text{DFI} = f\,\{\text{GDP, POP, DIST, Asdum, EXP}\,(t, t-1, t+1)\}$$

where:
GDP = host-country gross domestic product, a proxy for market potential (supply side);

Pop = host-country population, a proxy for potential market demand;

DIST = distance between the investor and host countries, a proxy for transactions costs;

Asdum = a regional dummy variable for the ASEAN countries;
EXP   = contemporaneous, lagged, and 'forward-loaded' Korean exports, a proxy
         for transactions costs and for market receptivity for the source country's
         products.

The leads and lags in exports were estimated as a means of avoiding the inherent
simultaneity problems. However, as trade and investment decisions are undertaken
simultaneously, it is unlikely that the simultaneity problem can be avoided entirely.
Predictably, lag structure made very little difference in the results of the regressions.
    The Korean DFI data are sufficient for regressions at the aggregate manufactures
level and for labour-intensive manufactures. While it would have been useful to
have further disaggregation, paucity of data precluded such analysis. The results
are presented in Table 7.2 for both single-year (1992) and pooled data (1992 and
1995).

Table 7.2   Determinants of Korean DFI

Independent variable	All manufactures		Labour-intensive manufactures	
	DFI 1992	Pooled[a]	DFI 1992	Pooled[a]
Constant	11681[b]	−1033[b]	−1707	−1768
GDP	−0.14	−1.2	0.46	−0.1
Pop	49.92[d]	7.9[c]	5.2[d]	6.6[d]
Distance	0.36	1.7[d]	0.43	0.35
ASEAN	2084[d]	985	1850[b]	3476[d]
Exp.^{2}	0.001[d]	0.001	0.01[b]	0.02[d]
Adj. R^2	0.19	0.06	0.19	0.13
N	67	155	37	83

Notes:
a In the pooled observations, a time binary variable was added in order to capture any difference between
years. It was statistically insignificant except in the case of labour-intensive manufactures, where the estimated
coefficient came to 1503 and was statistically significant at the 95 per cent level.
b Significance at the 85 per cent level.
c Significance at the 90 per cent level.
d Significance at the 95 per cent level.
Lag structure of exports makes little or no difference in the results of the regressions.

    Several general results obtain. First, the R^2s are fairly low; in all cases, the model
explained less than 20 per cent of the variance in the dependent variable. This is
probably to be expected, given the relatively few degrees of freedom in the regressions
and the complicated nature of outward Korean investment, in which the government
continues to play an important regulatory role. Estimated coefficients on the size
variables (GDP and population) tend to be of the expected sign (where statistically
significant), suggesting that size does, indeed, matter. The positive estimate coefficients for the distance variable give credence to the argument that firms will choose
to invest abroad – rather than export directly – over longer distances. Further, the

regression results support the importance of the trade-investment link; exports are positively correlated with DFI. The ASEAN binary variable is statistically significant in three out of the four reported regressions and is always estimated to be positive (and tends to be larger) in the case of labour-intensive manufactures.

Regional and corporate integration in East Asia

Increasingly, developing countries have been placing a stronger emphasis on technology transfer in their multilateral and bilateral relationships. The evidence of this is ubiquitous, from the preponderance of requests for technical assistance in development aid and cooperation programmes to the 'virtuous cycle' of policy liberalization stemming from the desire to promote DFI capital inflows as a means of private-sector-led technology transfer. Regional economic integration accords can promote DFI inflows through reductions in transactions costs (whether they are border or non-border in origin); in doing so, they are able to establish an attractive business environment within which multinationals can easily profit from a vertical division of labour, as well as facilitating the emergence of multinationals within the developing region itself.[14] Of course, the same is true for developed countries. Also, as is noted in the theoretical model above (p. 194), DFI inflows can set in motion a virtuous cycle of policy reform that will support the liberalization process.

Hence, regional economic integration accords can help to enhance the locational attractiveness of a region. In fact, particularly in the highly integrated world economy of the 1990s, the 'externalities' associated with good or bad policies in one country often spill over to its neighbours. Lower transactions costs in the region, by freeing up trade and investment, will through, say, a free-trade area and ancillary agreements not only make for a more attractive regional business environment but also highlight the importance of one country's investment policies for the rest of the region. Regional economic integration can help to internalize this externality by providing regional rules as well as constant dialogue and peer pressure.

Developing countries tend to place a stronger emphasis on technology transfer than, say, developed countries because of the greater technological gap which may be evident in not only production technologies, but also management techniques, other business practices, corporate culture and various training programmes. The ASEAN free-trade area (AFTA), for instance, was created mainly as an instrument to attract more DFI to the region at a time when competition for such flows was deemed to be increasing (especially from China, but also from South Asia and Latin America). Some have even described AFTA as more of an investment pact than a trade pact (Ariff 1996).

Although the link between DFI and technology transfer has been firmly established, the relationship between trade and technology transfer is less well known. Through trade liberalization, countries are also able to stimulate technological development. For example, trade leads to the adaptation of new technologies from abroad by increasing the potential for success in using these technologies to crack foreign markets; also, increased competition forces domestic firms to place a higher priority on creating their own or importing new technologies (Pissarides 1995). This implies a strong incentive for developing countries which emphasize technology transfer (for example, all East Asian countries) to liberalize even unilaterally.

Moreover, in order to take best advantage of these new technologies, countries find that they must establish strong intellectual property protection laws and means of enforcement. Without an attractive, protective environment in which multinationals can operate and in which domestic firms can invest in new innovations, the process of technology transfer is significantly inhibited. Formal regional economic integration agreements can help in creating a strong underlying framework for the protection of intellectual property, and peer pressure in the implementation of associated laws.[15]

While there exists a substantial literature on the advantages and disadvantages of formal regional economic integration accords, the debate ultimately centres on the effect of such accords on domestic policy formation. For example, the North American Free Trade Agreement (NAFTA) was sold in the United States more as a means of encouraging further economic reform in Mexico than for its trade creation/diversion merits or de-merits. Most scholars, policy-makers, and business people would support formal regional integration if it leads to a more favourable policy environment. In Asia, where *de facto* formal accords did not exist until 1992 – when AFTA was formed – regional economic integration programmes were being developed as part of a *process* of economic reform, rather than as a separate policy strategy. There is a strong emphasis on 'open regionalism' in AFTA; the Philippines has tabled a proposal (backed by Singapore and Indonesia) to multilateralize intraregional tariff cuts. Moreover, the only region-wide arrangement in the Asia-Pacific, the Asia-Pacific Economic Cooperation (APEC) organization, appears to be committed to forming a region of 'open trade and investment' in a non-discriminatory way. This will lead to a more open environment in which to do business, particularly since most of the inter-action in APEC and increasingly in AFTA regards nuts-and-bolts policies related to trade and investment facilitation measures, which often constitute the most important 'taxes' on regional trade and investment (Cecchini 1988).

Overseas Chinese have played a critical role in bringing the region together through trade and investment. It is likely that, as China continues to liberalize and Korea and Taiwan lift restrictions on outward and inward DFI, this will continue to be the case. In this chapter, we have reviewed the nature of Chinese corporate interactions and, more generally, the role of DFI originating from the NIEs, using the case of Korea as a (non-Chinese) example of a non-triad, new source of DFI in the region. However, the analysis was mainly at the macro level; to get the best picture of corporate inter-action, alliances and strategies in developing Asia, one must rely on micro data and case studies. We have cited a number of studies which have shed some light on the many issues involved, but clearly more work remains to be done.

Notes

1. The political implications of a large foreign investment presence are especially important in the case of developing countries which are at early stages of building their nation-states (for example, in Asia) or those which have had a history of political and economic excesses in their relationship with a developed country (for Latin America, the United States; for Africa, Europe). The import-substitution paradigm becomes popular in such an environment even independently of any theoretical claims to economic effectiveness.
2. This body of analysis, most elegantly articulated by the 'immizerating-growth' literature, finds a key theoretical contribution in Bhagwati (1971).
3. A related point applied to the context of regional economic integration is found in Petri and Plummer (1996).
4. Of course, this will also be true of domestic firms. But foreign affiliates will tend to be more conscious

of the problem and, in any event, more dependent on this global network of which they are a necessary part.

5. We would like to thank Professor Shigeyuki Abe for pointing out this possibility.
6. Hence, Froot and Yoffie (1993) approach the liberalization incentive from the *national* perspective; in this chapter we argue that foreign firms will play an important (though by no means unique) role in moulding this incentive.
7. While the existing endogenous protection literature also makes this assumption as a means of proxying costs from the *economy-wide* perspective (discussed below), we focus here on the firm: a more distorted environment makes doing business more costly on the supply side, and chokes off sales on the demand side.
8. This is because efficiency losses of protection are assumed to be increasing in special preferences.
9. We assume non-negative ERPs here because: (a) it is not clear in this model why a foreign firm would opt to enter into a country giving it a negative ERP; and (b) firms would certainly find it in their interests to lobby for liberalization in the case of negative ERPs, as the protective environment works to their detriment.
10. In theory, the change in the international division of labour could just lead the foreign firms to lobby for more protection, possibly creating an additional round of protection increases (particularly if product *j* is used as an intermediate input). But if we assume non-zero costs to lobbying and the general equilibrium effects of such reaction, the probability of this response is lower.
11. Yoshihara (1988) is the most exhaustive book in the literature and surveys not only the origins of ethnic Chinese in the region but also histories of the more important families.
12. These data are from ADB (1997) but should be treated with caution. As is noted elsewhere in this volume, DFI data are notorious for being inaccurate in both developed and developing countries. None the less, they serve as important indicators.
13. For a closer examination of the trade–investment nexus and the Korean regressions in a cross-country context, see Kreinin *et al.* (1999; Chapter 8 in this volume), on which this section draws.
14. ASEAN multinationals, for example, have been increasing in number and importance since the creation of AFTA. In fact, some of the largest investors in Vietnam are ASEAN-based, with ASEAN DFI accounting for fully 20 per cent of the country's total.
15. Having recognized this, the ASEAN countries have developed a regional framework or intellectual property protection.

References

Ariff, Mohamed (1996), 'Outlooks for ASEAN and NAFTA externalities', in Shoji Nishijima and Peter H. Smith (eds), *Cooperation or Rivalry? Regional Integration in the Americas and the Pacific Rim*, Boulder, Col.: Westview Press, pp. 209–24.

Asian Development Bank (ADB) (1997), *Asian Development Outlook 1997 and 1998*, Manila: Asian Development Bank.

Baldwin, Richard E. and Elena Seghezza (1996), 'Testing for trade-induced, investment-led growth', NBER Working Paper 5416, Washington, DC: NBER.

Bhagwati, Jagdish N. (1971), 'The generalized theory of distortions and welfare', in J. Bhagwati *et al.* (eds), *Trade, the Balance of Payments, and Growth*, Amsterdam: North-Holland.

Cecchini, Paolo (1988), *The Costs of Non-Europe*, Brussels: Commission of the European Communities.

Chen, Edward K.Y. and Teresa Y.C. Wong (1997), 'Hong Kong: foreign direct investment and trade linkages in manufacturing', in Wendy Dobson and Chia Siow Yue (eds), *Multinationals and East Asian Integration*, Ottawa: International Development Research Centre, ch. 4.

Dunning, John H. (1988), 'The eclectic paradigm of international production: a restatement and some possible extensions', *Journal of International Business Studies*, **19**(1), 1–31.

Froot, Kenneth A. and David B. Yoffie (1993), 'Trading blocs and the incentives to protect: implications for Japan and East Asia', in Jeffrey A. Frankel and Miles Kahler (eds), *Regionalism and Rivalry: Japan and the United States in Pacific Asia*, Chicago: University of Chicago Press, pp. 125–53

Kim, Si Joong (1995), 'Structural change in the Korean economy and Korean investment in China and ASEAN', in Sumner J. LaCroix, Michael G. Plummer and Keun Lee (eds), *Emerging Patterns of East Asian Investment in China: From Korea, Taiwan, and Hong Kong*, New York: M.E. Sharpe.

Kreinin, Mordechai E., Michael G. Plummer and Shigeyuki Abe (1997), 'Motives for Japanese DFI', mimeo.

Kreinin, Mordechai E., Michael G. Plummer and Shigeyuki Abe (1999), 'Export and direct foreign investment links: a three-way comparison', in Mordechai E. Kreinin, Michael G. Plummer and Shigeyuki Abe (eds), *Asia-Pacific Economic Linkages*, Oxford: Pergamon.

Lardy, Nicholas R. (1994), *China in the World Economy*, Washington, DC: Institute for International Economics.

Lee, Hiro and David Roland-Holst (eds) (forthcoming), *Economic Development and Cooperation in the Pacific Basin: Trade, Investment, and Environmental Issues*, New York: Cambridge University Press.

Lee, Keun and Michael G. Plummer (1992), 'Competitive advantages, two-way foreign investment, and domestic capital formation in Korea', *Asian Economic Journal*, **4**(2), 93–11.

Pan, Yigang and David K. Tse (1996), 'Cooperative strategies between foreign firms in an overseas country', *Journal of International Business Studies*, **27**(5), Special Issue.

Petri, Peter A. and Michael G. Plummer (1996), 'The determinants of direct foreign investment', Brandeis University Working Paper.

Pissarides, Christopher A. (1995), 'Trade and the returns to human capital in developing countries', mimeo, October.

Plummer, Michael G. and Manuel F. Montes (1995), 'Direct investment in China: an introduction', in Sumner J. LaCroix, Michael Plummer and Keun Lee (eds), *Emerging Patterns of East Asian Investment in China: From Korea, Taiwan, and Hong Kong*, New York: M.E. Sharpe.

Rodrik, Dani (1986), 'Tariff, subsidies, and welfare with endogenous policy', *Journal of International Economics*, **21**, 285–300.

Rodrik, Dani (1996), 'Understanding economic policy reform', *Journal of Economic Literature*, **xxxiv**, March, 9–41.

Rugman, Alan M. (1980), 'Internalization as a general theory of foreign direct investment: a re-appraisal of the literature', *Weltwirtschaftliches Archiv*, **116**(2), 365–79.

Rugman, Alan M. (1981), *Inside the Multinationals: The Economics of Internal Markets*, New York: Columbia University Press.

Rugman, Alan M. and Richard Hodgetts (1995), *International Business: A Strategic Management Approach*, San Francisco: McGraw-Hill.

Thoburn, John T., H.M. Leung, Esther Chau and S.H. Tang (1990), *Foreign Investment in China under the Open Policy: The Experience of Hong Kong Companies*, Aldershot, UK: Avebury.

Tu, Jenn-hwa (1997), 'Taiwan: a solid manufacturing base and emerging regional source of investment', in Wendy Dobson and Chia Siow Yue (eds), *Multinationals and East Asian Integration*, Ottawa: International Development Research Centre.

United Nations (1995), *World Investment Report 1995*, New York: United Nations.

Yamazawa, Ippei and Alcihito Asano (1996), 'Trade–investment and productivity nexus in Asia-Pacific: review of existing studies', Working Paper APEC/SC/HIT/DP, no. 7, March.

Yoshihara, Khnio (1988), *The Rise of Ersatz Capitalism in South-East Asia*, Singapore: Oxford University Press.

Zhang, Hai Yan and Daniel van den Bulcke (1996), 'International management strategies of Chinese multinational firms', in John Child and Yuan Lu (eds), *Management Issues in China*. Vol. II: *International Enterprises*, London: Routledge.

Zhang, Zhaoyang and Chen Kang (1997), 'China: a rapidly emerging light-manufacturing base in Guangdong Province', in Wendy Dobson and Chia Siow Yue (eds), *Multinationals and East Asian Integration*, Ottawa: International Development Research Centre.

[14]

The multilateralization of regional preferences: evidence from the Asia-Pacific[1]

The economic analysis of trade policy has traditionally assumed that most-favored-nation (MFN) liberalization and regional preferential agreements were distinct roads leading to different ends. Regional liberalization was discouraged and narrowly circumscribed by the framers of the GATT system. The original Agreement and subsequent amendments left room only for exceptions expected to be rare, specifically customs unions and free-trade areas that would completely remove internal barriers to trade (Article XXIV).

In the event, recent experience with preferential trading agreements (PTAs) has proved more positive than the framers of the GATT presumed. GATT's own remarkable growth has been paralleled by the rapid expansion of Europe's preferential relationships, creating the most successful customs union in history. While the European Union (EU) and its predecessors were expanding and liberalizing internally – at times breaking new ground in the degree of integration attempted – they also continued to play a central role in GATT negotiations. In light of this experience, Lawrence (1991) and others have raised the possibility that preferential agreements may be the 'building blocks' rather than the 'stumbling blocks' of global liberalization.

There are several mechanisms that appear to causally link preferential trading arrangements to global liberalization. Research on these issues is in an early stage, and some of the linkages identified here have not been adequately treated in previous literature. Three types of linkages can be distinguished. One set involves changes in *payoffs* to policy choices that come about as a result of a PTA. Specifically, a PTA's preferences for inefficient internal producers create incentives for member countries to reduce barriers toward third countries. Another set of linkages operates through changes in the *political economy* of protectionism. As a result of changes set into motion by a PTA, pro-trade interests expand, while the voice of specific anti-trade lobbies is diluted. Still other mechanisms involve changes in *outsiders'* behavior: countries excluded from an agreement become increasingly interested in joining, or at least in negotiating lower mutual barriers.

The complementarity of global and regional liberalization is especially striking in the Asia-Pacific. East Asian countries have simultaneously pursued regional and multilateral liberalization, and are designing their future regional arrangements with the global system in mind ('open regionalism'). These trends reflect East Asia's outward-looking policies, which encourage trade with both neighbors and distant partners, as well as dynamic factors that help to speed the multilateralization of regional liberalization measures. East Asia's *positive* experience is consistent with the *negative* experience of several African and Latin American countries, which failed to liberalize multilaterally, and then also failed to survive as viable regional blocs (McCulloch and Petri 1995).

The dynamics of preferential trade areas [2]

Unlike most analyses of PTAs, this study does not deal with immediate welfare consequences of PTAs, but rather with their effects on subsequent policy choices. This dimension is critical in interpreting the current trend toward regional agreements. Even if PTAs reduce current world income due to trade diversion, they could still benefit global welfare by triggering dynamic forces that favor multilateral liberalization.

We analyze the endogenous, dynamic consequences of regional PTAs in terms of seven specific linkages. Each proposition suggests a mechanism that leads to changes in the membership of the PTA and/or the policies of member countries toward non-member countries. Some, but not all, of these linkages unambiguously favor multi-lateral liberalization. A few, depending on parameters and circumstances, could lead to increased protectionism as well as further global integration. On balance, the theoretical arguments, as well as accumulating experience in East Asia and elsewhere, suggest that the dynamics of PTAs favors global liberalization.

Proposition 1: Reductions in trade barriers within a PTA make it more attractive to reduce external barriers, in effect 'MFN-izing' regional concessions.
The members of a PTA have good reason to avoid diverting their own imports from outside producers to regional partners, because this implies buying products at higher prices than could be found on world markets. To the extent that a country can do so given its domestic policy constraints, it will therefore reduce global barriers that protect its partners' less-than-globally-competitive products. Moreover, if countries anticipate these consequences, they will avoid forming PTAs that are attractive primarily because of their trade-diverting features.

As will be shown below, the members of Asia-Pacific trading arrangements generally lowered external barriers in parallel with internal barriers. Indeed, it is hard to find any successful regional trading bloc that has offered high extra-bloc protection for regional trade diversion. Two parallel scenarios are responsible for this result: either the members of a PTA reduce their extra-bloc barriers, or they back away from implementing regional preferences. In NAFTA and the ASEAN Free Trade Area (AFTA), reductions in regional barriers were either preceded or accompanied by reduction in extra-bloc barriers. In several unsuccessful regional blocs of Latin America and Africa, however, the members did not reduce extra-bloc barriers, but then also failed to implement regional preferences. Many of these arrangements then fell apart.

How quickly and effectively these forces work depends on whether the PTA is a free trade area (FTA) or a customs union (CU). The former allows each country to set barriers toward third countries; the latter requires joint decisions. It is easier for countries to avoid import trade diversion in FTAs than in CUs, because in the latter the partner benefiting from diversion plays a role in setting the PTA's external barriers. These considerations offset arguments against FTAs which are based on their ability to develop protectionist rules-of-origin policies (Krueger 1993). Most regional arrangements in recent years have taken the form of FTAs, and most have accompanied regional liberalization with reductions in extra-bloc barriers.

Proposition 2: The effects of a PTA on a country's production structure make the political economy of trade liberalization more favorable over time.
As a PTA opens an economy's industry to competition, sectors that cannot compete

within the region shrink, while those that can expand. In this process, the political balance tends to shift toward more trade-oriented interests. These changes may have enabled the EU and its predecessors, for example, to tackle an increasingly wide range of obstacles to the movement of goods, capital and labor, and generally reduced trade barriers facing non-members. Lawrence (1991) suggests that the European customs union allowed liberalization to move more rapidly than it would have had member countries retained their individual, nationalistic economic policies.

A formal model can be developed to reflect these considerations, along the lines proposed in McCulloch and Petri (1995). The model demonstrates that PTAs create a shift toward pro-trade politics by increasing the importance of pro-trade interest groups. As in other political economy models, trade policies are assumed to be determined not by general welfare considerations (which would yield free trade), but by a median voter. Each voter's interests are assumed to be tied to his or her role as a producer, which in turn are defined in terms of a specific-factor model. When trade is liberalized, sector-specific assets in import-competing industries depreciate, and those in export-oriented industries appreciate. This determines voting outcomes in the short run.

Over time, factors migrate from import-competing to export-oriented industries. Because even an increase in regional trade shifts capitalists and workers out of uncompetitive activities, the median producer becomes more trade-oriented over time. This story is consistent with the view that regional agreements can dominate (and possibly preempt) global agreements in the short run (Levy 1994), but it suggests that regional agreements also help to lay the foundations for global agreements down the road.

To demonstrate how this model works, consider a simple specification with Ricardian production. Here each sector's productivity is assumed to vary arbitrarily relative to the same sector in other countries. Then the only industries that would benefit from moving from autarky to free trade are those in which the country has lowest production costs (at the new equilbrium factor prices) relative to all partners. Since other industries, which make up the bulk of an autarkic economy's production structure, would decline with free trade, general liberalization will not be attractive to the median producer.

Although global free trade will not be acceptable in this setting, it may be possible to design viable regional trade agreements. What is needed is a regional partnership that is attractive to the median producer – presumably an industry that is regionally, but not globally, competitive. The PTA would thus divert trade to industries with median productivity, while 'weeding out' those industries that are even regionally uncompetitive. In turn, these shifts help to lay the groundwork for more trade-oriented decisions in the future.

This logic is illustrated below. To operationalize the random distribution of Ricardian productivity levels, we assume that the economy consists of six equal-sized sectors (labelled *a* through *f*), each of which bears a different productivity relationship *vis-à-vis* the rest of the world, as shown below. In the initial autarkic situation, Country 1 is assumed to produce in all six sectors, with 1/6th of demand and production involved in each. But Country 1 is not equally efficient in all six sectors, and in particular we assume that its costs (in labor units) vary relative to costs in Country 2 and the rest of the world (*w*) across the six sectors as follows:

Product a: $c_1 < c_2 < c_w$
Product b: $c_1 < c_w < c_2$
Product c: $c_2 < c_1 < c_w$
Product d: $c_2 < c_w < c_1$
Product e: $c_w < c_1 < c_2$
Product f: $c_w < c_2 < c_1$

If costs are constant, and Country 1 establishes free trade with both Country 2 and the rest of the world, it will most likely shift all of its resources into producing a and b and will import c through f. This will depreciate the sector-specific assets of two-thirds of all industries (c through f) which will be opposed to this policy. (Although somewhat different specialization patterns are also possible, depending on the relative sizes of the different economies, they would not change substantially the political economy calculus.)

Even if Country 1 is unwilling to liberalize globally, it may be willing to liberalize preferentially with Country 2. Under this narrower agreement, Country 1 will produce a, b and e, and import c, d and f. Only half of its producers will be opposed to the regional deal, and any other factor favorable to trade will tilt the median producer toward the agreement. For example, consumer gains, or even some previous trade with the partner before the agreement, which would have diminished the importance of industries that are likely to shrink under the agreement, would be enough to make the PTA attractive.

The most interesting implication, however, is the effect of the PTA on subsequent liberalization possibilities. The bloc will shift each country's industrial structure toward more efficient sectors. Starting from the post-bloc industrial configuration, even MFN liberalization will have a good chance at passing. Two-thirds of each country's industries (a and b in Country 1 – that is, those industries that are globally as well as regionally competitive) will agree to free trade, with only those industries opposed that were kept alive by trade diversion. Thus the regional PTA offers a feasible path from autarky to free trade. It 'divides and conquers' the opposition to liberalization by keeping alive industries that are regionally but not globally competitive.

Since the industries benefitting from trade diversion in a regional agreement will be ultimately eliminated under global free trade, one might expect that they will oppose the PTA in order to prevent the erosion of their political power. But because global free trade will not take place until after the regional agreement (it will take time for the political structure to change and for the broader agreement to be negotiated), this need not be the case. If the PTA lasts long enough, and/or discount rates are high enough, then the temporary 'diversion gains' of industries scheduled for later elimination may be large enough to earn their support. This dynamic perspective puts trade diversion into a new light. In the right circumstances, trade diversion is the payoff needed to muster political support for eventual open markets.

Proposition 3: *The membership of PTAs tends to expand and to become more diverse over time.*

In the course of its evolution, a typical PTA gradually enlarges its membership by bringing in increasingly diverse partners. In the case of Europe, for example, the six expanded to nine in 1973, and Greece, Spain and Portugal all joined in the 1980s. The last three, with economies quite different from the original six, brought with them opportunities for trade flows along stronger lines of comparative advantage. The US–Canada agreement, similarly, led to the inclusion of Mexico, the prospects for adding of Chile, and eventually including other Latin American countries.

The dynamics of blocs appears to favor a larger and more diverse membership for two reasons. First, along lines already argued, the establishment of a PTA changes the balance of producer interests in favor of greater international competition, and this will favor the admission of new, competitive countries. In addition, as Baldwin (1993) has argued, countries outside a bloc will lobby increasingly hard for membership in an expanding trade bloc (and will, perhaps, offer very attractive terms to be included) in order to avoid trade diversion and missing the benefits associated with participating in a larger market.

The attraction of membership is further intensified if other, parallel blocs begin to gain members, raising the possibility that a country will be discriminated against in most of its important trading relationships. Even if an economy favors a particular bloc (for example the EC rather than EFTA), it may decide to join a less desirable bloc rather than be left outside of all agreements. Taken together, these forces favor the expansion of blocs, despite predictable opposition from industries and countries that were initially bribed with diversion gains.

Pressures for expanding bloc membership are clearly operating in most of the Asia-Pacific's regional arrangements. As discussed below, AFTA has accepted Vietnam, and Cambodia and Laos are lobbying for early membership. APEC's membership has also expanded, and the organization has had to call a brief moratorium to resist pressures for admitting Russia, South Asia and Latin American countries while it pursues a 'deepening' of its regional liberalization strategy.

Proposition 4:   The establishment of a PTA dilutes the influence of protectionist interests in the bloc's decision-making processes.
Even those protectionist interests that manage to survive inside a PTA will find their influence diminished. De Melo and Panagariya (1992) have noted that protectionist interests will be diluted due to the expansion of the size of the political decision making entity. In their terms, the influence of any one interest group will be diminished since the group will have less influence on the area's decisions than on the decisions of its own country. Such dilution may mean that a larger area is less constrained by lobbying than a smaller area – as confirmed by the relatively liberal position of national vs. state and local governments in the United States.

Proposition 5:   The establishment of a PTA encourages other countries and blocs to liberalize.
A preferential trading scheme adopted by a group of countries also changes the policy incentives facing other countries and blocs. An important aspect is the coercive power of a large bloc: third countries may go out of their way to accommodate a bloc or to avoid confrontations with it. If the prospect of trade diversion is sufficiently threatening to countries outside a bloc, then they may be willing to join international agreements that limit a bloc's internal advantage by reducing barriers worldwide. Indeed, the

threat of a bloc may serve to hasten negotiations with outsiders. For example, American perceptions that the multilateral liberalization process had stalled in the late 1980s partly explains US interest in bilateral talks with Canada and other potential partners; the US hoped that these initiatives would increase enthusiasm in Europe for the GATT round.

Whether a world consisting of large blocs will have higher or lower trade barriers than a world without preferential arrangements is subject to some theoretical controversy. On one hand, Krugman (1991) argues that the greater market power of a bloc will give it more incentive to apply high 'optimal' tariffs. On the other hand, an environment that includes a small number of 'large' players is more likely to lead to negotiations that avoid globally suboptimal trade wars than an environment of more numerous smaller players.

The idea that blocs can 'ratchet up' the pace of global liberalization has been prominently argued by proponents of APEC, potentially the largest regional trading arrangement. For example, C. Fred Bergsten, the chair of APEC's Eminent Persons Group (EPG), has argued that the meeting of 15 APEC leaders in Seattle in 1993 played an important role in motivating European concessions in the waning days of the Uruguay Round. The ratchet theory was incorporated into the EPG's report calling for regional liberalization through APEC.[3] There is also evidence that the rapid progress of AFTA was prompted in part by liberalization in NAFTA.

For the sake of completeness, an effect working against global liberalization should be also noted. Specifically, the political economy of structural change will work against liberalization in countries left out of blocs. As blocs reduce the outsider's exports (due to trade diversion) they force that country toward an autarkic production structure with more weight on inefficient industries. Over time, in a mirror image to the structural changes taking place inside blocs, the excluded country's protectionist interests will grow relative to its liberal interests. These unfavorable dynamics, however, are likely to be offset by ratchet effects, that is, greater concessions by excluded countries.

Proposition 6:   The foreign investments attracted by a PTA will generate additional pressures for multilateral liberalization.
Several recent PTAs, including the case of AFTA discussed in more detail below, were developed in part to create an environment that attracts foreign direct investment from countries outside the region. This motivation is particularly important in the case of developing countries. Once these investors arrive, they are likely to become a force that favors additional liberalization both inside the region and toward third countries.

To be sure, foreign investors have mixed interests; they benefit from the protection afforded to regional producers, but they also pay discriminatory tariffs on inputs purchased from their third-country parents. In general, there is strong empirical evidence that foreign investment and trade are complementary, in part because intrafirm trade makes up an important share of total trade. Global production strategies increasingly call for a flexible network of trade among a firm's foreign subsidiaries. These subsidiaries and their parents, in turn, are likely to become an active lobby for general liberalization.

These issues are central in the decision-making of Asia-Pacific countries. In general, as the importance of foreign investment grows within a PTA, policy makers become increasingly sensitive to the factors that attract investment. These include reductions in barriers toward third countries, especially the home countries of investors. The parallel trade and investment liberalization initiatives of most Asia-Pacific countries, described below, confirms that the needs of foreign investors are important regional priorities, and generally lead to more liberal policies.

Proposition 7:   'New' liberalization measures adopted by PTAs pave the way for global agreements.

Because of their close economic relationships and greater capacity to negotiate complex agreements, PTAs can address a more ambitious liberalization agenda than is possible in global negotiations. Examples of such 'deep integration' include the harmonization of product standards, regulatory policies, government procurement, dispute resolution methods, and so on. In time, such measures could encourage global liberalization by offering models for worldwide agreements. In the interim, deep integration can also improve market access for non-member producers, since it increases the effective scale of PTA markets. It has been argued, for example, that harmonization in Europe ultimately benefitted US and other third-country companies by allowing them to enter Europe as a single market, without fighting for a beachhead in any one economy.

There is a danger, however, that harmonization within a PTA will be inconsistent with standards adopted elsewhere. This could happen whether or not regional agreements exist, but PTAs may make it easier for a group of countries to ignore others, or even to attempt to gain advantage by creating standards which favor internal producers. In the worst case, competing standards established by significant blocs could impede the development of global standards. Despite these possibilities, East Asian blocs have not appeared to use harmonization for competitive impediments, while diverging standards have emerged in the past without regional blocs (for example for television transmission).

Empirical evidence from the Asia-Pacific

The endogenous processes outlined so far tend to push trading blocs toward greater liberalization, or else hasten their demise. Rather than competing with global liberalization, regional agreements thus lead to the same ends. The Asia-Pacific region's experience confirms these propositions: those regional cooperation initiatives that survived have been motivated by the need to enhance international competitiveness and have led countries and regions to interact more effectively with the global economy.

ASEAN economic integration

ASEAN was established in 1967 mainly for political objectives, although economic cooperation – termed regional 'resource pooling and market sharing' – was among its original goals. Some early measures for cooperation were launched in the 1970s with modest effect, but in the 1980s economic objectives became a top ASEAN priority. Economic reforms in China, the resolution of the war in Indochina, rapid growth throughout East Asia and ASEAN, intensified international competition for foreign investment, and a shift in the region's domestic policies from import-substitution to export promotion all helped to make the environment favorable for ambitious co-operative efforts.

The decision to create an ASEAN Free Trade Area (AFTA) at ASEAN's Fourth Summit in January 1992 was a milestone in regional economic cooperation. While the original AFTA agreement had an extensive list of exclusions and a long implementation horizon, subsequent amendments made the agreement more comprehensive and shortened its time horizon (it will now be completed by 2003 or possibly even 2000). All ASEAN countries are slated to reduce the tariffs facing ASEAN partners to 0–5 percent. The ASEAN leaders have also committed themselves to other forms of cooperation in 'non-border areas', including trade facilitation. For example, 'action plans' in infrastructure, transport and communications are being formulated specifically to support the AFTA process, and the economic ministers will begin discussions on the regional liberalization of services in 1996 (ASEAN Update, October 1995).

The progressive escalation of AFTA's objectives exemplifies the complementarity of regional and MFN liberalization efforts. As is generally the case, it is hard to tell whether the momentum for MFN liberalization is a product of AFTA, or whether both are manifestations of a more open and competitive policy regime. But it is clear that regional and MFN liberalization efforts are being pursued in parallel, and that the regional approach alone would not be attractive to most ASEAN countries.

AFTA is not a 'natural bloc' and would make little sense without a broader liberalization strategy. Only one-fifth of ASEAN trade is intra-regional, and much of this trade is entrepot trade through Singapore. With Singapore excluded, only about 5 percent of ASEAN's trade is intra-regional. By traditional criteria, AFTA is a not a promising PTA because the prospects for trade creation are modest, and for trade diversion significant (Singapore aside, ASEAN economies are similar in their production structures and have relatively inefficient producers in many important industrial fields). Thus the goal of AFTA is not an inward looking bloc, but rather an economic zone that encourages foreign investment in competition with other regional groupings.

Because of its broader objectives, AFTA has warmly embraced 'open regionalism' by making it easy to multilateralize regional tariff reductions. Singapore and Indonesia have already announced that they intend to make all of their AFTA tariff reductions MFN (PECC 1995). In addition, the AFTA agreement itself encourages the MFN-ization of regional concessions by counting MFN liberalizations as contributions toward a country's AFTA obligations under the CEPT.

AFTA's experience also confirms the benefits of expanding bloc membership. AFTA has recently admitted Vietnam, where economic integration with ASEAN has become a powerful motive for economic reform. After agreeing to accede to AFTA in July 1995, Vietnam has pledged complete liberalization by 2006. Laos is slated to join in two years, and Cambodia has indicated that it also plans to apply for admission in a few years' time.

Table 1 provides evidence on ASEAN's impressive MFN trade liberalization during the time when it developed plans for AFTA. The first data point shows protection levels in the mid-1980s (1984–87), before the birth of AFTA, and the second provides data for more recent years (1991–93), after the Third and Fourth ASEAN Summits. The data clearly show that substantial MFN progress was made in parallel with developing the preferential AFTA agreement.

Table 1   Tariffs and Non-Tariff Barriers in ASEAN: Weighted Averages, 1984–87 and 1991–93

| | INDONESIA | | | | MALAYSIA | | | | SINGAPORE | | | | THAILAND | | | |
| | Tariffs | | NTBs | | Tariffs | | NTBs | | Tariffs | | NTBs | | Tariffs | | NTBs | |
Commodity	84/87	91/93	84/87	91/93	84/87	91/93	84/87	91/93	84/87	91/93	84/87	91/93	84/87	91/93	84/87	91/93
PRIM PDTS.	10.4	8.5	98.4	11.2	6.4	5.3	6.3	1.6	0.7	1.9	12.6	2.1	16.5	26.4	28.6	12.0
Food	18.4	14.7	99.8	21.7	8.3	7.5	12.2	4.0	0	0	21.6	5.0	30.3	41.1	40.3	25.9
Agric Raw Mat	9.3	8.2	84.8	0	8.1	7.2	8.3	0	0	0	13.8	1.3	15.1	21.3	25.5	1.1
Crude fert/ores	2.8	2.1	99.6	1.3	2.5	2.8	2.4	0.7	0	4.2	3.6	0	8.4	11.7	29.2	19.0
Min. Fuels	3.7	3.7	100	5.8	3.0	3.0	0	0	2.1	0	4.3	0	1.5	25.0	18.6	2.3
Non-Fer. Met	9.0	10.2	100	4.7	11.1	11.6	0	0	0	0	0	0	15.6	18.9	0.6	2.1
MANU. PDTS.	21.7	14.7	89.8	5.3	17.7	14.1	9.1	7.0	1.4	1.9	12.8	0	30.4	41.6	16.3	6.2
Chemicals	11.0	9.2	94.2	0.8	7.0	7.7	2.4	2.1	0	0	52.6	0	26.3	32.4	6.7	1.1
Iron & Steel	10.3	9.3	98.1	28.9	8.9	10.5	11.5	6.9	0	0	0	0	20.1	20.7	12.6	0.1
Mach & Equip	24.1	13.1	86.5	5.6	20.1	13.5	12.4	9.9	2.5	3.5	7.0	0	29.7	42.5	23.1	8.2
Non-Elec Mach	13.4	14.6	95.6	1.5	9.2	8.0	4.4	1.7	0	0	1.8	0	20.3	32.5	8.6	3.1
Elect Mach	19.5	18.3	75.9	0.5	19.0	18.8	8.9	0.5	0	0	18.3	0	32.5	40.7	19.6	1.8
Trans Equip	40.4	7.1	82.9	14.7	35.0	17.0	25.3	27.8	7.7	10.6	5.2	0	39.8	57.1	44.2	19.8
Other Manuf	26.6	22.9	91.8	1.0	20.7	19.9	5.4	3.8	0.3	0.3	5.1	0	36.2	46.1	9.1	6.7
Leath & Travel	24.0	13.1	100	0	25.0	23.0	0	0	0.2	0.2	0	0	43.3	64.7	0	0
Rubber Pdts	14.3	13.4	40.1	0	39.1	27.8	0	0	0	0	0	0	35.2	49.6	0	0
Wood Pdts	28.6	27.0	100	0	25.8	25.5	0	0	0	0	0	0	22.3	48.0	90.9	0
Paper Pdts	25.6	21.6	79.9	6.8	10.9	12.8	0	0	0	0	0	0	30.7	26.4	10.4	6.2
Text & Clothing	39.0	28.3	90.2	1.3	27.3	27.0	0.5	0.2	1.0	1.1	5.7	0	50.8	69.3	2.0	2.7
Non-met Min	26.0	21.8	95.8	0	19.6	19.6	33.7	27.9	0	0	0	0	34.0	27.3	12.1	27.5
Furniture	40.9	34.9	100	0	37.8	29.3	0	0	2.4	2.8	0	0	53.9	71.8	0	0
Footware	59.2	39.5	100	0	38.3	41.2	0	0	0	0	0	0	59.8	99.4	0	0
Prof. Equip	11.7	11.9	98.2	0	5.6	5.5	0	0	0	0	2.1	0	22.2	35.5	0.5	0.2
ALL PDTS	18.2	12.6	92.5	7.3	14.7	11.2	8.2	5.1	1.2	1.9	12.9	0.7	26.9	36.9	20.2	8.2

Notes:
(1) NTBs are calculated on a coverage basis.
(2) No data were available for Brunei, the Philippines, and Vietnam.
Source: UNCTAD, 1994, Directory of Import Regimes, as cited in PECC (1995).

As Table 1 shows, virtually all members of AFTA have implemented ambitious multilateral liberalization programs. Already quite open at the start, Singapore essentially abolished its non-tariff barriers. Indonesia reduced mean tariffs from 18 to 13 percent and the incidence of NTBs from 93 to 7 percent. Malaysian tariffs and NTB incidence were already low at the start of this period, but each fell by a further 20 percent. Thailand's average tariffs in manufactures increased from 30 percent to 40 percent, but much of this increase can be attributed to the 'tariffication' of NTBs, whose incidence declined from 20 to 8 percent.

In sum, AFTA and global liberalization are moving in parallel. AFTA probably helped ASEAN countries move more ambitiously on both regional and MFN liberalization by ensuring a receptive regional market and helping to coordinate their policies. The possibility of costly trade diversion due to the region's incomplete production structure undoubtedly contributed to the multilateralization of CEPT cuts. In addition, AFTA recently admitted a new member (Vietnam), and contributed to the acceleration of its liberalization efforts. And AFTA's own liberalization efforts may have been encouraged by competition from other regional blocs such as NAFTA. Acknowledging these developments, AFTA has committed to rapid and deep liberalization in part to 'move faster than any other free trade area'[4] in the world.

Australia–New Zealand closer economic relations
Signed in 1983, the Australia–New Zealand Closer Economic Relations Trade Agreement (CER) is one of the most comprehensive economic cooperation initiatives in the world and provides further evidence of the consistency of regional agreements and overall economic liberalization. The CER followed several earlier attempts at economic integration (for example the New Zealand–Australia Free Trade Area – NAFTA – in 1965) which were piecemeal efforts at cooperation, similar to ASEAN's first initiatives (Cobban, 1992). Over the period in which the CER was implemented, New Zealand and, to a lesser extent, Australia underwent radical economic liberalization programs. Tariffs, quotas and investment restrictions were liberalized, and domestic fiscal and monetary policies were reformed. Today, these two economies are among the most open in the world.

Table 2 presents comparable disaggregated data on tariffs (weighted average) and NTBs (frequency index of core NTBs calculated by the OECD) for Australia and New Zealand over the period 1988 to 1993. Average tariffs in New Zealand fell from 15 to 9 percent, and in Australia from 16 to 9 percent. These cuts were across-the-board, with tariffs falling in virtually every commodity category. The incidence of NTBs also fell sharply. In Australia the frequency index fell from 10 to 1 percent, and NTBs were all but phased out in New Zealand.

It would be hard to argue that the CER was the primary reason for comprehensive liberalization in Australia and New Zealand, or for these countries' intensified interest in global ties. Clearly, the CER was consistent with these policy changes. And the possibility of a positive, causal effect – along the lines suggested in the theoretical section of this paper – should not be dismissed. According to a recent report by the Pacific Economic Cooperation Council,

the demonstrated success of [CER] and of the ability of firms to gain export experience and to compete in export markets through expansion of trans-Tasman trade, have had a significant

Table 2 Tariffs and Non-Tariff Barriers in Australia and New Zealand: Weighted Averages, 1988 and 1993

Commodity	Australia Tariffs 1988	Tariffs 1993	NTBs 1988	NTBs 1993	New Zealand Tariffs 1988	Tariffs 1993	NTBs 1988	NTBs 1993
Live Anim and Prod	0.7	0.7	3.1	7.7	4.3	2.6	0	0
Veg. Prod	3.3	1.3	1.6	0.4	6.3	3.7	2.6	0
Fats and Oils	5.5	3.9	0	25.5	9.1	4	4.6	0
Prepared Foods	8.9	5.9	2.9	1.5	15.6	8.6	10	0.9
Mineral Prod.	3.1	0.9	1.9	0	2.9	1.7	0	0
Chemicals and Prod	8	3.4	1.6	0	4.6	2.1	0.4	0
Plastics and Rubber	20.3	12.1	4.7	0	17.6	10.2	39.9	0.3
Hides and Skins	15.3	8.4	1.1	0	15.5	8	11.3	0
Wood and Articles	11.1	5.8	0.6	0	12.4	7	0	0
Pulp, Paper, etc.	15	7.8	0.5	0	22.1	10.9	0.5	0
Textiles and Art.	28	20.1	26.6	0	21.6	15.8	54	8.1
Footware, Headgear	29.7	19	25.2	0	24.4	20.7	34.9	0.8
Articles of Stone	14.7	8	0	0	17.1	8	9.6	0
Precious Stones	8.4	3.3	0	0	9.3	4.2	0	0
Base Metal and Prod	11.9	7.5	11	0	13	7.3	7.3	0
Machinery	17.3	8.6	7.3	0	20	9.6	3.8	0.8
Transport Equip	24.4	10.3	3.4	5.6	25.2	11.4	20.6	0
Precision Instruments	9.6	4.2	1.2	0	8.3	3.5	0.4	0
Arms and Ammun.	6.6	3.6	0	0	1.1	7	0	0
Misc Manufactures	18.7	11.5	2.8	0	2.9	12.8	8.8	0.3
Works of Art, etc.	1.9	0	0	0	0	0	0	0
Total	15.6	9	4.5	0.9	14.9	8.5	14.5	0.4

Note: NTBs calculated as frequency indices.

Source: PECC (1995).

effect in shifting the balance of business opinion in both economies to take a more favorable view of trade liberalization and deregulation. Firms in both countries have adjusted and specialized to develop their international competitiveness.[5]

Far from interfering with Australia and New Zealand's efforts to pursue broader economic cooperation initiatives, the CER has even become something of an instrument of international cooperation. As discussed below, Australia has been a leading proponent of Asia-Pacific Economic Cooperation. Australia and New Zealand are also dialogue partners of ASEAN, and have pursued closer relationships involving development assistance and other bilateral economic issues. The CER and ASEAN have recently initiated a CER–AFTA dialogue, in which further types of economic cooperation and facilitation are being explored.

Asia-Pacific economic cooperation
The Asia-Pacific Economic Cooperation began in 1989 as a 'forum' without a clear mandate and modest ambitions. In little more than five years, it has turned into an 18-member organization representing all major Pacific Rim markets, complete with a secretariat in Singapore, several working committees and task forces, an annual heads-of-state summit, and a compelling long-term mission. At the 1994 Summit in Bogor (Indonesia), APEC leaders dedicated themselves to creating a region of 'free and open trade and investment in the Asia-Pacific no later than 2010 in the case of industrialized economies and 2020 in the case of developing economies'.[6] The Osaka summit of 1995 and the immediate future summits are pledged to working out the details of this ambitious goal.

Unlike all other regional groupings, APEC is explicitly outward-looking; its members have agreed to pursue economic integration based on the principle of open regionalism. While the meaning of this concept is still subject to debate, it generally suggests that the organization is sensitive to the interests of outside parties. At one extreme, this may mean adopting policies that do not discriminate against outsiders (for example, by 'MFN-izing' liberalization measures adopted within APEC), and at the other, developing agreements that, while discriminatory, allow any outside country to join as long as it offers reciprocal concessions. The Leaders' Declaration from the 1995 Osaka meetings reaffirmed this position:

> We emphasize our resolute opposition to an inward-looking trading bloc that would divert from the pursuit of global free trade, and we commit ourselves to firmly maintaining open regional cooperation. We reaffirm our determination to see APEC take the lead in strengthening the open multilateral system. ... Ensuring that APEC remains consistent with the WTO agreement, we will achieve trade and investment liberalization progressively. (Point 4, November 19)

Important economic reasons underlie APEC's commitment to open regionalism. ASEAN and other developing countries are uncomfortable with any arrangement that would provide special privileges – trade and investment diversion – to the United States and Japan, the group's dominant developed countries. They are therefore insisting that all APEC commitments be made, from the outset, on an MFN basis. The United States has argued, however, that it does not want Europe to be a free rider on APEC agreements, and insists that concessions be offered only on a reciprocal basis. While 'voluntary, concerted' approaches are preferred by many of APEC's members, it is likely that political imperatives will eventually require reciprocity (perhaps applied only in some APEC countries). APEC's becoming the 'Pacific Chapter of the WTO' would please many economists, but it may be hard to sell to Congress. But even in this case many APEC concessions are likely to be rapidly extended on a multilateral basis.

The competition for membership in APEC is a second factor that is likely to keep the organization aligned with international liberalization objectives. Russia, India and some other South Asian countries, several South American countries and Indochina have all expressed interest in joining APEC. Although a two-year moratorium on membership is now in effect, it seems likely that the organization's membership will be expanded. Entry into APEC, in turn, is likely to have beneficial effects, much as entry into ASEAN has led to the acceleration of reform in Vietnam.

Any APEC agreements are thus likely to be designed from the outset to minimize trade diversion and to lay the groundwork for the inclusion of new members and perhaps any country willing to offer reciprocity. One reason why APEC can afford to be so generous is that its trade is already predominantly intra-regional. In the 1991–93 period, the share of APEC partners in total trade was about two-thirds for North America and three-fourths for other APEC economies.[7] The comparable figures for the European Community in 1957 were only about one-third. Thus, APEC economies can extend concessions multilaterally without risking significant transfers to free-riding outsiders.

East Asian economic group
A final regional grouping, which did not manage to get off the ground, also offers interesting lessons. In December 1990, shortly after APEC was established, Prime Minister Mahathir of Malaysia proposed an East Asian Economic Grouping (EAEG) that would be an Asia-only trade bloc. One rationale offered for the proposal was that the EAEG would be a counterweight to emerging regional blocs in Europe and North America. The United States was, of course, strongly opposed to the idea.

But interestingly the EAEG was coolly received also within East Asia. The ASEAN countries were against it because they envisioned a discriminatory trade bloc that would 'isolate' their economies and make them even more heavily dependent on Japan and other regional partners. Japan was against it because its stake in the US markets was too large to risk. In other words, the potential diverting aspects of the EAEG were quickly recognized by most potential members, and the organization received little support. Eventually the EAEG was demoted to a face-saving East Asian Economic Caucus (EAEC) at the ASEAN-leaders Fourth Summit.

Evidently, as long as world markets remain relatively open, East Asian countries are not interested in pursuing narrow and exclusive regional arrangements. Their primary goal is parallel regional and global liberalization, that is, open regionalism.

Conclusions
Reminded of the fragmentation of the world economy in the 1930s, many observers greeted the recent resurgence of regional trading arrangements as a threat to the integration of the world economy. In fact, regionalism and globalism may not be

mutually exclusive. The benign behavior and evolution of recent PTAs, particularly in East Asia, suggests that some positive policy dynamics may systematically lead PTAs to become more liberal toward third countries. A PTA makes a country's remaining global barriers more expensive, since it threatens trade diversion to inefficient regional producers. In addition, as a PTA exposes an economy to external competition, it shifts the production structure toward more efficient, internationally-oriented players. If producers play a role in determining trade policy, such shifts favor further regional and multilateral liberalization programs.

The experiences of several different East Asian regional institutions provide evidence for these hypotheses. In each case, a strong positive association can be noted between the implementation of the PTA and global liberalization. It is harder to show, of course, that the PTA was causally related to global liberalization (rather, both the PTA and MFN liberalization may reflect a common shift toward a more open policy regime). Nevertheless, the detailed policy positions of countries accord with some of the conceptual linkages outlined earlier in this chapter. In addition, the observations of close observers of these arrangements also sometimes describe causal relationships between regional and global liberalization.

Overall, East Asia's regional experience has contributed innovations for aligning regional and MFN liberalization efforts. The concept of open regionalism, for all its ambiguities, has given rise to several strategies for extending the benefits initially derived from regional actions to a wider constituency. These approaches formalize what many countries involved in regional arrangements were already doing, namely, extending the preferences they offered to partners on a multilateral basis. It helps that the East Asian PTAs are generally free trade agreements, which allow countries to remove external barriers that would result in trade diversion.

In evaluating PTAs, therefore, special attention has to be paid to the dynamics of PTA membership and the effect of the structural shifts brought about by a PTA on subsequent policy. The evidence suggests that contemporary PTAs provide an important transition point between protection and global liberalization. In this light, they are an important positive development in the history of global economic integration.

Notes

1. The authors gratefully acknowledge valuable comments by Professor Mordechai Kreinin.
2. This section draws extensively on McCulloch and Petri (1995).
3. The EPG plan for APEC was initially a conditional MFN strategy: it proposed participation to any country willing to accept the terms of the agreement. This is, in effect, an automatically expanding FTA. The conditional MFN feature raised controversy, as some Asian countries interpreted the strategy as an effort by the United States (and perhaps Japan) to build a bloc which they could dominate. The final EPG compromise suggested that each country could determine whether the concessions it offered would be restricted regionally or extended to all outside partners on an MFN basis.
4. Address by the Sultan of Brunei to the ASEAN Economic Ministers' meeting, September 1995 (ASEAN Update 1995).
5. PECC (Draft Report), *Milestones in APEC Liberalization: A Map of Market Opening Measures by APEC Economies*, mimeo November 1995, p. 112.
6. Summary taken from *APEC Economic Leaders' Declaration of Action*, Osaka, Japan, November 19, 1995.
7. APEC Economic Committee (1995), op. cit.

References

Baldwin, Richard E. (1993), 'A domino theory of regionalism', CEPR Discussion Paper No. 857.

Cobban, Murray (1992), 'The Australia–New Zealand Economic Relationship: The Role of CER', Chapter 7 in Richard W. Baker and Gary R. Hawke (eds), *ANZUS Economics*, Westport: Praeger.

de Melo, Jaime and Arvind Panagariya (1992), 'The new regionalism', *Finance and Development*, **29**, 30–47, December.

Krueger, Anne (1993), 'Free Trade Agreements as Protectionist Devices', prepared for a conference in honor of John Chipman, University of Minnesota, processed.

Krugman, Paul (1991), 'The Move Toward Free Trade Zones', in *Review*, Federal Reserve Bank of Kansas City, December.

Lawrence, Robert Z. (1991), 'Emerging Regional Arrangements: Building Blocks or Stumbling Blocks', in Richard O'Brien (ed.), *Finance and the International Economy: 5*, Oxford: Oxford University Press.

Levy, Philip I. (1994), 'A political–economic analysis of free trade agreements', Yale University, processed.

McCulloch, Rachel and Peter A. Petri (1995), 'Alternative paths toward open global markets', revised version of paper presented at a Festschrift Conference for Robert M. Stern, University of Michigan, November 18–20, 1994.

Pacific Economic Cooperation Council (PECC) (1995), *Survey of Impediments to Trade and Investment: Summary Report*, Singapore: PECC.

Name index